New Caribbean Studies

Series Editors
Kofi Campbell
Department of English
Wilfrid Laurier University
Waterloo, ON, Canada

Shalini Puri
Department of English
University of Pittsburgh
Pittsburgh, PA, USA

New Caribbean Studies series seeks to contribute to Caribbean self-understanding, to intervene in the terms of global engagement with the region, and to extend Caribbean Studies' role in reinventing various disciplines and their methodologies well beyond the Caribbean. The series especially solicits humanities-informed and interdisciplinary scholarship from across the region's language traditions.

More information about this series at
http://www.palgrave.com/gp/series/14752

Alison Klein

Anglophone Literature of Caribbean Indenture

The Seductive Hierarchies of Empire

Alison Klein
Thompson Writing Program
Duke University
Durham, NC, USA

New Caribbean Studies
ISBN 978-3-030-07561-3   ISBN 978-3-319-99055-2 (eBook)
https://doi.org/10.1007/978-3-319-99055-2

© The Editor(s) (if applicable) and The Author(s) 2018
Softcover re-print of the Hardcover 1st edition 2018
This work is subject to copyright. All rights are solely and exclusively licensed by the Publisher, whether the whole or part of the material is concerned, specifically the rights of translation, reprinting, reuse of illustrations, recitation, broadcasting, reproduction on microfilms or in any other physical way, and transmission or information storage and retrieval, electronic adaptation, computer software, or by similar or dissimilar methodology now known or hereafter developed.
The use of general descriptive names, registered names, trademarks, service marks, etc. in this publication does not imply, even in the absence of a specific statement, that such names are exempt from the relevant protective laws and regulations and therefore free for general use.
The publisher, the authors and the editors are safe to assume that the advice and information in this book are believed to be true and accurate at the date of publication. Neither the publisher nor the authors or the editors give a warranty, express or implied, with respect to the material contained herein or for any errors or omissions that may have been made. The publisher remains neutral with regard to jurisdictional claims in published maps and institutional affiliations.

Cover illustration: 'Mersey' by Allan C. Green. Image courtesy of State Library Victoria, Australia.

This Palgrave Macmillan imprint is published by the registered company Springer Nature Switzerland AG
The registered company address is: Gewerbestrasse 11, 6330 Cham, Switzerland

Acknowledgments

I am deeply grateful to Ashley Dawson for his vital guidance and support, which began years before I conceived of this manuscript and continues to this day. I would also like to thank Herman Bennett, Barbara Webb, Lyn Di Iorio, and Mikhal Dekel for their formative assistance in the early stages of this project.

The CUNY Graduate Center's Doctoral Student Research Grant Program and The Center for Latin American, Caribbean, and Latino Studies Summer Research Travel Fellowship funded my research, and the Graduate Center English Department's Millennium Fellowship gave me much needed time to write the first draft of this project. Research funding from Duke University's Thompson Writing Program assisted in the completion of the manuscript.

The rich archives in the West Indiana and Special Collections Division at the University of the West Indies, St. Augustine, and in the Caribbean Research Library at the University of Guyana deepened my understanding of indenture. The staff at both libraries were unfailingly kind and helpful. While I was conducting research at the University of the West Indies, Brinsley Samaroo, Patricia Mohammed, Gabrielle Jamela Hosein, Bridget Brereton, Shaheeda Hosein, Kumar Mahabir, Lomarsh Roopnarine, and Robert Waters generously took the time to discuss my project and my research, and I am especially grateful to Dr. Samaroo for his practical assistance. On research trips within the United States, Donette Francis, Tim Watson, and Samantha Pinto helped me frame my ideas. Margriet Fokken and Maurits Hassan Khan pointed me toward useful resources on Munshi Rahman Khan and provided important perspectives on his life and work. Peggy Mohan graciously took the time to speak with me about her novel *Jahajin*, which deepened my understanding of that text.

Many thanks to the publishing team at Palgrave Macmillan, particularly Camille Davies and Tomas René, whose patience and practical guidance I deeply appreciate.

I am profoundly thankful to Ira, Kim, Melissa, and Hilary Klein for their various forms of support during this process, ranging from reading drafts to brainstorming titles to hosting me in New York City. Liam O'Loughlin, Sachelle Ford, Matthew Pavesich, Danielle LaLonde, and Ian Foster read drafts and offered vital feedback. It was a delight and an honor to share my work with the members of the Caribbean studies seminar: Ashley Williard, Nicole Burrowes, Ryan Mann-Hamilton, and Gordon Barnes. Sameena Mulla and Benjamin Holtzman aided me with practical advice on the publishing process. I also feel fortunate to have met and shared ideas with Asha Jeffers, Radica Mahase, and Kavita Singh at conferences. Finally, a special thanks to Anne Donlon, who has been a constant and steady source of calmness, humor, and intellectual stimulation.

Contents

1 Introduction: The Ties That Bind   1

2 To Have and To Hold: The Role of Marriage in Nonfiction Indenture Narratives   25

3 Tying the Knot: Early Depictions of Indenture   59

4 Tangled Up: Gendered Metaphors of Nation in Contemporary Indo-Caribbean Narratives   103

5 Family Ties: Embodiment of Female Laborers in the Poetry of Indenture   145

6 At the End of Their Tether: Women Writing about Indenture   181

7 Conclusion: Loose Threads   225

Index   235

CHAPTER 1

Introduction: The Ties That Bind

LIMINAL LABORERS

For English speakers, so many metaphors that relate to marriage, intimate connections, and family relationships involve rope in some way: "tying the knot," "family bonds," "the ties that bind." The same is true of terms and metaphors having to do with indentured labor. In the nineteenth and early twentieth centuries, Indian indentured laborers were referred to as "bound coolies," and woodcuts and caricatures of the laborers, such as the one below, often show immigrants with their hands tied in order to demonstrate their indentured status (Fig. 1.1). It seems to me that this is not a coincidence; ties of love and ties of labor are not as separate as we might imagine. Exploring the literature of indenture, we see that sexual relationships are used as metaphors for struggles between nations, while imperial hierarchies of gender, race, and class impact even supposedly private relationships such as that of a husband and wife.

The short story "Boodhoo," by Alfred Mendes, is a prime example of this. Published in 1932 in *The Beacon*, the first literary magazine of Trinidad and Tobago, it is a striking piece, depicting a sexual relationship between the British wife of a planter and her servant. Written shortly before the fracturing of the British Empire, "Boodhoo" challenges the view of the British as a noble, civilizing force, and it draws attention to the complex interactions of gender, race, and labor in the colonies of the

© The Author(s) 2018
A. Klein, *Anglophone Literature of Caribbean Indenture*,
New Caribbean Studies,
https://doi.org/10.1007/978-3-319-99055-2_1

Fig. 1.1 A woodcut depicting indentured laborers on an estate in British Guiana. Image from: Jenkins, Edward. 1871. *The Coolie, His Rights and Wrongs*. New York: George Routledge & Sons.

Caribbean, as well as the impact of the British imperial indenture system of the late nineteenth and early twentieth centuries. Minnie, who has come to Trinidad as the wife of Henry, a plantation owner, is initially "nauseated" when she hears talk of planters having children by their Indian laborers (Mendes 1979, 145). Yet, she is lonely and isolated, and is drawn into a love affair with her half-Indian, half-British servant, Boodhoo. In the course of this affair, she learns that Henry is actually Boodhoo's father, while Boodhoo's mother was a laborer on Henry's plantation. The story ends with these issues unresolved: Minnie dies in childbirth, terrified that her child will be dark-skinned and give away her infidelity. "Boodhoo" is unusual for its time in several ways: it offers a sympathetic depiction of a woman's infidelity, it features a love affair between a British woman and a half-Indian man, and it highlights the ways that planters often abused their power over their laborers. Most importantly, it demonstrates the destruction created by imperialism and indenture, not just to the colonized, but to the colonizers as well. Henry's liaison with an Indian woman in his youth leads to his wife's affair and death, illustrating the cross-generational damage of these systems of power.

This book addresses these systems of power, what I call "the seductive hierarchies of empire." The term "seductive" applies in three respects to the ideologies of gender, ethnicity, and class that developed under imperialism and indenture. Firstly, this book deals with the intimate relationships, often sexual in nature, between colonizers and colonized, and between colonized citizens. It explores the ways that those relations reflected and wrestled with issues of nationalism, colonial and anti-colonial sentiment, and struggles for power. Secondly, the term refers to the lure that such hierarchies held for colonizers. The belief in one's eminent superiority and fitness to rule over others, thereby justifying the domination of millions of people, must have held great appeal indeed. Finally, and perhaps most importantly, the term refers to the pervasiveness with which these hierarchies are replicated within the colonized and formerly colonized peoples, for generations after the end of imperialism. The categorization of people, it seems, is a hard lesson to unlearn.

To consider the role that indenture played in the British Empire and the Caribbean, and the role of gender and racial dynamics in imperial and anti-imperial discourse, I examine novels, autobiographies, interviews, and poems that depict the system of indentured labor in the Caribbean. In these texts, tensions around colonialism and race are often mediated through gender, and particularly through the absence or presence of South Asian and Chinese women. Representations of women and their relationships in these narratives demonstrate that for British authors, power over women laborers bolstered the masculinist enterprise of empire; for anti-colonial authors, the abusive treatment of women laborers acted as a catalyst for nationalist arguments; and for feminist authors, relationships between women offered an escape from concentric cycles of patriarchal oppression and suppression.

In the texts that effectively challenge these destructive hierarchies, what emerges is a poetics of kinship, a focus on the importance of building familial ties across generations and across classifications of people. Novels such as Cristina García's *Monkey Hunting* (2003) and poems such as Lelawattee Manoo-Rahming's "Incarnation on the Caroni" (2000) advocate a deep engagement with one's kin as a way of acknowledging the trauma of the past, recognizing the hierarchies that helped perpetuate those traumas, and moving forward—shaking off the bonds, so to speak, of empire. I differentiate here between "family," which generally refers to ties of blood or marriage, and "familial," or, "kinship," which I use to refer to the consciously chosen ties that arise sometimes from shared genes but sometimes through shared experience. There are family ties, such as between an abusive husband and his wife, that are just as damaging and repressive as colonialism and indenture.

These and other patterns emerge most clearly when analyzing texts across time periods and geographic boundaries, and so I compare works by authors writing at the time of indenture to works by contemporary authors, works from Trinidad, Guyana, Jamaica, Suriname, Cuba, Britain, and the United States, and works that depict both Indian and Chinese indenture. Authors writing at the peak of indenture, such as Edward Jenkins, depict it as a system that benefits all involved parties, while authors writing after the collapse of British colonialism, such as David Dabydeen, focus on indenture as one of imperialism's cruelest forms of control. Authors depicting Indian indenture, such as A.R.F. Webber, tend to focus on relations between the British managers and the Indian laborers. By contrast, authors who focus on Chinese indenture, which in some places existed coterminously with slavery, devote more attention to the associations between the Chinese laborers and the Afro-Caribbean citizens, as in García's *Monkey Hunting*. Indenture played a less formative role in the development of Jamaican society than that of other Caribbean nations such as Trinidad and Tobago and Guyana, which is reflected in its lack of representation in literature about Jamaica. When indenture does appear in such texts, such as in Patricia Powell's *The Pagoda* (1998), it plays a relatively minor role. My analysis is also comprehensive, considering, to the extent possible, each Anglophone novel, poem, and nonfiction text that directly depicts the colonial system of indenture in the Caribbean. My hope is that this undertaking will draw attention to the importance of this time period and the literature that imagines it.

Much attention has been paid, with good reason, to the role of slavery in imperial history. Indentured labor, which, for 75 years was the primary movement of people to the colonies and the primary labor force on the plantations, receives much less attention, especially in literary theory. Between 1838 and 1918, approximately 500,000 Indians and 200,000 Chinese were brought to work in the Caribbean, a massive movement of people at a time when the voyage took three months (Roopnarine 2009, 71; Look Lai 2006, 9). This immigration is a critical aspect of colonial history, as it dramatically altered the ethnic makeup of the Caribbean, the cultural norms and traditions of those who migrated, and the structure of British imperialism. Yet, the history of indenture and its effects remain invisible in many ways; those outside of the Caribbean generally think of it as a region populated by people of African descent, yet in some nations, including Trinidad and Tobago and Guyana, Indo-Caribbeans make up the largest ethnic group.

A crucial aspect of this migration is the way that gender roles shifted under indenture. As indenture migration was, in theory at least, voluntary, far fewer women than men indentured, with the disparity ranging from 2:1 to 5:1 for Indian laborers (Mohammed 2002, 37–39), while hardly any Chinese women migrated. Initially, women who traveled under indenture from traditional societies like India may have gained some freedoms. As they were able to earn wages, they had more economic independence, and their scarcity meant that they could choose a mate. As a result, migrants adapted some gender-related traditions: dowries were reversed, so that money went from the groom's family to that of the bride, rather than the other way around (Mohammed 2002, 47).

At the same time, the few women who traveled to the colonies were seen as the protectors of Indian civilization, culture, and tradition, which led to limitations on their freedom. Historian Patricia Mohammed notes that most cultures view men's honor as dependent upon the control of women's sexuality, and, as a result, conflicts between ethnic groups often play out as men attempting to protect women against the perceived threat of other men (Mohammed 2002, 9). This was especially true far from home, when one's culture seemed in peril. As a result, women's access to education was restricted, and once their period of indenture had ended, they were often confined to the home. The majority of indentured Indians lived in barracks on the estates. After they had completed their contracts and had chosen to remain permanently, villages and communities were reconstituted, and, with this, the reemergence or consolidation of many of the customs and traditions brought from India.

Perhaps the most disturbing aspect of these shifts is the increased level of violence against women during this time period: a man who believed his wife had consorted with another man often chopped off her arm or nose, or murdered her. Colonial authorities blamed this and many of the other ills of the system on the gender disparity, citing men's sexual frustration and jealousy as a cause for the violence. They also blamed the quality of women, claiming that the only women who were willing to indenture were of low moral character and therefore more likely to choose more than one mate and stir hostilities.

Due to these factors, women, especially women of Indian, Chinese, and African descent, take on a metaphoric weight in the narratives of indenture, acting as a site of contestation. Feminist scholars such as Gayatri Spivak and Anne McClintock have pointed to the symbolic position that women hold in imperialism, noting that one of the major justifications for empire has been the protection and civilization of colonized women. However, during Caribbean indenture, colonized women took on an even greater representational significance for both the British and the colonized peoples, due to the disparity in the ratio of male to female laborers. In power struggles between the British managers and the laborers, as well as between different ethnic groups in the colonies, gaining control over the female laborers was a demonstration of dominance and superiority. Authors writing in favor of indenture and colonialism often use female laborers as scapegoats, the cause of the ills of the system. Authors writing against indenture and imperialism depict colonized women as the bearers of culture and tradition and portray colonizers desiring female laborers as an indication of their greed. By contrast, female authors writing about indenture veer away from such metaphors, emphasizing instead the cyclical nature of various forms of oppression.

As with slavery, a major justification for indentured labor was the improvement of inferior races. Laborers would not only enjoy good food, medical care and an escape from the poverty of their home country, they would be exposed to Christianity, morality, and the technological and organizational advancements of the West. In reality, the civilizing mission was a justification for the economic exploitation of the laborers, and indenture, which developed directly out of slavery, extended the life of the plantation economy that was a major source of Britain's wealth. The system was brutal and corrupt at nearly every stage: planters typically provided inadequate food and housing, worked the laborers far beyond the hours set out in the contracts, and cheated them of their wages. As abuses became public, indentured labor became a controversial topic in Britain and its colonies, and after some temporary halts, the system ended for good in 1920.

Within the indenture system, the laborer occupied a liminal space, not quite a slave but not quite free, not at home but not quite foreign.[1] Europeans viewed the Chinese and Indians as a buffer between themselves and the Africans, inferior to the white races but superior to those of Africa. Their labor was used as a weapon against formerly enslaved Africans; the abundance of workers kept wages low and prevented laborers from negotiating for better conditions. Through the system of indentured labor, Britain, whose empire was beginning to fracture, maintained control of its colonies and its wealth for a little longer, and also bolstered the conviction of white male superiority.

To justify slavery and indenture, British imperialists developed a teleological view of labor that was linked to hierarchical views of civilization and race. In keeping with Hegel's understanding of history as a linear evolution of cultures, African, Asian, and European nations represented stages in a progression of civilization. Similarly, slavery, indentured labor, and wage labor were depicted as progressive steps necessary to civilize undeveloped races. The stagist view of civilization has been effectively attacked and dismantled, but the teleological view of labor still permeates many discourses on labor. To suggest that systems of labor have become increasingly humane as we have moved from slavery to indenture to wage labor ignores the forms of exploitation that exist in each system. While it should be noted that there were significant differences between these forms of labor, Hugh Tinker calls indenture "a new system of slavery" (Tinker 1993), and Cedric Robinson suggests that indentured labor, "wage slavery…peonage, share-cropping, tenant-farming, forced labor, penal labor, and modern peasantry" (Robinson 1983, 219) all share qualities of slavery.

In addition, far from occurring in stages, these systems have existed coterminously. Indentured servants traveled from Germany, Ireland, and England to the United States and the Caribbean before and during slavery, and forms of indenture and slavery continue to exist in the present. Although there are no longer official, state-sanctioned systems of slavery or indenture, human trafficking and other forms of economic oppression have grown out of these networks of mass labor migration. Studying indentured labor helps us understand how those systems of exploitation and domination develop, and literature offers a unique window into this

---

[1] See Lisa Yun, *The Coolie Speaks* (2008), and Moon-Ho Jung, *Coolies and Cane* (2006).

development. Literature reveals a society's views and prejudices on an intimate level; it both shapes and is shaped by the prevailing norms and values of a people.²

There is a growing body of novels and poetry about the indenture system, and these texts draw attention to the damaging hierarchies of labor and race that indenture perpetuated. By my count, only two novels were written in English about indenture between 1834 and 1917, the peak of the system: Edward Jenkins' *Lutchmee and Dilloo* (1877) and A.R.F. Webber's 1917 novel *Those That Be in Bondage* (1988). However, 12 novels have been written between 1976 and today, not to mention the many novels that touch on indenture or its aftereffects.³ Poetry about indenture also blossomed in this time period: in the last 60 years, Rajkumari Singh, Mahadai Das, David Dabydeen, and Lelawattee Manoo-Rahming all wrote verses reflecting on the labor of their ancestors. As third- and fourth-generation South Asian and Chinese diasporic citizens explore their history and the reasons for the migration of their ancestors to the Caribbean, Africa, and the Pacific Islands, indentured labor is becoming a more and more common topic of literature. This interest has been fueled by the rise in the last few decades of Caribbean-centered publishers like Peepal Tree Press, and the expanded publishing opportunities that these presses offer. Unfortunately, there are few texts by the laborers themselves, who tended to lack the education or leisure time necessary to record their experiences, and so we must rely on interviews and testimonials to hear their stories directly. As part of this project, I explore these oral narratives in order to bring attention to such underrepresented accounts and the insights they offer.

---

² Elizabeth E. Weber summarizes the argument of literary intellectual Liang Qichao, who suggested in 1902 that literature had the power to move the masses: "In the creation of provocative...and enchanting fictional worlds, authors could stealthily inculcate with particular social values those readers who might be less receptive to more overtly political tracts and nonfiction essays" (Weber 2016, 304).

³ Deepchand Beeharry: *That Others Might Live* (1976); Sharlow: *The Promise* (1995); David Dabydeen: *The Counting House,* published in 1996 (2005); Roy Heath: *The Shadow Bride* (1996); Patricia Powell: *The Pagoda* (1998); Cristina García: *Monkey Hunting* (2003); Helen Atteck: *Bound for Trinidad: An Historical Novel* (2004); Ron Ramdin: *Rama's Voyage* (2004); Ryhaan Shah's *A Silent Life* (2005); Peggy Mohan: *Jahajin* (2007); Amitav Ghosh: *Sea of Poppies* (2008); Khalil Rahman Ali: *Sugar's Sweet Allure* (2013).

Theorizing Indenture

The Caribbean is a growing but still underrepresented area in the field of postcolonial studies, as scholars tend to focus on Southeast Asia and Africa, and the role of indentured labor in both Caribbean history and worldwide migration is relatively understudied. This is especially true in literary criticism; indenture narratives are not generally included in the canon of Caribbean literature, and almost all of the work being done on indenture is in the field of history. For example, Patricia Mohammed's *Gender Negotiations among Indians in Trinidad, 1917–1947* (2002) examines the ways that gender roles shifted in the new environment, while in *Coolies and Cane* (2006), Moon-Ho Jung notes that after emancipation, Chinese indentured laborers in Louisiana were used to strengthen notions of whiteness and white supremacy. Walton Look Lai's seminal book *Indentured Labor, Caribbean Sugar* (1993) offers a comprehensive historical overview of Indian and Chinese indenture in the Caribbean, while Lisa Yun's *The Coolie Speaks* explores written and oral testimonies of indentured laborers in Cuba and notes ways that these testimonies challenged dominant paradigms such as racial hierarchies. Lisa Lowe's *The Intimacies of Four Continents* (2015) demonstrates that nineteenth- and twentieth-century European liberal notions of freedom, wage labor, and free trade were inextricably tied to oppressive practices of colonialism, slavery, and indenture. Gaiutra Bahadur's book, *Coolie Woman* (2014), part memoir and part history, is a thorough exploration of the experiences of indentured women, built around Bahadur's research into the story of her own great-great-grandmother, who indentured in British Guiana from India.

Mariam Pirbhai is one of the few scholars to conduct an extended analysis of literary depictions of indentured labor. In *Mythologies of Migration, Vocabularies of Indenture* (2009), Pirbhai emphasizes key themes in indenture narratives, such as the tension between forming alliances with other oppressed races versus seeking strength in one's community. While her examination centers on Indian diasporic texts from across the globe, this book concentrates on literature depicting Caribbean indenture of both Indian and Chinese laborers. Such a focus allows for an exploration of the shifting significance of indenture in literature across time periods, as well as of the parallels and divergences between the experiences of Indian and Chinese migrants.

Other critics who have explored indenture have built theoretical frameworks to draw attention to the contributions of different ethnic groups to

Caribbean culture. Shalini Puri introduced the term "dougla poetics" (Puri 1997, 143), borrowing a word used to identify a person of mixed Indian and African descent. The theorization of "dougla poetics" is meant to acknowledge and increase acceptance of cultural hybridization, but some have argued that the term elides other groups, such as those of Chinese or Amerindian descent.[4] On the subject of Chinese contributions to the Caribbean, Ann-Marie Lee-Loy describes the way that poets such as Easton Lee have created "a new creole melody" (Lee-Loy 2010, 114), adding Chinese music to the cultural melody of Jamaica, so that Chineseness "no longer represents alien or outsider; rather it is just another way of 'being Jamaican'" (Lee-Loy 2010, 115).

Feminist critics have further built on the model of dougla poetics with the concepts of "*kala pani* discourse," "*jahaji*-hood," and "post-indentureship feminisms." Brinda Mehta, who coined the term "*kala pani* discourse," draws on the Hindu belief that those who crossed the *kala pani*, the dark waters of the ocean, lost their caste (Mehta 2004, 10). She does so to highlight the vital role of Indian women in Caribbean culture and to build a transnational feminist framework based on the shared experience of migration and struggle rather than ethnicity. Similarly, Mariam Pirbhai employs the phrase "*jahaji*-hood," which refers to the familial bond that develops between those on the same ship voyage, to evoke "the labor diaspora's shared sense of bondage, cultural affinity, and spiritual fraternity as it was initiated by the traumatic and perilous journey" (Pirbhai 2012, 25). Finally, Gabrielle Jamela Hosein and Lisa Outar offer the framework of "post-indentureship feminisms," which draws on the shared experience of indentureship and its aftermath rather than national identity (Hosein and Outar 2016, 9).

These approaches highlight the importance of building solidarity across traditional lines of classification such as nationality and ethnicity, but the texts discussed in this book offer a vital addition: the importance of building solidarity across *time*. Equally imperative to crossing spatial and societal borders is the need to cross temporal ones, to develop a sense of kinship with previous and future generations. Ramabai Espinet's novel *The Swinging Bridge* offers a useful demonstration of this in the character of Bess, the narrator's cousin: "Bess had a notion of family that transcended the immediate: she dealt in lineage and posterity and generations and

---

[4] Puri has stated that she "had not intended (indeed, had cautioned against) constructions of douglaness that were idealizing, paradigmatic, or prescriptive" (Puri 2016, 322).

descendants. Family was not just breeding and reproducing—it was a work of art in itself, as carved and sculpted as any other legacy one could leave behind" (Espinet 2003, 123). This quote is particularly meaningful, referring as it does to a character who is a marginal figure in her own family because she is the child of an extramarital affair. With her growing awareness of Bess' emphasis on posterity over blood ties, Mona, the narrator of *The Swinging Bridge*, begins to acknowledge the importance of this approach in remembering the past and preventing it from repeating, and begins to rediscover her own sense of self.

My analysis of the narratives of indenture also builds on Foucault-inspired postcolonial critics who challenge the notion that public and private domains are divisible. For example, Robert J.C. Young's *Colonial Desire* (1995) suggests that the imperial obsession with racial classification and miscegenation is a result of the colonizer's suppressed desire for the colonized, Ann Laura Stoler's *Carnal Knowledge* (2002) examines the connections between colonial policies around child-rearing and intimate relationships and imperial views of a racial hierarchy, and Alys Eve Weinbaum's *Wayward Reproductions* (2004) argues that discourses of biological reproduction have been employed to support ideologies of racism, nationalism, and imperialism. Additionally, in *The Anarchy of Empire in the Making of U.S. Culture* (2002), Amy Kaplan shows that domestic issues are closely linked to foreign policies in the United States. These theorists tend to focus on the colonizers, using these relationships to explore the colonial mindset or the implementation of colonial power. While this is an important aspect of understanding imperialism, it brushes aside the experience of the colonized. I examine relationships between the colonizers and the colonized, as well as between the colonized people themselves, which reveals the insidious ways that imperial rhetoric impacted these connections.

Exploring literature from a range of authors, we see the ways that intimate relationships act as metaphors for larger conflicts of ethnicity and class. In most indenture narratives, particularly those written by men, the central conflict revolves around a female laborer involved in a sexual relationship (either consensual or nonconsensual) with a man outside of her ethnic group. An especially frequent trope is a relationship between a British man and a female Indian laborer. By most accounts, such connections between managers and laborers were common, but this does not explain the prevalence of this trope. These relationships act a focal point, a catalyst within the plot for tensions around colonialism, both by pro-imperial authors advocating Britain's power and civilizing influence, and by anti-imperial authors attempting to demonstrate the selfishness and brutality of the colonizers. Writing at the time of indenture, Edward Jenkins and A.R.F. Webber use this relationship as a stand-in for Britain's relationship with India, suggesting that Britain was raising India out of darkness and into civilization. The metaphors in these texts equate Indian women with children or animals, vulnerable beings who need to be protected: in *Lutchmee and Dilloo*, Craig thinks of Lutchmee, "Was she not a pretty animal?" (Jenkins 2003, 130). Later authors Dabydeen and Sharlow use this same relationship to attack imperialism, showing Britain taking advantage of India. Yet, in these texts, women are still depicted as possessions to be controlled: they are compared to treasure, or land being pillaged by other ethnic groups. When Vidia suspects Rohini of sleeping with an African man, he screams, "Niggerman digging in your belly for gold that belong to me" (Dabydeen 2005, 87).

When viewing fictional characters as allegories for their nation, we run the risk of reducing the complexity of the work. In his controversial essay, "Third World Literature in the Era of Multinational Capitalism," Fredric Jameson does just that, suggesting that "Third-world texts, even those which are seemingly private…necessarily project a political dimension in the form of national allegory" (Jameson 1986, 69). Aijaz Ahmad famously attacked this essentialist view, arguing that it makes sweeping generalizations based on a binary view of a capitalist first world versus a precapitalist third world, and that it defines third world nations by their experience of colonialism. It is the aim of this project to avoid such overgeneralizations while still drawing attention to the ways that authors themselves sometimes rely on such essentializing allegories.

An investigation of these texts also demonstrates that the complex, interwoven hierarchies of race, class, and gender within the indenture system permeate literature by both European authors and authors of Indian and Chinese descent, authors writing a century ago and contemporary authors. For example, early authors Edward Jenkins and A.R.F. Webber, but also the contemporary author Sharlow, describe their Indian protagonists as high-caste, light-skinned, and European-featured, while the Indian villains are invariably dark-skinned. Helen Atteck's novel *Bound for Trinidad* (2004) criticizes the racism faced by Chinese laborers, but the characters of African descent veer toward stereotypes and appear only in servant roles. Such hierarchies appear in the nonfiction texts as well. In

Munshi Rahman Khan's autobiography, he is proud of his high status as a scholar, and he shows great respect for European women and Indian women with wealth and high caste, whereas African women and the Indian women of the working class are described as greedy, dishonorable, and coarse.

Further, the bleakness of the narratives points to the violence that is often inherent in the creation of diasporic populations. Authors who focus on literary depictions of emerging nationalisms, as Doris Sommer does in *Foundational Fictions: The National Romances of Latin America* (1991), offer a somewhat romantic view of these movements, suggesting that there is a redeeming quality to the violence of nation-making. Indenture narratives tend to deny this sense of redemption, ending in tragedy and destruction. Death is a common theme in these texts: *Lutchmee and Dilloo*, *Those That Be in Bondage*, *The Counting House*, and *The Promise* all include the violent death of one of the main characters. In addition, the prevalence of children dying suggests a lack of hope for the future. In *Lutchmee and Dilloo*, Lutchmee has a miscarriage because she is forced to continue working in the fields, while in "Journey Across the Black Waters," a woman named You throws her baby overboard on the voyage to Trinidad rather than have it suffer the experience of being the child of a single female laborer (Bain 2013).

The content of indenture narratives shifts over time from supporting imperialism to promoting nationalism in former colonies, from perpetuating hierarchies to attacking them. The form of the narratives and the authors' styles shift as well, which can be attributed in part to changes in literary techniques over the 150 years that the texts cover, but also to the differing purpose of each author. Early authors Jenkins and Webber write in a third-person omniscient point of view, aiming for a sense of objectivity as they capture the benefits of imperialism on the Indian laborers. Their stories are chronological, moving from cause to effect to show the rationality of the plantation and the inevitableness of imperialism. In *Lutchmee and Dilloo*, Dilloo becomes an agitator and rebels against management, and so he must die. Lutchmee recognizes the worth of the Scottish overseer and supports the management against Dilloo, and so she lives.

David Dabydeen, on the other hand, employs a fragmented storyline to show the damaging effects of imperialism. *The Counting House* moves back and forth between Rohini and Vidia's lives in India before they indentured and their experiences as laborers in British Guiana. These shifts emphasize the ways that British colonialism weakened the Indian economy and led to an increase in indenture and also the forms of oppression that laborers faced once they arrived on plantations. The novel follows the perspective of three different characters in order to capture the full experience of the colonized peoples: Rohini, a female Indian laborer; Miriam, a black servant; and Kampta, an unbound Indian laborer. Two sections of the novel are told in third-person point of view, while the third is in first person. These techniques, which jar the reader, defamiliarize the text and force the reader to consider his or her own subject position while reading haunting descriptions of the trauma of colonialism.

The novels and poetry by women authors tend even further toward fragmentation, reflecting their desire to demonstrate the insidious effects of indenture on the descendants of laborers. Both *Monkey Hunting*, by Cristina García, and *Jahajin* (2007), by Peggy Mohan, follow several generations of a single family. The storyline cuts back and forth between an indentured laborer and his or her descendants in order to capture the ongoing impact of indenture and imperialism and repeating patterns of oppression. These novels, like *The Counting House*, each focus on three different storylines; three seems to be a common choice by contemporary authors, perhaps seeking to avoid binaries and trouble neat categorizations. Similarly, poems by Mahadai Das and Lelawattee Manoo-Rahming intersperse their own experiences living in Guyana and Trinidad, respectively, with the traumatic experiences of their female ancestors who migrated as indentured laborers. They employ enjambed lines, disjointed imagery, and synaesthetic descriptions to convey the horrors of indenture and the distance the poets must reach across to understand the lives of these ancestors.

The differences that arise in the texts by male versus female authors point to the differences in the lived experience of men and women in post-indenture nations. The male authors tend to work metaphorically, using intimate relationships as a symbol to demonstrate the impact of imperialism. Female authors such as Cristina García and Peggy Mohan, on the other hand, tend to hone in on the intimate relations as subjects in and of themselves, with the structures of imperialism and indenture as a backdrop for these interactions. They seem to work from the public to the private, rather than the other way around, focusing on how issues of nationalism and imperialism play out in close quarters, rather than using intimate relationships to make statements about larger issues of colonial rule. This suggests that Caribbean women, who have gained many public rights in the last century, but who are still at high risk for domestic violence in private, may be more concerned than men with how issues of domination play out in the domestic sphere.

The nonfiction narratives, by contrast, reflect the challenges of penning one's story when one lacks education, or time to write. Munshi Rahman Khan, the only known Caribbean laborer to write an autobiography, was a well-educated Muslim man who came from relative wealth and indentured out of a sense of adventure and an attempt to escape his family obligations. His tone is formal and didactic, and his autobiography is multigenre, equal parts journal, poetry chapbook, and history lesson. He shares his experiences as a laborer in order to solidify his reputation as an intellectual and tell the Muslim side of the Muslim-Hindu conflicts that erupted in Suriname in the mid-twentieth century. Alice Singh, whose journal provides interesting insights into women's experience of indenture, was not a laborer herself. Her father and grandmother were Brahmins who indentured when they became separated from their family in India, and with their education and high caste, they had little trouble entering the middle class of Suriname. Singh wrote her journal without the intention of publication, hoping more to share her experiences with her family, and so it is casual in style and content, reflecting largely on domestic matters. The interviewees, who were uneducated and never escaped a subsistence lifestyle, succinctly describe the challenges of indenture decades later. They tend to concentrate on issues of survival, which highlights the reason that so few laborers recorded their experiences.

Yet even the nonfiction texts contain metaphors around intimate relationships that reveal much about the laborers' views. Rahman Khan, who had been an indentured laborer in Suriname, describes marriage as a binding force, much more so than indenture itself. Upon arriving in Suriname, a female laborer claims to be his pregnant wife, and the estate manager forces Rahman Khan to support her financially. When he manages to move out of his lodging with her, he writes, "The chains that had bound me broke and I was set free" (Rahman Khan 2005, 96). The manager's insistence that Rahman Khan take responsibility for the woman reflects imperial anxiety about single women laborers, and Rahman Khan's response indicates his view of women as little more than a burden. By contrast, Alice Singh, whose parents had a cross-caste marriage, describes their marriage as "a ship sailing smoothly across the sea" (Singh 2011) indicating that marriages were sometimes viewed as a way of breaching religious and caste divisions, and also that metaphors of the ocean and of boats hold a strong place in the Indo-Caribbean imaginary.

Comparing these nonfiction texts to slave narratives, a genre that may be more familiar to North American readers, we see that Caribbean indenture narratives serve a fairly different purpose. Autobiographies by formerly enslaved persons like Frederick Douglass in the United States, and Mary Prince and Olaudah Equiano in the Caribbean, tend to describe the horrors of slavery as a call to arms to end the practice, and often follow the narrator's journey from slave to fugitive to free person. While such testimonials about indenture exist, such as Totaram Sanadhya's *My Twenty-One Years in the Fiji Islands* (1991), there are no known equivalents in the Caribbean. Munshi Rahman Khan's *Autobiography of an Indian Indentured Laborer* details some of the abuses of the system, but does not attack the practice of indenture. This may be because indentured laborers who were educated, like Munshi Rahman Khan, may have had a less brutal experience of indenture, as their skills allowed them to reach positions of management. In addition, they were better placed than their uneducated counterparts to enter the middle class after their period of indenture was over. Thus, the educated immigrants might have had less interest in abolishing the system and less incentive to record their stories, though they had more ability to do so. Early novels depicting indenture illuminate problems with the system but do not call for its end, and these texts tend to focus on the time of the laborer's indenture. It is only in later fictional texts, such as Sharlow's *The Promise* (1995), that we see an excoriation of the system itself and the same progression from bound laborer to freedom that appears in many slave narratives.

While there is important historical work being done on indenture, literature offers a unique view of this imperial system of labor and migration in the Caribbean. Particularly enlightening are the moments when the depictions in literature differ from the reality of the time. For example, commissions of inquiry indicate that the majority of women who traveled to the Caribbean under indenture were single, yet in almost every literary representation, the female characters travel with their husbands, suggesting that the authors view men as laborers and women as wives. Such moments enrich our understanding of individuals' experience of indenture, offering glimpses into the lives of both the laborers and the management, the colonizers and the colonized.

Chapter Summaries

Chaps. 2, 3, and 4 address the pervasiveness of the hierarchies of empire within both colonial and anti-colonial writings. Chap. 2 focuses on nonfiction narratives from the laborers and their descendants—autobiographies, testimonials, and interviews. I begin with these texts in order to reverse the tendency to treat with primacy the voice of the colonizers, and to demonstrate the ways that laborers suffered under, perpetuated, and resisted categorizations along gender, ethnic, and class lines. In particular, I examine colonial legislation around marriage and the impact of that legislation. Marriage, the publicly recognized institution of a private relationship, was a flashpoint for religious, ethnic, and class tensions in the Caribbean colonies. To explore the broader implications of these tensions, I analyze Rahman Khan's *Autobiography of an Indian Indentured Labourer*, the only published first-person account of indenture, and *Autobiography of Alice Bhagwandy Sital Persaud* (2011), by the daughter of an indentured laborer. I also examine the few available interviews with and testimonials by indentured laborers, including an unpublished interview (held by the University of the West Indies, St. Augustine) with a 109-year-old woman named Doolarie. These texts demonstrate that the British legislation of marriage, meant to impose Victorian ideals and justify imperialism, tended instead to support the view of women as contested property and to solidify existing class and racial hierarchies in both the colonizers and the colonized. Further, these texts demonstrate a colonial anxiety around single female laborers, who challenged the justification that colonialism brought comfort and safety to the helpless and victimized colonized women.

The third chapter examines two novels by authors writing at the time of indenture, Edward Jenkins' *Lutchmee and Dilloo* and A.R.F. Webber's *Those That Be in Bondage*. In both, a British man in power develops a relationship with a beautiful young Indian woman, raising her out of the degradation and harsh life of field labor and into a world of civilization and refinement. This represents the primary justification of colonization: Britain would protect its helpless colonies and civilize them. Both authors wrote their novels to suggest that the system of indenture needed corrections, but was generally beneficial to Britain, India, and the Caribbean nations involved in the system. Yet Jenkins and Webber reveal more than they perhaps intended. The tragic ending of *Lutchmee and Dilloo*, for example, in which a noble Indian man is turned vicious by the evils of the system, counters Jenkins' argument that indenture benefits the Indian people. In *Those That Be in Bondage*, Webber, who was of African and European descent, reveals an ambivalence toward empire. Though he was an advocate of Guyanese independence, the depictions of his characters suggest that he accepts the colonial notion of a racialized hierarchy of civilization, with Britain at the top.

In the fourth chapter, I turn to contemporary anti-colonial texts that nonetheless replicate some of the ideologies of empire, David Dabydeen's *The Counting House* and Sharlow's *The Promise*. Both novels contain the same trope that appeared in the earlier texts, a British man in power developing a relationship with a young Indian woman. However, these authors deploy this trope to attack empire; the British male takes advantage of the Indian female, using her for sexual favors and giving little in return. This again represents the relationship of Britain to India, suggesting violent, greedy motivations for imperialism, as opposed to noble, altruistic ones. While Dabydeen and Sharlow restructure the metaphor of the British man/Indian woman relationship, they fail to dismantle the traditional patriarchal view of gender that underlies this metaphor. By using female characters to represent India, they support the notion that women are the bearers of tradition and culture, that they are not individuals in their own right, and that their sexuality must be controlled and protected. As a counterpoint to these novels, I consider depictions of a similarly exploitative relationship in Patricia Powell's *The Pagoda*, which touches on Chinese indenture in Jamaica. Rather than using her characters as representatives of their nation, Powell explores the ways that colonized individuals were trapped within yet transgressed repressive gender and racial categorizations, offering a critique of imperialism without perpetuating the ideologies that underpin it.

The fifth chapter focuses on the poetry of indenture, and acts as a transition of sorts. In it, I examine the work of five contemporary authors: Guyanese poets Rajkumari Singh, Mahadai Das, and David Dabydeen; Jamaican poet Easton Lee; and Trinidadian poet Lelawattee Manoo-Rahming. Woven through their poems are images of the female ancestors who voyaged to the Caribbean under indenture, particularly images of their bodies: eyes, feet, foreheads, and wombs. For Das and Singh, who wrote in the 1970s, this focus on the body demonstrates anti-colonial, nationalistic sentiments, while for Dabydeen, Lee, and Manoo-Rahming, whose poems were published in 1988, 1998, and 2000, respectively, the emphasis on the body shows a sense of displacement. Poems written by

Rajkumari Singh and Mahadai Das in the early, still hopeful days of Guyanese independence, draw attention to the colonial view of female migrants as mere bodies, useful for labor or sexual gratification, but also celebrate the fertile possibilities of the people and the land. That they do so through the metaphor of Indo-Guyanese women's capacity for reproduction is at times problematic. In contradistinction, for authors David Dabydeen and Lelawattee Manoo-Rahming, writing in the wake of violent and dictatorial political movements in Guyana and Trinidad, the sense of hopefulness has dissipated. These authors, disillusioned by the political upheaval and autocratic regimes that followed independence, seek to reembody their ancestors as way of grounding themselves, finding a connection to the land of their birth by strengthening a sense of lineage. Tracking the images of the female laborer across decades, we thus see a move away from the often-problematic nationalist sentiments and toward a poetics of kinship.

In the final chapter, I extend this exploration of the poetics of kinship, considering how such an approach can be used to recognize and move beyond the hierarchies of empire. I examine the cyclical nature of trauma as depicted in two novels by contemporary women writers: Cristina García's *Monkey Hunting*, and Peggy Mohan's *Jahajin*. While Monkey Hunting focuses on Chinese indenture in Cuba and Jahajin explores Indian indenture in Trinidad, both novels weave together narrative strands from different time periods in order to demonstrate the ongoing impact of indenture on generations of a single family and the dangers of a nostalgic approach to the past. Additionally, both novels draw parallels between family dynamics, such as unhappy marriages and parents abandoning their children, and national upheavals, such as revolutions and uprisings. I argue that García and Mohan use these parallels to advocate an active engagement with the past in order to break cycles of trauma on both an individual and a national level. While García depicts the dangers of erasing the past, Mohan primarily warns against romanticizing the past in the form of nostalgia.

BOUNDARIES OF THE PROJECT

This exploration is limited to Anglophone texts about Caribbean indenture in order to examine the changing role of indenture and gender roles in a single geographic location, as much as one can call the Caribbean such a thing. Novels written about the British imperial system of indenture in other parts of the world are equally significant but not discussed in this project. These include Deepchand Beeharry's *That Others Might Live* (1976), a prototypical indenture narrative that focuses on Indian indenture in Mauritius, and Amitav Ghosh's *Sea of Poppies* (2008), also about Mauritius. To hone in on issues of language and metaphor, I primarily examine literature written in English, with the exception of the translated *Autobiography of an Indian Indenture Laborer*. A future study of indenture narratives might include *Le "Kooli" de Morne-Cabri* (2007) by Laure Moutoussamy, which deals with indenture in Martinique. I also primarily concentrate on texts that deal directly with indenture. Several novels touch on aspects of contract labor, such as Roy Heath's *The Shadow Bride* (1996), which follows a doctor working on an indenture plantation, or on the aftereffects of indenture, including Edgar Mittelholzer's *Corentyne Thunder* (1970), Sam Selvon's *A Brighter Sun* (1953), and Jan Lo Shinebourne's *The Last English Plantation* (1988). These texts are certainly worthy of examination, but my goal is to understand the changing significance of literary depictions of indenture across time periods and geographic locations, as well as the reasons for the increasingly frequent treatment of indenture in literature depicting the Caribbean.

While I explore both Indian and Chinese indenture, most of the texts included in this book deal with the Indian experience for the simple reason that there are fewer texts about Chinese indenture. This is, at least in part, attributable to the lower numbers of Chinese who migrated to the Caribbean, which in turn may have led to less of a cultural consciousness around Chinese identity than there is for, say, Indians in Trinidad. Ann-Marie Lee-Loy explores possible reasons for the lack of literary representation of the Chinese-Caribbean experience, as discussed by two authors of Chinese descent, Willi Chen and Easton Lee. Chen has explained that his choice of subject is impacted by the proportionally small numbers of Chinese in Trinidad, his home nation. Jamaican-born Lee, on the other hand, suggests that Caribbean citizens of Chinese descent were "'made to feel ashamed' of those aspects of their culture and experiences that differed from those of the more dominant West Indian culture(s) within which they lived," and that "the political and cultural marginalization of the Chinese communities of the West Indies might have sent them the message that other West Indians would not have any interest in what the Chinese had to say" (Lee-Loy 2010, 103–104). Both authors thus acknowledge that the lower numbers of Chinese migrants led to a smaller body of Chinese-Caribbean literature, but Lee focuses more on a sense of rejection within the Caribbean community. It seems that "Out of many, one people," Jamaica's idealistic motto, and, perhaps also, "All ah we is one," the unofficial motto of Eric Williams' party in Trinidad and Tobago, have not rung true for all ethnic groups in those nations.

Drawing Together the Threads

In the course of my research, I came across an unpublished interview with Doolarie, a 109-year-old formerly indentured woman. This is a rare example of a female laborer describing her experience of indenture. Doolarie conveys the degrading experience of indenture: the laborers were loaded into trucks "like flour bags" (Doolarie 1982) and taken to the plantation, and she shows the scar on her head where her husband beat her with a hoe for talking to another man. In the next chapter, I explore the oppressive gender and racial dynamics revealed in this interview, as well as its omission from the existing body of literature. This work reflects the mission of my project: to draw attention to the underexamined experiences of the Indian and Chinese diaspora in the Caribbean and the ways that intimate relationships reflect larger issues of gender, class, and ethnicity in literature by both the dominant and the oppressed groups.

The repressive gender and racial ideologies of the British Imperial system of indentured labor continue to impact the Caribbean. Female laborers were triply vulnerable due to their ethnicity, class, and gender, and the dramatic gender disparity meant that women laborers took on an added significance in struggles between ethnic groups. These conditions led to disturbing rates of sexual and domestic abuse that persist today and, in some cases, to limitations on women's education and freedom. While women have gained significant access to education and public positions of power, there has been less progress in domestic issues, such as violence against women. All of the Caribbean islands have higher rates of sexual violence than the world average, and the Indo-Caribbean community's comparative lack of awareness of government measures against domestic violence suggests that these women are still highly vulnerable to such abuse; in 1999, 77.3% of Indo-Guyanese women did not know about the Domestic Violence Act that had passed in 1996, the highest percentage of any ethnic group in Guyana (Red Thread 2000).

Imperial ideologies still poison race relations as well. Colonizers promoted a view of the superiority of European races over Asian races, and Asian races over African races, and encouraged conflicts between colonized groups in order to prevent solidarity and rebellion. This led to clashes between ethnic groups that persist today: as recently as 1998, violence erupted in Guyana between Afro-Caribbeans and Indo-Caribbeans in response to tensions between ethnically divided political parties. Poetry and prose depicting the Caribbean indenture system offer glimpses into the viewpoints of authors who defended and challenged imperialism and indenture, and awareness of these views can help us deconstruct the lingering, damaging effects of these systems.

Bibliography

Atteck, Helen. 2004. *Bound for Trinidad – An Historical Novel*. St. Catherines, ON: Wanata Enterprises.
Bahadur, Gaiutra. 2014. *Coolie Woman: The Odyssey of Indenture*. Chicago: The University of Chicago Press.
Bain, Kimberly. 2013. The Journey Across Black Waters. https://ghostsinthewater.wordpress.com/. Accessed 7 Mar 2018.
Beeharry, Deepchand. 1976. *That Others Might Live*. New Delhi: Orient Paperbacks.
Dabydeen, David. 2005. *The Counting House*. Leeds: Peepal Tree Press.
Doolarie. 1982. Interview with Noor Kumar Mahabir. St. Augustine, September 18.
Espinet, Ramabai. 2003. *The Swinging Bridge*. Toronto: HarperCollins.
García, Cristina. 2003. *Monkey Hunting*. New York: Knopf.
Ghosh, Amitav. 2008. *Sea of Poppies*. New York: Picador.
Heath, Roy. 1996. *The Shadow Bride*. New York: Persea Books.
Hosein, Gabrielle Jamela, and Lisa Outar. 2016. Introduction: Interrogating an Indo-Caribbean Feminist Epistemology. In *Indo-Caribbean Feminist Thought: Genealogies, Theories, Enactments*, ed. Gabrielle Jamela Hosein and Lisa Outar, 1–19. New York: Palgrave Macmillan.
Jameson, Fredric. 1986. Third World Literature in the Era of Multinational Capitalism. *Social Text* 15: 65–88.
Jenkins, Edward 2003. *Lutchmee and Dilloo: A Study of West Indian Life*. Edited by David Dabydeen. Oxford: Macmillan Education.
Jung, Moon-Ho. 2006. *Coolies and Cane: Race, Labor, and Sugar in the Age of Emancipation*. Baltimore, MD: The Johns Hopkins University Press.
Kaplan, Amy. 2002. *The Anarchy of Empire in the Making of U.S. Culture*. Cambridge: Harvard University Press.

Lee-Loy, Ann-Marie. 2010. *Searching for Mr. Chin: Constructions of Nation and the Chinese in West Indian Literature*. Philadelphia: Temple University Press.
Look Lai, Walton. 1993. *Indentured Labor, Caribbean Sugar: Chinese and Indian Migrants to the British West Indies, 1838–1918*. Baltimore: The Johns Hopkins University Press.
———. 2006. Introduction: The People from Guangdong. In *Essays on the Chinese Diaspora in the Caribbean*, ed. Walton Look Lai, 1–10. St. Augustine: University of the West Indies Press.
Lowe, Lisa. 2015. *The Intimacies of Four Continents*. Durham: Duke University Press.
Manoo-Rahming, Lelawattee. 2000. *Curry Flavour*. Leeds: Peepal Tree Press.
Mehta, Brinda. 2004. *Diasporic (Dis)locations: Indo-Caribbean Women Writers Negotiate the Kala Pani*. Kingston: University of the West Indies Press.
Mendes, Alfred. 1979. Boodhoo. In *From Trinidad: An Anthology of Early West Indian Writing*, ed. Reinhard W. Sander, 142–172. Teaneck: Holmes & Meier Publishers.
Mittelhölzer, Edgar. 1970. *Corentyne Thunder*. London: Heinemann.
Mohammed, Patricia. 2002. *Gender Negotiations Among Indians in Trinidad, 1917–1947*. New York: Palgrave.
Mohan, Peggy. 2007. *Jahajin*. New Delhi: HarperCollins and The India Today Group.
Moutoussamy, Laure. 2007. *Le 'Kooli' de morne Cabri*. Matoury: Ibis Rouge.
Pirbhai, Mariam. 2009. *Mythologies of Migration, Vocabularies of Indenture: Novels of the South Asian Diaspora in Africa, the Caribbean, and Asia-Pacific*. Toronto: University of Toronto Press.
———. 2012. Recasting Jahaji-Bhain: Plantation History and the Indo-Caribbean Women's Novel in Trinidad, Guyana, and Martinique. In *Critical Perspectives on Indo-Caribbean Women's Literature*, ed. Joy A.I. Mahabir and Mariam Pirbhai, 25–47. New York: Routledge.
Powell, Patricia. 1998. *The Pagoda*. New York: Harcourt Brace & Company.
Puri, Shalini. 1997. Race, Rape, and Representation: Indo-Caribbean Women and Cultural Nationalism. *Cultural Critique* 36: 119–163.
———. 2016. Afterword. In *Indo-Caribbean Feminist Thought: Genealogies, Theories, Enactments*, ed. Gabrielle Jamela Hosein and Lisa Outar, 321–329. New York: Palgrave Macmillan.
Rahman Khan, Munshi. 2005. *Autobiography of an Indian Indentured Labourer*. Translated by Kathinka Sinha-Kerkhoff, Ellen Bal, Alok Deo Singh. Delhi: Shipra Publications.
Ramdin, Ron. 2004. *Rama's Voyage*. San Juan, Trinidad and Tobago: Chakra Publishing House.
Red Thread. 2000. Women Researching Women. http://www.hands.org.gy/download/wom_surv.htm. Accessed 17 Aug 2013.

Robinson, Cedric J. 1983. *Black Marxism: The Making of the Black Radical Tradition*. London: Zed Press.
Roopnarine, Lomarsh. 2009. The Repatriation, Readjustment, and Second-term Migration of Ex-Indentured Indian Laborers From British Guiana and Trinidad to India, 1838–1955. *NWIG: New West Indian Guide/Nieuwe West-Indische Gids* 8 (1): 71–97 http://www.hands.org.gy/download/wom_surv.htm.
Sanadhya, Totaram. 1991. *My Twenty-one Years in the Fiji Islands; And, The Story of the Haunted Line*. Edited By John Dunham Kelly and Uttra Kumari Singh. Suva, Fiji: Fiji Museum.
Selvon, Sam. 1953. *A Brighter Sun*. New York: The Viking Press.
Shah, Ryhaan. 2005. *A Silent Life*. Leeds: Peepal Tree Press.
Sharlow. 1995. *The Promise, Or, After All We've Done for You*. Longdenville: S. Mohammed.
Shinebourne, Jan Lo. 1988. *The Last English Plantation*. Leeds: Peepal Tree Press.
Singh, Alice Bahadur. 2011. *Autobiography of Alice Bhagwandy Sital Persaud (1892–1958)*. http://mosessite.blogspot.com/2011/05/autobiography-of-alice-bhagwandy-sital.html. Accessed 19 Mar 2012.
Sommer, Doris. 1991. *Foundational Fictions: The National Romances of Latin America*. Berkeley: University of California Press.
Stoler, Ann Laura. 2002. *Carnal Knowledge and Imperial Power: Race and the Intimate in Colonial Rule*. Berkeley: University of California.
Tinker, Hugh. 1993. *A New System of Slavery. The Export of Indian Labour Overseas 1830–1920*. London: Hansib Publishing Limited.
Webber, A.R.F. 1988. *Those That Be in Bondage: A Tale of Indian Indentures and Sunlit Western Waters*. Wellesley: Calaloux Publications.
Weber, Elizabeth E. 2016. Reimagining Coolie Trajectories: The Triumphant Return as Political Statement in Late Qing 'Coolie Fiction. *Literature Compass* 13 (5): 300–310.
Weinbaum, Alys Eve. 2004. *Wayward Reproductions: Genealogies of Race and Nation in Transatlantic Modern Thought*. Durham: Duke University Press.
Young, Robert J.C. 1995. *Colonial Desire: Hybridity in Theory, Culture and Race*. New York: Routledge.
Yun, Lisa. 2008. *The Coolie Speaks: Chinese Indentured Laborers and African Slaves in Cuba*. Philadelphia: Temple University Press.

CHAPTER 2

To Have and To Hold: The Role of Marriage in Nonfiction Indenture Narratives

Introduction: Prescribing Monogamy

During the 1870 Commission of Inquiry into the Treatment of Immigrants in British Guiana, William Frere, the president of the Commission, asked, "With regard to the marriages of Coolies, there is a law prescribing monogamy: is there not, in this Colony?" (British Guiana 1870, 338). James Crosby, immigration agent-general, responded that there was the strikingly named Heathen Marriage Ordinance, which put forth the terms under which Hindu and Muslim immigrants could register their marriage. As indicated by Frere's question, the act was intended to encourage monogamous relationships, and to achieve this purpose, it also set forth punishments for anyone who committed adultery with a married woman. Crosby gives an example of what he considers a positive outcome of this law: "In a late case which took place with regard to two parties, and which was likely to lead probably to serious consequences on the *Herstelling* estate...I was enabled to put an end to the dispute in a satisfactory manner under section 11. The woman was restored to her husband" (British Guiana 1870, 339). His response indicates that the ideal resolution in such situations was the return of the wife to her husband, regardless of her wishes. Historian Lisa Yun notes that Spanish colonizers imposed similarly intrusive laws on Chinese indentured laborers in Cuba. These include a law from 1860 that required laborers to obtain permission from their employer before marrying, a legislation that bears troubling echoes of the 1842 slave codes (Yun 2008, 5). These examples indicate the significance that legislation around marriage played in colonial attempts to control the colonized populations and indoctrinate them with European values.

We can also see from these statements that colonial views on the role of marriage in the immigrant population were recorded extensively in official documents, letters, and commissions of inquiry. Yet, this is only one half of the story—missing are the laborers' responses to these issues. Even when immigrant advocates like James Crosby testified about the laborers' experiences, they filtered those experiences through an imperial lens. Nonfiction texts by laborers and their descendants help us understand the role that marriage played in conflicts between the colonizers and the colonized, and the impact of colonial legislation around marriage. Unfortunately, few laborers directly recorded their experiences, as those who are focused on survival have little spare energy to devote to documenting their experiences. Even rarer are first-person accounts of how the female laborers viewed migration and indenture. Women were less likely to be literate than men, and due to the expectation in Indian and Chinese culture that women remain in the private domain, less likely to give testimony in court. Lisa Yun notes with regret that of the nearly 3000 Chinese laborers who testified to their experience of Cuban indenture in 1874, none were female (Yun 2008, 62).

To help fill this gap, I explore the few direct accounts by Caribbean indentured laborers and their descendants. These include two written texts: *Autobiography of an Indian Indentured Labourer*, published in 1948 by Munshi Rahman Khan,[1] a rare firsthand description of Caribbean indenture by a well-educated Indian man who recorded his experiences in Suriname; and *Autobiography of Alice Bagwandy Sital Persaud*, the handwritten diary of the daughter of an indentured laborer. I also examine interviews with three female indentured laborers in the Caribbean, Maharani, Doolarie, and Achamma, and include excerpts from Lisa Yun's analysis of the testimonials of Chinese laborers in Cuba. These autobiographies and interviews offer critical counternarratives in a discourse that has generally been dominated by accounts from the colonizers.

The laborers' accounts of indenture reveal critical and underexplored aspects of colonial legislation. Firstly, the laws, meant to impose Victorian values, in many cases codified existing caste, class, and gender hierarchies

---

[1] The term "Munshi" is a sign of respect, translated as "teacher."

in the laboring population. The colonizers' emphasis on recruiting higher-class women strengthened the degrading view of working-class women as immoral and uncivilized, while the laws intended to promote monogamy reinforced the supremacy of the husband in the marriage, even in cases where the woman faced deadly violence. Secondly, these narratives demonstrate an imperial anxiety about single women in the colonies, as these women challenged the argument that colonialism civilized the colonized peoples and promoted marriage, monogamy, and family. For example, plantation policies aimed to pair a woman with a husband as rapidly as possible and keep her with him regardless of how happy she was.[2] Finally, we see women pushing against colonial anxiety and resisting stereotypes, making use of the systems of justice available to them and relying on other women for support.

Many postcolonial critics have pointed to the ways that British colonizers legislated the treatment of colonized women as a means of justifying imperialism and maintaining control in the struggle for power with colonized men. Varsha Chitnis and Danaya Wright write that in colonized India, the "tussle over legal and political power was fought on the backs of Indian women because it was the alleged degraded position of Indian women and the barbaric actions of Indian men that justified the colonial mission in the first place" (Chitnis and Wright 2007, 1318). An early example of this is Britain's 1861 abolition of sati, the practice in which a widow immolated herself on her husband's pyre. In "Can the Subaltern Speak?" feminist literary critic Gayatri Spivak explores how the abolition of sati translated the act of widow immolation into an example of the barbaric characteristics of Hindu society, while the Indian nativist response might be that the woman wanted to die. In both of these views of sati, Spivak notes, the woman's voice is lost. She argues that by abolishing the practice, the British continued to limit women's agency and that "if, in the contest of colonial production, the subaltern has no history and cannot speak, the subaltern as female is even more deeply in shadow" (Spivak 1999, 274).

There has been less critical attention to colonial laws regulating the Indian and Chinese diaspora. Marina Carter, one of the few historians to examine British legislation of indentured immigrants, argues that imperial laws in Mauritius, the first colony to employ Indian indentured labor on a large scale, created "a united front of men, employers, and officials, against

[2] See Marina Carter and Shaheeda Hosein for explorations of these themes.

the independent will of women, particularly those who wished to leave unhappy and restrictive relationships" (Carter 1994, 238). At various points in this chapter, I refer to legislation or events from Mauritius in order to indicate the scope of the legislative policies of British imperialism in the age of emancipation. Studying the laws imposed upon diasporic citizens, as well as the response to those laws, reveals that marriage, the publicly recognized institution of a private relationship, was a flashpoint for religious, ethnic, and class tensions in the colonies.

For example, in the Caribbean colonies, as in Mauritius, British, Indian, and Chinese citizens used the mistreatment of colonized women to support imperial or anti-imperial ambitions. One of the major justifications for British colonialism in India was that it would promote the sanctity of the family and that Indian women would be saved from barbaric practices such as child marriages and widow immolation. In fact, many of the laws passed under British colonialism had the opposite effect, forcing women to stay in unhappy, violent relationships. The interviews in particular demonstrate women's brutal experiences of indenture, challenging the argument that colonialism "saved" Indian women from lives of degradation. Similarly, Indian men often used the treatment of women as an argument against colonization, pointing to the overwork and sexual abuse of women. Yet Indian men also petitioned for (and often gained) laws that would protect their sovereignty over women. This suggests that for both the British and the Indians, attempts to legislate morality were often thinly veiled means of maintaining control of colonized women, and thus maintaining some level of power in the colonial/anti-colonial struggle.

In understanding the role that marriage and its legislation plays in the contestations between colonial officials and laborers, it is helpful to remember that these laws evolved directly out of the slave codes that preceded them. The Barbados Slave Code of 1661, one of the first sets of laws around slavery in the Caribbean colonies, infamously described its purpose: "To protect slaves as we do men's other goods and Chattels" (Barbados 1661), denying enslaved Africans and Amerindians their own humanity or the right to legal protection under English laws. Slaves generally lacked legal rights to form families and marry, although this varied from colony to colony. In Danish colonies, Christian slaves could marry with their owner's permission, and under a 1755 law married slaves could not be sold or parted, although this law was not enforced until the 1800s (Hall and Higman 1992, 61). Virginia Bernhard suggests that in the English colony of Bermuda, "masters recognized marriage as a binding, if not a legal institution" (Bernhard

1999, 42). *The History of Mary Prince*, an autobiographical account of slavery in Bermuda, offers a harsher view of the subject. Prince reports that when she married, her master furiously demanded of her husband, "who gave him a right to marry a slave of his?" (Prince 1997, 84), while her mistress whipped Mary for marrying. The violence of these responses indicate that Mary's masters felt threatened by any actions that indicated her sense of agency or her status as a human being with the right to and desire for companionship. This disdain for human rights seeped into the laws regarding indentured workers.

In most ways, indentured laborers had more rights than enslaved peoples. One of the most frequently cited differences between the two forms of labor is that under indenture families were, if at all possible, kept together. Yet the notion that Britain was bringing civilization to a barbaric people remained, and continued to impact policies and legislation around intimate relationships. In particular, Britain argued that they were rescuing colonized women from oppressive, barbaric practices. In 1817, James Mill praised the British governor-general of Bengal for enacting the abolition of sati when the Indian rulers were too timid to do so: he called sati "a barbarous superstition which had prevailed from antiquity…which, however repugnant to the feelings and creed of the rulers of the country, the tenure by which they held power rendered them for a long time averse and afraid to interfere" (Mill and Wilson 1858, 185). Family relationships, and in particular, control over women's sexuality, became contested ground between the colonizers, who sought to impose Victorian notions of propriety, and the colonized, who struggled to uphold their culture's norms around intimate relationships.

Background and Context

I begin my analysis with background information on the laborers whose narratives I explore. Munshi Rahman Khan, author of *Autobiography of an Indian Indentured Labourer* (Rahman Khan 2005), did not indenture because he needed the money—he came from a relatively wealthy family and had a job, as well as a family. He was well educated, and although he was Muslim, he was very familiar with Hindu teachings. In 1897, while traveling in Kanpur, he was approached by two *arkatis*,[3] who persuaded him to indenture by telling him stories of the flourishing plantation system in Suriname and flattering

[3] Recruiter.

him with praise for his high level of education. He labored on plantation Lust en Rust[4] for five years, where he was made a *sardar*[5] against his wishes. He describes various conflicts with the managers of the plantation over unfair labor practices, but seems to have had a positive relationship with Horst, the plantation owner. While still under indenture, Rahman Khan married again, and the birth of his first son kept him in Suriname after his contract ended. He and his family experienced poor health at various times, but he lived to the age of 96, dying in 1972. In photos, he appears as a slender man, serious but not grim. The portrait on the cover of the Dutch version of his book shows him sitting, dressed in white, with his five sons behind him. His hands are on his knees, and he looks straight at the camera, neither smiling nor frowning.

The autobiography, originally titled *Jivan Prakash*, or *Life's Light*, was completed in 1943 and is based on a day-to-day diary that he kept as a laborer. It is a mix of genres, including history, memoir, poetry, and political treatise. The first section begins with his family lineage, including the story of an ancestor who fought tigers with only a dagger, and a detailed account of his own education and teaching experience before being recruited. He thus testifies to his authority as a storyteller, placing his indenture narrative in the context of his status as a scholar. The second section details his life as a laborer and ends with the death of his close friend Subhan. In this section, he focuses primarily on his interactions with Subhan and his own rise to a position of authority, minimizing the field labor that he performed. The third section describes his life after indenture, while the final section details the conflicts that arose between Hindus and Muslims in the 1930s and his own role in trying to end the conflict. The autobiography seems intended to cement Rahman Khan's reputation as a literary figure in Suriname, while the poems in honor of the Dutch queen, Wilhelmina, align him with the educated elite of the colony.

Suriname, where Munshi Rahman Khan indentured, was primarily a Dutch colony, though at times it fell under British control. The Dutch system of indenture was similar to that of the British. After the emancipation of the enslaved population in Suriname in 1863, the government brought in workers from China, Java, Madeira, the Netherlands, and Barbados, but soon struck a deal with the British in which they exchanged old forts in West Africa, remnants of the slave trade, for the right to recruit Indian labor.

---

[4] Pleasure and Rest.
[5] A headman or driver.

This kind of imperial bargaining, in which forts, the machinery of war, were traded for the contracted labor of people, indicates the values that drove imperialism—military might, economic strength, and a disregard for human rights.

The first ship carrying Indian indentured laborers arrived in Suriname in 1873, followed by six more ships that year. Indentured labor in Suriname officially ended in 1916, but as late as 1931 laborers who had renewed their contract were still working under indenture. Today, as in Trinidad and Tobago, and Guyana, those of Indian descent make up the largest portion of the population—37%. As in the British colonies, the male to female ratio was approximately five to one, which led to the same issues of violence against women and the fraught negotiation of gender roles. For instance, indentured women in Suriname may have gained some level of freedom to earn wages and choose a mate, but were highly vulnerable to sexual and economic abuse. In fact, scholars such as Ruben Gowricharn argue that the Indian populations in Suriname and Guyana developed in very similar ways, which is not surprising given that they share a border (Gowricharn 2013).

To some extent, the autobiography follows the conventions of slave narratives like *The Interesting Narrative of the Life of Olaudah Equiano*, in which the author describes being kidnapped, traveling to a distant country, laboring for years, and eventually achieving freedom. However, in writing his autobiography, Rahman Khan does not seek to attack indenture or imperialism. He describes various injustices that he experienced, but does not fault the system as a whole. In fact, he had a positive relationship with the Dutch plantation owners and even served as a success story for indenture, a laborer who rose through the ranks and was able to buy his own land after his indenture period ended. His goal in writing seems to be primarily to memorialize the important moments of his life and to capture the experience of the Indians living in Suriname.

The tone of the book is by turns humble and boastful. Describing his interactions with others, he seems self-effacing: to a commissioner who says that he has heard Rahman Khan is well read, he replies "Sir, I cannot say so" (Rahman Khan 2005, 128), showing a deference to colonial authority. On the other hand, he has no compunctions about repeating praise that he received from others. Regarding the plantation owners who are considering hiring him as manager, he writes, "An enquiry had convinced them of my spotless character. I was a unique person, they thought" (Rahman Khan 2005, 141). Rahman Khan states that he wrote the book at the request of his son, but the fact that he sought out translators so that his book could be published in English indicates that he wanted as wide an audience for it as possible (Sinha-Kerkhoff and Bal 2005, 196).

The autobiography is an important book, offering a rare glimpse into the migrants' view of their lives as contract laborers, but critical response to it has been mixed. Presenting on the autobiography at a conference, Mohan Gautam stated that it offered insights into the assimilation of Indians in Suriname: "Knowledge for [Rahman Khan] was an ongoing process which combined the Indian past of his Indian roots and the unknown future of Suriname. Traditional continuity combined with a proper conscious integration was the only way to survive in an unknown surroundings" (Gautam 1995, 18). In a review of the translated book, R.L. Singal praises the text: "His narration presents a vivid picture of the social intercourse and ethnic relations that existed in a colonial society among the indentured labourers in Suriname. Both subject matter and style of his narration is quite stirring and gripping" (Singal 2005). By contrast, V.S. Naipaul, himself the descendant of Indian indentured laborers, calls the text "a primitive piece of book-making" (Naipaul 2007, 85). Naipaul concedes that "his narrative tools are suited to his vision…He deals in wonders: men who fight tigers, men who suffer from dreadful maladies and are then cured by wise healers" (Naipaul 2007, 86–87), but feels that there is an incompleteness and a lack of reflectiveness in Rahman Khan's descriptions (Naipaul 2007, 86).

The gender norms depicted in Rahman Khan's book are indicative of the low status given to women in Rahman Khan's society. The translators write in their introduction that "his world was clearly a man's world" (Sinha-Kerkhoff and Bal 2005, xxxi) and regret that the book "teaches us less to nothing about how Hindostani women experienced life on the plantations at the time" (Sinha-Kerkhoff and Bal 2005, xxxi–xxxii). We do, however, get a sense of the attitudes that some Indian men held toward women. Rahman Khan does not seem to see women as individuals, indicated by their interchangeable nature in his book. He does not name either his first wife in India or his second wife in Suriname, nor does he mention his daughters, though his autobiography is dedicated to his sons.

As there is little illumination of women's experiences of indenture in Rahman Khan's autobiography, and there are no published accounts from women who indentured in the Caribbean, I turn to a diary by a woman whose grandmother was an indentured laborer. Feminist critics have noted, "An extensive literary tradition of [women's writing] had existed for centuries, especially if one turned to supposedly 'marginal' genres—memoir, journal, diary, the many modes of private autobiographical writing" (Smith and Watson 1998, 6). Unlike Rahman Khan, Alice Bahadur Singh[6] wrote an autobiography that was not intended for publication.[7] Alice, born Alice Bhagwandie Sital Persaud, lived from 1892 to 1965, and wrote her autobiography in the last decade of her life. Sadly, it is incomplete—the text ends after she describes moving to England with her husband and children as a young woman, and does not detail her return to British Guiana or the active role she or husband took in the Indo-Guyanese community. Alice's diary was written for her family, reflecting the public/private gender division of traditional Indian culture, in which men were identified with the public sphere, and women with the domestic.

Further emphasizing this divide, the diary fits into a convention of women writers framing their experiences through their home even when they have led highly public lives. Alice begins her text with a domestic scene: "Today is Sunday the 27th of April, 1958…I am sitting in my chair in my room while the radio is playing pleasant music" (Singh 2011). Feminist historian Antoinette Burton notes: "The frequency with which women writers of different nations have made use of home to stage their dramas of remembrance is a sign of how influential the cult of domesticity and its material exigencies has been for inhabitants of structurally gendered locations like the patriarchal household" (Burton 2003, 6). Alice continues by articulating her position as a wife and mother and adopts an unassuming approach to her own experiences: "I am about to start to write about events of my life as far back as I can remember. I trust that my children and their children will at some time, when they have nothing better to do, read through the pages" (Singh 2011).

As can be seen in these examples, Alice's diary is very different in tone and subject matter from that of Rahman Khan. It focuses primarily on domestic matters—her parents, her siblings, her husband, and her children. She, like Rahman Khan, wrote the autobiography at the request of one of her children, Hardutt Singh. She writes, "For years now he has been reminding me to make a start" (Singh 2011). Her purpose seems to have been to share her life with her family, rather than with a wider audi-

---

[6] I refer to Alice Singh henceforth by her first name in order to distinguish her from her family members, who share her last name.

[7] Her handwritten diary is available at the University of Guyana library, and was typed up and published online by Sushila Patil and Moses Seenarine.

ence. She implies that her recollections will be of little interest to anyone other than her family, and that even they will only bother to read them "when they have nothing better to do."

The Indo-Caribbean women, including Alice herself, tend to remain invisible in this diary. Feminist critics Sidonie Smith and Julia Watson note that before publishing options were readily available to women writers, they described their lives in diaries and letters, and that even in these seemingly private accounts of their lives "their writing of daily selves reproduced gendered ideologies which they both trouble and reproduce" (Smith and Watson 2001, 98). Alice does describe her mother and grandmother in some detail, but she says little about her own public life, and when recounting her childhood, she describes her two brothers in depth but makes no mention of her sister. In this way, she seems to minimize the importance of her own contributions and those of her female peers to Indo-Guyanese society. If one were to read only her diary, one would suspect that her adult life consisted primarily of marrying and having children, when in reality she was very engaged in the community, founding several cultural and charity organizations.

While Alice was not a laborer herself, her life and her descriptions of the experiences of her parents and her grandmother, a feisty, outspoken woman, offer a valuable counterpoint to those of Rahman Khan. Alice's grandmother, Phularjee, was originally from Bengal, India, the daughter of a Brahmin priest and the widow of a wealthy landowner, and so she, like Rahman Khan, was not representative of the average indentured laborer. Alice indicates that "her in-laws were just farmers, but they had plenty of land" (Singh 2011). According to family lore, several members of the family, including Phularjee (Alice's grandmother) and Sital (Alice's father), were traveling together on a pilgrimage when Phularjee, her son, and two others got separated from the rest of the family in a large crowd. After they had been stranded for days, a recruiter promised to help her find her relatives but instead signed her up for indenture on a ship bound for Suriname (Bahadur 2014, 38).

Describing Phularjee, Alice emphasizes the European qualities of her appearance: "She was a small woman, light red brown complexion, with a straight nose…On the whole, she was a very pretty woman" (Singh 2011). Phularjee was widowed at a young age, and appears to have been quite strong-willed, even difficult. Alice writes, "When I knew Mai she was not young, but even in those days she was very haughty, so I can well imagine what she must have been in her younger days" (Singh 2011).

This description also offers an interesting counterview to depictions of indentured women as subservient wives or immoral prostitutes. Alice's husband, Jung Bahadur Singh, was closely connected to the system of indenture, as well. The son of indentured immigrants from India, he also served as a compounder, or ship's doctor on immigrant voyages. They had seven children, and one of their daughters, Rajkumari Singh, became one of the first published female Indo-Guyanese authors, and her poetry is treated in Chap. 5. In photos, Alice is round-faced and smiling slightly, her hair pulled back from her face in a bun, her eyes soft and clear. Her grandson describes her wearing the traditional peasant dress of East Indian immigrants, from the Central Province of British India, not a sari but skirt and blouse and veil with silver jewelry (Singh n.d.).

Alice and her husband were prominent members of the Indo-Caribbean community of Guyana. Alice founded the British Guiana Dramatic Society, which produced plays from Indian culture, and she was very active in social welfare projects, such as the Red Cross and the YWCA. Karna Bahadur Singh, Alice's grandson, writes:

> Alice Bhagwandai was of cosmopolitan background from education and experience. Convent educated, open to the varied influences of her mother and father, a gifted linguist…she exerted a strong influence on her husband with her more sophisticated background. She also worked with her father in the Immigration Office, Paramaribo for some time and her developed social consciousness and experience in East Indian affairs was useful when she and her husband began similar work in British Guiana. She was an early type of the East Indian emancipated woman. (Singh n.d.)

This affectionate description suggests that Alice was one of the Indo-Caribbean women who helped shift views on gender roles, taking an active part not only in her community, but also in her marriage. Thanks in large part to an increased access to education, in the early twentieth century, Indo-Caribbean women like Alice began taking on more public roles and shifting views of a woman's place in society.

As noted, Rahman Khan and Phularjee, who were well educated and came from wealth, were atypical of the majority of laborers, most of whom were poor. Unfortunately, because most laborers lacked education, they were unlikely to record their experiences, and so we know little about their lives from their perspective. There are exceptions, such as testimonials and letters written to commissions of inquiry, but these tended to be given by males. This makes interviews a useful counterpoint to understanding women's experience of indenture. This chapter includes analysis of interviews given by three formerly indentured female laborers in the Caribbean, Maharani, Doolarie, and Achamma. Finally, I include excerpts from Lisa Yun's comprehensive exploration of written and oral testimonies given by Chinese laborers in Cuba in 1874 to a commission tasked with investigating the conditions of "coolie" labor in Cuba. As noted, the perspectives offered by these speakers is somewhat one-sided as they were all men, but their testimonials offer important insights into the Chinese experience. By nature, interviews and testimonials are briefer than autobiographies, and so these narratives contain less information than the texts by Rahman Khan and Alice Singh. In addition, the answers are shaped by the questioner and, in some cases, by the interpreter, as many of the interviews and testimonials are in languages other than English. As a result, the content is filtered somewhat through these other speakers.

At the same time, the act of writing is in itself an interpretation, and Rahman Khan and Alice Singh would have shaped their narratives according to their intended audience. By contrast, the interviews, and, to a lesser extent, the oral and written testimonies, would have come out more or less spontaneously. Maharani, Doolarie, and Achamma's responses are often blunt, referencing violence and degradation that is only alluded to by Rahman Khan and Alice. The Chinese laborers certainly had a more targeted purpose than the three interviewees in sharing their stories, as they sought to broadcast the extent of their suffering and seek redress. Yet their narratives also have a degree of spontaneity, spoken or written as they were with little time for preparation.

Maharani is one of five Indian migrants that Noor Kumar Mahabir interviewed about their experiences indenturing in Trinidad and Tobago. Without changing the wording, he shaped the testimonies into poetry form in the book *The Still Cry*, published in 1985. Mahabir transcribed the interviews phonetically, capturing the rhythms and syntax of the speakers' Creole. For instance, when Maharani describes her departure from the depot in India, it is recorded as follows:

> when e coming ship
>   everybody gone inside
>   an dem people watching an telling me not to go. (Maharani 1985, 80)

Kumar thus validates the Creole language as a dialect rather than a "pidgin" form of English. Maharani also shares her experiences in an unpublished interview with Patricia Mohammed from 1990.

Born a Brahmin, Maharani was 5 when she married, and widowed at 12. Shortly after, her brother-in-law took her to a magistrate's office to turn over her inheritance to him (Bahadur 2014, 48). After cooking and cleaning for her in-laws for years and suffering many beatings, she finally decided to run away. At a well, she met a recruiter with one foot who offered her a job sifting sugar, and she accepted. This was a common tactic, deceiving potential migrants about the nature of their work. When Maharani arrived in Trinidad, she was set to challenging tasks such as cutting cane and weeding fields. As a Brahmin widow, she would have been of a higher caste than the average laborer, but she did not have the extensive education that Rahman Khan did, and, as a young girl, she did not have the familial support or the confidence that Phularjee had. The backbreaking labor that she performed as a result was probably more typical of the laborers' experience.

Doolarie, who was also interviewed by Noor Kumar Mahabir, traveled to Trinidad out of economic necessity.[8] Doolarie's Certificate of Exemption from Labour, the only surviving documentation of her life, tells us little about her life experience or her family, only that she had a scar on her right knee. In a sense, then, this scar, perhaps acquired while laboring on the plantations, is all that remains of Doolarie in the archives of indenture. We do know that Doolarie began her indenture in 1913 and was 109 when she was interviewed in 1982,[9] meaning she would have been thirty years old when she indentured. She indentured with her father because there were no jobs for them in India, but he died on the journey, leaving her to fend for herself. Doolarie, unlike many of the laborers described here, seems to have been of low caste, and she describes the hand-to-mouth existence that she experienced before, during, and after indenture.

Like Maharani, Achamma ran away from her family, including her husband, and indentured alone. This would have been a dangerous choice, as the Indian Emigration Act of 1883 stated that no married woman could migrate without her husband's permission. The law was intended to stop women from running away from their husbands and posing as widows or

---

[8] The interview transcript and the Certificate of Exemption are held by the University of the West Indies, St. Augustine. The Certificate of Exemption reports that she served her term at Plantation Brician Castle (most likely a misspelling of Brechin Castle) and that her name was Doolarie, of Brickfield Road, Central Trinidad.

[9] The interview is listed as taking place on September 18, 1992. However, as many other interviews in the series took place on September 18, 1982, it is likely that this is a typographic error, and this interview also took place in 1982.

single women, and to appease Indian men by upholding their sovereignty over their wives. Yet Achamma managed to escape her husband in spite of this law, and she, like so many others, was drawn in by a recruiter's promise of quick wealth and an easy return to India.

The stories of Chinese indenture are drawn from Lisa Yun's examination of oral and written testimonies given by 2841 migrants who worked alongside enslaved Africans on Cuban plantations. These testimonials were given to a three-member commission tasked with investigating the conditions of the Chinese laborers in Cuba. Li Chengxun and Ren Shizen, the two laborers quoted here, both indentured in 1874, were well educated, and tell distressingly similar stories of deception, abuse, and inhumane working conditions. Li was born into a poor family and became a teacher at age 18, but after returning home for the funeral of his father, lost his position. A recruiter convinced him to indenture, saying that he would be working as a private tutor for a wealthy family in Macao. When Li learned of his true destination, he resisted, but was forced at knifepoint to continue his journey. Ren, a feng shui expert, was also given false promises by the recruiter, and once on the plantation, he was whipped, held in shackles, and given insufficient food. He recorded his testimonial with the hope that one person would return to China with his message: "Don't be deceived into coming here" (Yun 2008, 98).

Codifying Existing Hierarchies

As the stated goal of imperialism was to spread the benefits of civilization to savage races, British imperialists sought to craft legislation that would encourage monogamous relations, protect colonized women, promote Christianity, and otherwise spread Victorian values. Laws such as the Age of Consent Act, which made sexual intercourse illegal for any girl under the age of 12, and the Heathen Marriage Ordinance, which implemented onerous procedures for non-Christian marriages, demonstrate the ways that colonial administrators attempted to impose Victorian notions of family relationships while also granting Indian men some measure of control over Indian women. Admittedly, some of these laws have commendable goals, such as preventing the sexual abuse of minors, but they often had unintended consequences. This section analyzes nonfiction indenture narratives to explore the ways that legislation around marriage tended to concretize existing prejudices around gender, class, and religion in the laboring population. I also note the ways that such legislation tended to increase rather than decrease the violence against colonized women.

As a Muslim, Rahman Khan did not belong to a caste, but his education and his relative wealth certainly placed him into a higher class than most of the laborers, a position that was preserved by his treatment on the plantation. As a result of his literacy and societal status, he rapidly moved from field laborer to overseer, indicating that higher-class laborers were granted some protections by planters and easier access to higher paying positions. Walter Rodney notes that once laborers had completed their indenture period, a much higher proportion of high-caste migrants were able to purchase land than those of low caste, indicating that Rahman Khan's experiences were not unique (Rodney 1981, 112). Rahman Khan himself expressed a sense of caste and class consciousness, describing his dismay at the Brahmins who threw away their signifiers of caste at the depot in Calcutta (Rahman Khan 2005, 80). Some of this was certainly due to his respect for Hindu religion, but he may have also felt that an erasure of caste was a threat to his own status as an educated man.

The benefits afforded to educated Indian men did not seem to extend to similarly educated Chinese men laboring in Cuba. Li Chengxun, who had been a teacher in China, testifies, "Since I arrived at the island of Cuba/I have been the same as slaves. The work is extremely heavy/Oxen and dogs are ten times better off than I am" (Yun 2008, 103). Li was not wealthy—he reports growing up in poverty and indenturing due to economic hardship. He was certainly literate, though, but neither this nor his status as a teacher seems to have saved him from much sorrow. Similarly, Ren Shizen, whose testimonial includes literary allusions that indicate a high level of education, reports: "There are shackles on my feet and chains around my neck…When I am alive, I work like an ox and a horse; when I am dead, I am worthless like crickets and ants" (Yun 2008, 97). It seems that, under the slave-like conditions of Cuban indenture, educated men were not given any special dispensation and may even have been considered a threat to be neutralized with chains and harsh treatment.

While British and Indian officials clashed on many subjects, in some areas their goals were in harmony, such as their mutual desire for the perpetuation of patriarchal control. Some colonial laws regarding marriage were designed to appease Indian men by upholding their sovereignty over their wives. Shaheeda Hosein argues, "Largely seen as a threat, [the Indian woman's] sexuality had to be controlled; and both the Indian male and the colonial authorities viewed marriage as the vehicle through which this could be done" (Hosein 2004, 201). The 1883 Indian Emigration Act stated that no married woman could migrate without her husband's permission, which was intended to stop women from running away from their husbands and posing as widows or single women. Section 32 also gave the depot official the authority to determine whether or not she was married: "The Registering Officer or Protector may also, in the case of any woman whom he believes to be married, refuse to decide whether he will register her until after the expiration of such time, not exceeding ten days, as he thinks fit" (India 1898). Even the suspicion that a woman was married gave the official the right to detain her in the depot and possibly refuse her emigration. Thus, a woman's ability to emigrate was dependent on the consent of an Indian man (her husband) or a British man (the depot official). Robert Mitchell, the colonial administrator responsible for gathering immigrants for British Guiana, strenuously objected to these rules on the grounds that they prevented working-class women from escaping terrible situations: "The fact is that the unfortunate women of the peasant class in this country are hardly removed from ordinary beasts of burden" (quoted in Bahadur 2014, 27).

Though she was not a member of the peasant class, Maharani's story indicates the level of familial and societal oppression that many women attempted to escape by migrating. Living with the family of her deceased husband, she had no wealth, little status, and few options. Running away, in spite of the laws against such behavior, seemed to be her only way to escape the endless beatings:

> i say dem go beat me
> well i run
> i no tell nobody i leaving
> only me modder-in-law. (Maharani 1985, 79)

Contrasting the stereotype of the Indian mother-in-law as cruel and controlling, Maharani's mother-in-law seems to be the only person she trusted. The legislation and rhetoric around indentured women suggests that Maharani's story of running away from an abusive relationship is a typical one. Achamma emphasizes over and over again that she indentured alone, which indicates the boldness of this move: "I came alone, I left my husband behind… left my parents…My husband didn't know that I was leaving India. I ran away" (Achamma). She does not offer a reason for running away, but the repetition of the family members she ran away from hints at an unhappy home situation.

Not all of the migrants fled from abusive families, though. Doolarie reports coming to Trinidad with her family, because they had no way of supporting themselves. In the interview, she says of her family, "Everybody came Trinidad…and my father died," later clarifying that he died on the voyage from India to Trinidad. Doolarie also indicates that her reasons for migrating were primarily out of economic need: "I didn't have anybody to stay with…In India it didn't have any food" (Doolarie 1982). Though many women certainly migrated to escape a marriage, the persistence of this image in rhetoric around indenture indicates that the runaway wife was a useful symbol for both imperialists and anti-colonialists. The British could claim that they were offering women an escape from their brutal marriages, while Indian men decried the erosion of the sanctity of their home.

Unsurprisingly, no law existed to prevent husbands from running away from their wives. Rahman Khan, like Maharani, entered an arranged marriage when he was young, though he was 18 years old as opposed to 5. When he was 17, Rahman Khan reports, he ran away and attempted to start a new life in the city of Charkhari. After he was forced to return home, his father "decided to chain me. He hoped that my marriage would prevent me from leaving home to seek greener pastures in the future" (Rahman Khan 2005, 46). His father's attempts to "chain" him with marriage failed, and Rahman Khan ran away again, this time emigrating to Suriname. Though he describes being deceived by the recruiters, it is clear that he was partially willing—he wrote a letter to his father from the depot but did not say where he was, afraid that his father would come and take him back.

Upon arriving in Suriname, Rahman Khan was frustrated to learn that there were rooms with provisions for a married couple. "Had I known about such a possibility, I would have brought with me a beautiful young *brahmin* or *kshtriya* girl from Kanpur of my own choice" (Rahman Khan 2005, 91). He does not seem to have considered bringing his own wife. Mohan Gautam reports from correspondence that when Rahman Khan told his father of his second marriage, "all sorts of questions were asked and he was also told that his first wife is still waiting for him in India" (Gautam 1995, 12). Women like Rahman Khan's wife, whose husbands left them to indenture, most likely suffered more economically than men whose wives left them, as women were generally dependent on their husbands for subsistence. Yet there was no legislation in place to prevent such migration, indicating the measure of control that Indian men had over choices in their own life, a control that many women did not share.

It is also important to note how the intertwining of colonial views on gender and class shaped policy, and how that intertwining supported traditional Indian views on gender and class. The women who were willing to indenture were generally of low caste and independent, often having run away from unhappy marriages. Yet, colonial authorities judged these women unfit to emigrate, considering them "immoral" or "indecent," and labeling them prostitutes. On this topic, in 1915 the Emigration Agent wrote:

> In considering this matter it must be borne in mind that genuine field labourers such as the planters require can be obtained only from the lower castes, i.e. from among the non-moral class of population. A more moral type is found higher in the social scale but such women would be useless in the fields. (Quoted in Reddock 1994, 30)

The agent promotes the view that lower-caste, laboring women were, by their very nature, less morally developed than women of higher caste. Doolarie adds that colonial officials denigrated behavior in Indian women that they connected to prostitution, stating, "In India if you sang or danced they called you bad people" (Doolarie 1982). This most likely refers to the fact that in India courtesans were often trained as entertainers, to sing and dance, and were given some degree of respect, but British colonizers attempted to impose puritanical Victorian values and decried all forms of prostitution as sinful and immoral.

Colonizers also blamed the low class of the indentured women for the conflicts between men and even the violence the women themselves experienced. A missionary in British Guiana wrote, "The great majority of women imported from Calcutta are very loose in their habits. They were bad in Calcutta and so they will…remain in Demerara" (quoted in Bahadur 2014, 118).[10] In an attempt to recruit a "better class" of women, the colonial authorities of Mauritius instituted a bounty system, under which men received a reward for bringing their wife with them

---

[10] The quota system, in which ships were required to include a certain proportion of women to men before they could sail from India to the colonies, was impacted by this debate. The government of India tried to set the ratio at 1:2, but emigration officials argued that this would only worsen the problem by bringing in more immoral women, and so the ration shifted from 1:3 in 1857 to 1:2 in 1868, then 1:4 in 1878–1879 (Reddock 1994, 28–29).

when they indentured. It is striking that the women did not receive the bounty themselves, a policy that led to many men bringing several "wives" with them to Mauritius and then selling or transferring them to other men shortly after arrival (Carter 1994, 69). In these cases, the system not only failed to bring more married women to the colony, it encouraged the treatment of women, particularly low-class women, as property to be bought and sold.

This poor treatment continued throughout the indenture period: Doolarie, who was lower class, and Maharani, who, as a young widow, would have had a similar status as a low-class woman, had a significantly more brutal experience of indenture than Rahman Khan and Phularjee. Doolarie describes the degradation of the laborers after they arrived in Port of Spain: "They brought [us] up in truck like bags...flour bag" (Doolarie 1982). Maharani reports being given work that was too difficult for her:

> ...i cyan wuk
> i cyan weed
> i cyan do nutting
> i crying
> but still i try. (Maharani 1985, 83)

Similarly, Achamma depicts her work as "Really hard. I used to wield a cutlass. I did tasks. I used to cut cane. I used to wash the paddy. Finish wash. All of that" (Achamma). Though women were supposedly given lighter work such as weeding, Maharani and Achamma describe endless hard labor such as cutting cane: "what wuk estate tell e to do/have to do" (Maharani 1985, 83).

The experiences of Phularjee, Alice's grandmother, suggest that higher-class women—the women that colonial officials hoped would indenture—had an easier indentureship. Phularjee felt entitled to complain about conditions on the ship, and she was shocked by the small quarters that were assigned to her and her son upon arrival. When asked to perform field labor, she refused: "When she was told to go and work in the fields and was handed a cutlass, she showed her soft small hands. She there and then sat down and refused to move" (Singh 2011). Luckily for her, her employers responded indulgently: "Because she was young, pretty and a fighter, the Barnett Lyon family were very lenient with her. She was made an assistant nurse in the estate's hospital" (Singh 2011). It is difficult to imagine the same circumstances occurring for someone of low caste.[11] Like Rahman Khan, she was given a leadership role, perhaps because of her high-caste status: "She was made responsible for all the unmarried women. Knowing Mai as I did, those women must have had a hard time!" (Singh 2011). Thus the caste differences of these women did not disappear after crossing the *kala pani*, but were in fact reinforced by colonial officials.

Similar patterns emerge in the observations of Rahman Khan. The majority of the women in Rahman Khan's book are either invisible, like his two wives, or burdensome troublemakers, like the woman who attaches herself to him upon arrival in Suriname. The few women for whom he expresses admiration suggest that he accepted colonial views of racial hierarchy and Hindu views of caste, as these women are primarily European and exclusively wealthy. For instance, he describes Mrs. Horst, the wife of the plantation owner Dolf Horst, as "a real Dutch lady…very considerate" (Rahman Khan 2005, 135), and he even goes so far as to name his daughter after her. This veneration is even more remarkable in his honorary poem to Queen Wilhelmina of the Netherlands, whom he calls "Maharani Queen Wilhelmina Sahab Bahadur"[12] (Rahman Khan 2005, 237). In a poem at the end of the book, he admires her intelligence and her generosity: "You are most loveable, caring and god loving/…We Hindostanis look upon you for your kindness and blessings" (Rahman Khan 2005, 237). The effusiveness of his descriptions places him as a loyal colonial subject, acknowledging the superiority of the noble white woman.[13]

By contrast, Rahman Khan shows little regard for non-European woman, especially those of low caste. He describes in detail the Creole mistress of the American man who owns the plantation after the Horsts,

---

[11] Gaiutra Bahadur similarly reports that her great-grandmother was given the job of minding the children because of her beauty and "'because her feet were soft'" (Bahadur 2014, 148).

[12] He mixes Western and Hindi terms of admiration: "Queen," as well as "Maharani," meaning princess, "Bahadur," a title conferred on Indians by the British to indicate respect, and "Sahab," perhaps a feminized form of the respectful term "sahib."

[13] Rosemarijn Hoefte notes that in spite of economic instability and political unrest in Suriname in the early twentieth century, the monarchy was much beloved—the king was given direct credit for positive developments, such as the end of slavery, whereas it was assumed that the only reason he had not interceded to end other abuses was because he did not know about them. All groups in Suriname, including the Creole population and those of Indian descent, saw the queen as "a protective mediator…the one person who transcended ethnic, class, and gender differences" (Hoefte 2014, 89).

and he blames the failure of the plantation on her spendthrift ways. Rahman Khan notes, "I have seen many big landlords falling prey to such acts of the fairer sex, rather the darker in this case" (Rahman Khan 2005, 186). This cutting comment suggests that Rahman Khan objects to the woman's race more than to her status as a mistress. Rahman Khan also recounts the fable-like tale of his close friend Subhan and Subhan's wife in India. Subhan was rewarded for his devotion to Islam by discovering a coin on the floor of the mosque on each of his visits there. He was warned in a dream not to disclose where he obtained these coins, but his wife pestered him until he told her the source of his income, after which the coins ceased to appear. Although the woman's concerns about supporting their family seem reasonable, she is depicted as a nag and a burden, a test of Subhan's faith and resolve.

Education was one of the major ways that colonized citizens, particularly women, were able to escape poverty and overcome caste and class barriers, yet it was a contentious issue. In the 1940s and 1950s, more and more girls' schools opened in Guyana, Trinidad, and Suriname, yet many families felt that educating girls ruined them for marriage. Interestingly, both Alice's father and grandmother objected to Alice attending school, and she reports that "Ma had to actually smuggle me out by a kind neighbor to the Louise convent in Gravenstaat" (Singh 2011). Alice does not explain exactly why her father and grandmother objected, but they seemed to believe it would prevent her from becoming the ideal Indian woman, modest and obedient:

> When my poor Pa heard that I had my first day at school, he was left with his mouth open. But when Mai heard, she did behave badly and she 'knew' this was a very bad beginning for me. And my poor Ma had a very bad time of it, but as I was her child, Mai could not dictate. (Singh 2011)

It is worth noting that both her grandmother and her father came from India, whereas her mother grew up in Suriname, which may suggest that gender roles had shifted within the Caribbean.

There were certainly some areas, such as religion, where colonial authorities did not so much codify existing hierarchies within the indentured population as seek to impose hierarchies from their own belief system. Under the Heathen Marriage Ordinance 10 of 1860, Christian marriages in British Guiana were automatically registered, but "heathen immigrants" had to endure a lengthy and costly process in order to obtain a marriage certificate.[14] Although this certificate was necessary for other legislative tasks such as bequeathing property to one's spouse or children, the process of acquiring one was so onerous that fewer than 100 couples a year bothered with the procedure (Bahadur 2014, 120). The practical result was that Christian immigrants in officially sanctioned relationships were rewarded with rights that were nearly inaccessible to other immigrants. This created significant logistical problems for the laborers, though. Partners could not inherit their spouse's money or land, and the children of such unions were considered illegitimate and also could not inherit, or even attend secondary school.[15] Additionally, this law, like the quota system, led to unintended and sometimes disastrous consequences. Some families sold girls into one unofficial marriage after another in order to get several bride prices. In the case of a woman named Goirapa, who was married to Yadakana in a traditional Indian wedding, this led to a fatal result. Yadakana began to suspect that her family was going to sell Goirapa again, and, realizing that he had no legal recourse to stop them, he killed her (Mangru 2005, 226).[16]

The descriptions of weddings within the nonfiction narratives convey the negotiations that Indo-Caribbean citizens made to accommodate colonial law and religious frictions. For example, Alice had three wedding ceremonies, demonstrating the different forces that she had to balance between: "I had my civil marriage, so this complied with law of the land, [and] my church blessing for Ma. But the real thing was in the evening my hindu marriage. This was a brilliant affair" (Singh 2011). Similarly, the courtship of Sital and Mary, Alice's parents, highlights the tensions that fractured the Indo-Caribbean community. These included religious conflicts, but also conflicts between those who wished to adopt the culture of the colonizers and those who wished to maintain traditional Indian values

---

[14] Couples were required to sign a declaration stating that no impediment existed, publish notice of the intended marriage, wait three weeks to ensure that there were no objections, obtain a certification from the District Magistrate, and then take that certificate to the Immigration Agent in Georgetown, who issued a marriage registration certificate for $2.

[15] The law also seems to have had little effect on the immigrants' views of marriage. In 1883, H.V.P. Bronkhurst, a Christian missionary wrote of the Ordinance, "The marriage ceremony gone through by them is a perfect farce...at least, the coolies have repeatedly told me so" (Bronkhurst 1883, 337).

[16] As in the British colonies, Dutch authorities in Suriname did not officially recognize Muslim and Hindu marriages, and over 90% of Indian children were considered illegitimate (Hoefte 2014, 65).

and culture. Both Sital and Mary's parents were against the marriage, because Sital was from a Hindu family who valued Indian culture and had traveled to Suriname under indenture, while Mary came from a wealthy Christian family that had integrated into colonial society. Religious and class tensions certainly existed in India before colonization, but colonial policies that legislated intimate aspects of the lives of the colonized citizens seem to have heightened these tensions.[17] In theory, marriage was a private, personal act, the joining together of two people amidst friends and families, but these examples demonstrate that marriages and weddings acted as a catalyst for simmering tensions.

COLONIAL ANXIETY

There was no official legislation forcing laborers into partnerships, but Rahman Khan's autobiography and the interviews with Maharani and Doolarie indicate that single women caused colonial officials deep discomfort. They blamed these women for creating conflicts between male laborers, and argued that women would be physically safer and more economically stable with the protection of a husband. Underlying these concerns is the fact that single women eroded the argument that imperialism protected colonized women, in part by promoting monogamous relationships. Colonial officials may have believed that they acted in the best interest of colonized women, as this is certainly a more pleasant rationalization for imperialism than a desire for wealth and domination. Yet their anxiety in this regard suggests that there were cracks in their own acceptance of this justification.

Single women, or women in multiple partnerships, made convenient scapegoats for the domestic violence that plagued the indenture system. In Trinidad, between 1872 and 1900, 87 murders of Indian women were reported, 65 of which resulted from suspected infidelity (Mohammed 2002, 45). In British Guiana, between 1859 and 1907, 87 Indian women were killed by a spouse or partner (Mangru 2005, 217). The rate of murder of women was six to seven times higher in British Guiana than in India (Hoefte 1987, 64). Colonial officials tried to blame this violence on the

---

[17] Rahman Khan's autobiography also describes religious conflicts flaring up around marriages, and weddings in particular. For example, a ten-year conflict between Hindus and Muslims in Suriname was sparked at the wedding of Rahman Khan's youngest daughter when a Muslim imam began arguing with a Hindu man.

gender disparity, on the low quality and promiscuity of the women who were migrating, or on the innate barbaric, violent tendencies of Indian men. However, Joseph Beaumont points out that violent crime was virtually nonexistent in the free, unindentured Indians of British Guiana (quoted in Faruqee 1996, 69). This violence was most likely a response to the brutal oppression that the male laborers faced, as well as a sense that far from home, their honor and ethnicity was vested in these women.[18]

The female interviewees certainly faced distressing levels of domestic violence. Maharani's husband, Ramgolam, beat her repeatedly and even killed her *jahajin*, or shipmate, out of jealousy. Doolarie reports, "The husband bad. They beat me" (Doolarie 1982), and explains that he hit her in the head with a hoe for talking to another man. Bharath, a formerly indentured male laborer who was also interviewed by Noor Kumar Mahabir, confirms the view that it was right and just for men to beat their wives: "If oman do wrong/must beat e" (Bharath 1985, 128). These examples demonstrate the pervasiveness of such violence, as well as the cultural acceptance of it.

Yet, in order to demonstrate that they were in fact bringing civilization to Indians, the European colonizers needed to prevent these attacks. Ordinance 10, passed in 1860, was intended to curtail the high rate of "wife murder," in which a man attacked or killed his wife for suspected involvement with another man. It attempted to deal with the problem by minimizing adultery, calling for a $24 fine or three months in jail the first time a man seduced another man's wife, and a $100 fine or one year in jail for each offense after. In addition to ignoring the more pressing problem of the pervasive acceptance of domestic violence, the ordinance was limited, as it applied only to officially sanctioned, Christian weddings, and, as noted, few immigrants bothered with these ceremonies. Unsurprisingly, this ordinance did little to prevent "wife murder."

Indian men sometimes reversed the British justification for imperialism, arguing (accurately) that colonialism and indenture led to the abuse of colonized women by British men. Yet in doing so, they often relied on the gender norms that a woman's role is to maintain her virtue for her husband, and a man's role is to protect women. In his passionate anti-indenture tract, *My Twenty-One Years in the Fiji Islands*, Totaram Sanadhya repeatedly offers the mistreatment of female laborers as a reason for ending the system. He tells the story of Kunti, a married woman who

---

[18] See Patricia Mohammed, *Gender Negotiations Among Indians in Trinidad: 1917–1947*.

jumped into a river and almost drowned in order to escape being sexually assaulted by an overseer. He writes, "With great difficulty, Kunti was able to protect her virtue for four years" (Sanadhya 1991, 44–45), and the book's editors note, "This 'virtue' is her sativa, the total devotion of a wife to her husband" (Kelly and Singh 1991, 43). Kunti's story became a rallying cry against indenture, indicating that one of the most effective critiques of the system was that it was a threat to a woman's devotion to her husband.[19] Similar arguments were made by Indian men in the Caribbean. In one of his many letters to colonial officials and the Indian government, Mohammed Ofry argued that Indian women were being "enticed, seduced, and frightened into becoming concubines, and paramours to satisfy the greed and lust of the male section of quite a different race to theirs. They have absolutely no knowledge whatever of the value of being in virginhood and become most shameless" (quoted in Reddock 1994, 44). These arguments indicate the extent to which clashes between different ethnic groups played out in control of women's sexuality.

As there were few Chinese women who migrated to the Caribbean, they play a less significant role in the anti-indenture testimonials given by Chinese laborers, but those testifying did reference women still living in China to emphasize the cruelty of indenture. After describing how he was tricked into bonded labor, Ren Shizen mourns, "Who will take care of my wife and children? Who will care whether they have enough food or clothes?" (Yun 2008, 96–97). His appeal echoes that of Sanadhya, as both allude to a man's duty to protect vulnerable women. Additionally, historian Juan Jiménez Pastrana documents Cuban newspapers that advertised the sale of Chinese girls, demonstrating that female Chinese migrants were not only present in Cuba; they were publicly trafficked (quoted in Yun 2008, 63).

Another argument that British officials gave for the promotion of marriage was that it offered women economic stability. It is certainly true that female laborers were often forced to seek a mate out of economic necessity, but scholars argue that colonial officials deliberately created this exigence. Rosemarijn Hoefte indicates that in Suriname, women earned half to two-thirds what men received, and that this was justified "by assuming

---

[19] Sanadhya also indicates that the treatment of these women brings shame to India in the eyes of other men, suggesting that Indian men are not truly men unless they protect the virtue of their women and punish those who seek to damage that virtue (Sanadhya 1991, 61–62).

that a woman was dependent on her husband, who was the main breadwinner" (Hoefte 1987, 59–60). Rhoda Reddock notes that even when women in Trinidad performed heavy, "men's tasks" like loading sugarcane onto carts or trucks, they were paid the same as other women (Reddock 1994, 37). Marina Carter even suggests that in Mauritius, planters deliberately kept women on lower wages so that the women were dependent on their employers and the indentured males (Carter 1994, 121).

Even when women attempted to remain self-sufficient, they were often forced into partnerships against their will. Maharani, possibly influenced by her first oppressive marriage, maintained an independent spirit, resisting the manager's attempts to marry her off. He argues:

> maharani you want de man
> ...
> when you fall sick an ting
> you have nobody
> you have to take somebody. (Maharani 1985, 84)

But she replies: "i no want nobody/...i stop alone" (Maharani 1985, 84), stating that she doesn't need anyone to take care of her. She wants to return to India, and if she marries, she will have to stay in Trinidad. Although she tells Ramgolam, her proposed husband, "me nuh like you" (Maharani 1985, 85), she finds herself partnered with him against her consent. She accuses him of drugging her, saying of the experience, "me eh know what happen/an e take me" (Maharani 1985, 85). In these ominous lines, the manager and Ramgolam conspired to force her into a partnership that she does not want. In the interview with Patricia Mohammed, however, Maharani's description has a different tone, pointing to the delicate task of extrapolating meaning from oral narratives. She reports, "Me not like him, but he, he put something in the food. I ate the food, then I start to like him." She laughs as she says this, and Mohammed laughs with her, suggesting a lighter version of the events than we see in the interview with Mahabir.

Regardless of the tone with which she describes her initial interactions with Ramgolam, it is clear that Maharani was pushed into a relationship that she did not want. Ramgolam was violent and controlling, and slept with other men's wives, yet she stayed with him and bore him nine children, highlighting the limited options for women of the working class. Doolarie, like Maharani, seems to have had little choice in her partnership, and suffered an equally violent experience of marriage. When asked whether her husband ever beat her, she initially evades the question, answering with resignation, "Husband and wife must marry" (Doolarie 1982). Achamma also remarried in Trinidad and had several children, although she does not express whether she did so as a result of her own desires or societal expectations.

The pressure to pair single woman meant that men, too, were sometimes unwilling partners, as in the case of Rahman Khan. He managed to escape the "chain" of his first marriage when he left India under indenture, but was shackled by another woman soon after his arrival in Suriname. When he arrived on the plantation with four other men and one woman, the manager assumed that the woman was married and asked who her husband was. In response, "she alleged that I was her husband. (Maybe she found me more youthful and handsome than the others)" (Rahman Khan 2005, 91). Gaiutra Bahadur writes of this moment:

> This much is clear: briefly, she had her pick of men, trading up to an educated man who regarded himself as high caste. This much is also clear and equally significant: she didn't think she could support herself and her possibly imaginary child, although indentured women worked and earned wages in every colony that imported them, except Mauritius. (Bahadur 2014, 86)

Despite Rahman Khan's protestations, the manager threatened to punish him if he did not live with the woman, indicating the colonizers' desire to have single women accounted for.

This circumstance was not unusual. A Javanese worker in Suriname reported, "You were allotted a room. Everybody also received a woman to share the room with. If no women were left you got a man. I got a woman, but didn't want her. A week later a man came who wanted a woman but hadn't received one. I gave her away. I didn't ask anything for her" (quoted in Hoefte 1987, 63). Speaking on this tendency, Rosemarijn Hoefte notes, "Women were often regarded as property to be sold, given, or gambled away" (Hoefte 1987, 63).

The next and last time we see Rahman Khan's reputed wife (who, like his official wives, remains nameless) is when he separates himself from her. Four weeks into his indenture, Rahman Khan takes the money he has saved and gives three-quarters of it to the woman as he moves out of their shared accommodation. This does not seem to satisfy her, though, and she complains to the manager that her husband had deserted her while she was pregnant with his child. The manager orders Rahman Khan to give her one-fifth of his earnings until her "expected son" was six months old. As the woman never gave birth, he never paid. Again, he refers to a woman as a shackle: "The chains that had bound me broke and I was set free" (Rahman Khan 2005, 96). The phrasing here is particularly interesting: he was under indenture, a state often referred to as "bound labor," yet he saw the woman who attached herself to him as his true form of bondage.

In addition to demonstrating anxiety over single women, authorities often valued keeping married couples together over the wishes or safety of the woman. Ordinance 4 of 1864 in British Guiana, which was initially meant to protect women, stated that if a man threatened an unfaithful wife or "reputed" wife, the magistrate had the power to transfer the husband, the wife, or the wife's lover. Under these laws, runaway wives were often returned to their husbands even when the husbands had threatened or injured them. This was a response, in part, to the pressure from colonized men upon colonial officials to confirm the men's sovereignty over their wives. In 1881, 274 Indians signed a petition requesting that British officials in Trinidad recognize Indian marriages to enable "any person…[to] prosecute an unfaithful spouse and their partner in guilt… for the imprisonment of the wife if she refused to return to her husband, and also for the continued prosecution of the parties if the offence be persisted in" (quoted in Weller 1968, 74). This petition thus requested that a woman's option be marriage or prison. The 1881 Ordinance, which extended the rights of marriage registration from Christian marriages to Muslim and Hindu marriages, was a direct response to these petitions.[20]

The impact of this bill was not only to limit a woman's options. Ashrufa Faruqee notes, "Because of the colonial plantocracy's concern with 'marital stability', the government favoured the transfer of the paramour, although he may not have been threatening the woman" (Faruqee 1996, 70), meaning that a woman was often left in the hands of a violent, jealous

---

[20] Marina Carter points to a similar petition of Telegu men to the governor of Mauritius, requesting that authority be returned to them, specifically by "establishing the legitimacy of Indian marriages and punishing abductors" (Carter 1994, 237). The government responded by passing the Indian marriage regulations of the 1850s, which "placed immigrant women under the legal authority of their spouses, effectively marshalling the forces of the state against runaway or adulterors, and criminalising disobedient or disaffected wives" (Carter 1994, 9).

husband. In at least one case, this led to the wife's death. In Mauritius, a woman named Podoo sought refuge in her neighbor's hut when her husband turned violent, but the overseer ordered her to return to her husband, who then gouged out her eyes and strangled her (Carter 1994, 77). This extreme violence is by no means an isolated incident and demonstrates the disregard for women's lives that permeated the system.[21]

Resisting the Hierarchies of Empire

As can be seen above, indentured laborers, particularly female laborers, faced repressive, brutal conditions and confining gender, caste, and class expectations. Yet, the laborers found ways to push back against these restrictive roles. As previously mentioned, Achamma and Maharani ran away from unhappy family situations and indentured alone, challenging the image of migrants as single men or women traveling with male family members. Maharani in particular strove to maintain her independence, defying pressures to marry and bear children for as long as possible. Maharani and the other laborers committed additional acts of defiance: small acts at times, but significant nonetheless.

In one such example, Maharani saw men drinking rum and smoking marijuana in the rum shop, generally an all-male space where men would gather and share stories. Intrigued, she decided to try rum, too: "i drink it/i start to roll" (Maharani 1985, 86). Members of her community objected to her enthusiastic partaking:

> dem gone an tell she fadder
> e say
> you have no right to drink out dat. (Maharani 1985, 86)

In spite of the disapproval of Ramgolam, her husband, she seems to have enjoyed the experience, stating, "i start to laugh" (Maharani 1985, 86). This moment demonstrates the web of restrictions that Indian women laborers faced, and the societal collusion to regulate their behavior. Bharath, a male laborer, describes a woman who broke gender expectations to an even greater extent. This feisty woman beat a man who attacked her husband and then "dat lady take e four bottle rum/drink out one time" (Bharath 1985, 102).

---

[21] See Carter, Bahadur.

The female interviewees also describe moments when they did not play the role of the modest and submissive family member. Doolarie, rather than being a passive recipient of violence, reported her husband to the police for hitting her in the head with a hoe. Unfortunately, they took no action against her husband, suggesting a lack of concern for such behavior. Maharani, when asked why she left India, says of her in-laws, "What have they got here? Wash their backside?" (Maharani). The delightful irreverence of her response demonstrates the lack of respect she felt for those she ran away from.

Even Rahman Khan, the traditionalist, defied gender norms in the homosocial bonds that he developed with another male laborer, Subhan. They divided the domestic tasks along traditional male/female lines: Rahman Khan took charge of their finances and Subhan did the cleaning and cooking, making "nice and soft roti, good enough to shame many ladies" (Rahman Khan 2005, 113). Rahman Khan seemed to feel it was his job to protect and instruct Subhan, describing with amusement times that he tricked Subhan by giving him incomplete or incorrect instructions to try to teach him common sense. When Subhan fell ill, Rahman Khan took tender care of him, washing his soiled clothes, bathing him, and feeding him until he died. Rahman Khan was shaken by his friend's death: "Subhan was my right hand in an alien land. Due to him I had feared nobody. I did not have to worry about my chores and household tasks...all my problems seemed small in Subhan's company" (Rahman Khan 2005, 119). In fact, the comfort and stability that their friendship brought him was remarkably similar to the arguments that many used to pressure Rahman Khan, as well as Maharani, to marry. The friendship between these two men seems to fit the traditional view of spouses more than either of the relationships that Rahman Khan had with his wives, indicating that the laborers did not strictly follow societal or colonial definitions of marriage or gender roles.

Conclusion: One More Knot

Rahman Khan, Doolarie, Maharani, Achamma, Alice Singh, and Phularjee's experiences of marriage were incredibly diverse, reflecting the diversity of their indenture experience. While Rahman Khan, Phularjee, and Alice were expected to marry, none were physically forced into it, as Maharani was, and Alice does not report the domestic violence that both Maharani and Doolarie experienced. (Although given that she wrote the diary for her family, it is certainly possible that she experienced abuse and did not report it.) Lacking education or high social status, Maharani, Doolarie, and Achamma were not lucky enough to be given nursing or managerial positions and performed the same hard labor as most indentures. Yet, these women also report resisting colonial and patriarchal forms of oppression—Maharani refused to marry and pushed against gender roles by drinking rum, while Doolarie reported her husband for his abuse.

These experiences help form a view of the impact of British legislation around marriage. To justify slavery and indenture, British imperialists developed a teleological view of labor that was linked to hierarchical views of civilization and race. African, Asian, and European nations represented stages in a progression of civilization; in the same way, slavery, indentured labor, and wage labor were depicted as progressive steps necessary to civilize undeveloped races. Similarly, colonizers held a hierarchical view of family structures and personal relationships. The Victorian, nuclear family with a husband, wife, and children in one household was seen as the height of civilization, and Christian marriage as the height of intimate relationships, followed by "heathen" Muslim and Hindu marriages, then partnerings that were not officially recognized and polygamous relationships.

Colonial views of marriage and contract labor were both used to maintain a sense of European superiority and justify imperialism. Lisa Lowe argues that after the abolition of slavery in 1838, British officials viewed as a vital aspect of emancipation the notion that slaves would have access to "this set of institutions constituting 'freedom':…wage labor, contract, marriage, and family would be the formal institutions through which modern freedom could be obtained and the condition of slavery overcome" (Lowe 2015, 26). The colonizers viewed marriage and wage labor as indicators of civilization, and the institutionalization of both in the lives of the colonized was an indication that Britain had successfully brought progress to the natives.

The autobiographies and interviews indicate that colonial legislation around marriage, meant to impose Victorian ideals and justify imperialism, tended instead to support the view of women as contested property and to solidify existing class and racial hierarchies in both the colonizers and the colonized. At times, measures meant to protect women actually placed them in more danger. It is ironic that Rahman Khan describes his purported wife in Suriname as "the chains that…bound me" (Rahman Khan 2005, 96), because for many laborers, particularly women, colonial legislation around marriage made it one more knot that bound them into constricting gendered, classed, and racialized roles.

Bibliography

Achamma. Interview with Peggy Mohan. "Trinidad Bhojpuri Speakers: Translations" 55, The Oral and Pictorial Records Programme, University of the West Indies, St. Augustine.
Bahadur, Gaiutra. 2014. *Coolie Woman: The Odyssey of Indenture*. Chicago: University of Chicago Press.
Barbados. 1661. *Act for the Better Ordering and Governing of Negroes*, September 27.
Bernhard, Virginia. 1999. *Slaves and Slaveholders in Bermuda, 1616–1782*. Columbia, MO: University of Missouri.
Bharath. 1985. *The Still Cry: Personal Accounts of East Indians in Trinidad and Tobago during Indentureship, 1845–1917*. Interview by Noor Kumar Mahabir. Tacarigua, Trinidad: Calaloux Publications.
British Guiana. 1870. *Evidence and Proceedings*, Commission of Enquiry into the Treatment of Immigrants, William E. Frere, Chairman. Georgetown, Demerara: "The Colonist" Newspaper.
Bronkhurst, H.V.P. 1883. *The Colony of British Guyana and Its Labouring Population*. London: T. Woolmer.
Burton, Antoinette M. 2003. *Dwelling in the Archive: Women Writing House, Home, and History in Late Colonial India*. New York: Oxford University Press.
Carter, Marina. 1994. *Lakshmi's Legacy: The Testimonies of Indian Women in 19th Century Mauritius*. Stanley-Rose Hill, Mauritius: Editions De L'Océan Indien.
Chitnis, Varsha, and Danaya Wright. 2007. The Legacy of Colonialism: Law and Women's Rights in India. *Washington and Lee Law Review* 64 (4): 1315–1348.
Doolarie. 1982. Interview with Noor Kumar Mahabir. St. Augustine, September 18.
Faruqee, Ashrufa. 1996. Conceiving the Coolie Woman: Indentured Labour, Indian Women and Colonial Discourse. *South Asia Research* 16 (1): 61–76.
Gautam, Mohan. 1995. Munshi Rahman Khan (1874–1972), An Institution of the Indian Diaspora in Surinam. Paper presented at *ISER-NCIC Conference on Challenge and Change: The Indian Diaspora in Its Historical and Contemporary Contexts*, The University of the West Indies, St. Augustine, Trinidad, August 11–18, 1995.
Gowricharn, Ruben. 2013. Ethnogenesis: The Case of British Indians in the Caribbean. *Comparative Studies in Society and History* 55 (2): 388–418.
Hall, N.A.T., and B.W. Higman. 1992. *Slave Society in the Danish West Indies: St. Thomas, St. John, and St. Croix*. Baltimore: Johns Hopkins University Press.
Hoefte, Rosemarijn. June 1987. Female Indentured Labor in Suriname: For Better or for Worse? *Boletin De Estudios Latinoamericanos Y Del Caribe* 42: 55–70.
———. 2014. *Suriname in the Long Twentieth Century: Domination, Contestation, Globalization*. New York: Palgrave Macmillan.

Hosein, Shaheeda. 2004. *Rural Indian women in Trinidad: 1870–1945*. PhD diss., University of the West Indies, St. Augustine.

India. 1898. *The Indian Emigration Act XXI of 1883 As Modified Up To 5th March 1897 and Rules and Regulations Issued Under Its Provisions*. Calcutta: Office of the Superintendent of Government Printing.

Kelly, John Dunham, and Uttra Kumari Singh. 1991. Introduction. In *My Twenty-One Years in the Fiji Islands; and, The Story of the Haunted Line*, 1–13. Suva: Fiji Museum.

Lowe, Lisa. 2015. *The Intimacies of Four Continents*. Durham: Duke University Press.

Mahabir, Noor Kumar. 1985. *The Still Cry: Personal Accounts of East Indians in Trinidad and Tobago During Indentureship, 1845–1917*. Tacarigua, Trinidad: Calaloux Publications.

Maharani. Interview with Patricia Mohammed. "East Indian Family and Gender Relations" 62-33-A, The Oral and Pictorial Records Programme, University of the West Indies, St.Augustine.

Maharani. 1985. *The Still Cry: Personal Accounts of East Indians in Trinidad and Tobago during Indentureship, 1845–1917*. Interview by Noor Kumar Mahabir. Tacarigua, Trinidad: Calaloux Publications.

Mangru, Basdeo. 2005. *The Elusive El Dorado: Essays on the Indian Experience in Guyana*. Lanham: University Press of America.

Mill, James, and Horace Hayman Wilson. 1858. *The History of British India*. London: Madden.

Mohammed, Patricia. 2002. *Gender Negotiations Among Indians in Trinidad, 1917–1947*. New York: Palgrave.

Naipaul, V.S. 2007. *A Writer's People: Ways of Looking and Feeling*. London: Picador.

Prince, Mary. 1997. *The History of Mary Prince: A West Indian Slave*. Edited by Moira Ferguson. Ann Arbor: University of Michigan Press.

Rahman Khan, Munshi. 2005. *Autobiography of an Indian Indentured Labourer*. Translated by Kathinka Sinha-Kerkhoff, Ellen Bal, Alok Deo Singh. Delhi: Shipra Publications.

Reddock, Rhoda. 1994. *Women, Labour and Politics in Trinidad and Tobago: A History*. London: Zed Books Ltd.

Rodney, Walter. 1981. *A History of the Guyanese Working People, 1881–1905*. Baltimore: The Johns Hopkins University Press.

Sanadhya, Totaram. 1991. *My Twenty-One Years in the Fiji Islands; And, The Story of the Haunted Line*. Edited by John Dunham Kelly and Uttra Kumari Singh. Suva: Fiji Museum.

Singal, R.L. 2005. Gripping Tale of Indian Worker Abroad. *The Tribune*, October 2. http://www.tribuneindia.com/2005/20051002/spectrum/book4.htm.

Singh, Alice Bahadur. 2011. *Autobiography of Alice Bhagwandy Sital Persaud (1892–1958)*. http://mosessite.blogspot.com/2011/05/autobiography-of-alice-bhagwandy-sital.html. Accessed 19 Mar 2012.
Singh, Karna Bahadur. (n.d.). Introduction. Jung Bahadur Singh Collection, *The Caribbean Research Library*. Turkmeyen: University of Guyana.
Sinha-Kerkhoff, Kathinka, and Ellen Bal. 2005. Introduction. In *Autobiography of an Indian Indentured Labourer*, xi–lii. Delhi: Shipra Publications.
Smith, Sidonie, and Julia Watson. 1998. *Women, Autobiography, Theory: A Reader*. Madison: University of Wisconsin Press.
———. 2001. *Reading Autobiography: A Guide for Interpreting Life Narratives*. Minneapolis: University of Minnesota Press.
Spivak, Gayatri Chakravorty. 1999. *A Critique of Postcolonial Reason: Toward a History of the Vanishing Present*. Cambridge: Harvard University Press.
Weller, Judith Ann. 1968. *The East Indian Indenture in Trinidad*. Rio Piedras: Institute of Caribbean Studies University of Puerto Rico.
Yun, Lisa. 2008. *The Coolie Speaks: Chinese Indentured Laborers and African Slaves in Cuba*. Philadelphia: Temple University Press.

CHAPTER 3

Tying the Knot: Early Depictions of Indenture

Introduction: "Reasonable Wear and Tear"

In 1915, 16-year-old Leslie Phillips arrived as an overseer on Plantation Cornelia Ida in British Guiana. Forty-five years later, in an essay titled "Single Men in Barracks" he described his sexual exploits with the female Indians who labored on the plantation. In a tone of amused nostalgia, he tells the story of an Indian woman named Rajama, "a comely but slightly promiscuous young Madrasi," and her husband, whom he calls "complacent and indolent" (Phillips 1961, 32). He writes:

> Rajama spent one Saturday night in my quarters, and daylight taking us unawares, we decided to let the next nightfall cover her journey home. About two o'clock on Sunday afternoon my house-boy brought the ominous news that Rajama's husband had arrived and wished to speak to her. To permit this would have placed me in open jeopardy, so I sought means to distract him. Learning of my predicament, Brown, a fellow Overseer, offered to get the man completely drunk if I would supply the liquor. I sent my boy with a chit to Fung-a Fat's Rum Shop, and he quickly returned with a large bottle of rum which Brown invited the man to share in his room. (Phillips 1961, 32)

The distraction worked temporarily, but the man returned, again asking to speak to his wife. Phillips sent him away, giving him "the assurance that when conniving Night again returned to cover such delicate manoeuvres, his property would be returned to him in good order, reasonable wear and tear excepted" (Phillips 1961, 32). Phillips describes this affair as one might describe a schoolboy prank, and his lack of concern for the feelings of the husband is matched only by his disturbing view of Indian women as property that may be borrowed at will by British men.

Phillips' intimacy with a female laborer, and his attitude toward it, is by no means unusual. This is demonstrated by the frequency with which British colonial officials sent out notices to plantation managers warning against these relationships. One British Guiana circular from 1869 condemned such managers for failing to set a high moral standard of behavior: "It appears there are some overseers on estates who, by their intimate relations with the female immigrants, are themselves fostering the laxity of morals which unfortunately obtains to a considerable extent amongst the Indian immigrants" (quoted in Bahadur 2014, 134). The implication is that overseers had an obligation to demonstrate the superior morality of the British and were failing to do so.

Some planters suggested that Indian women purposefully engaged in these relationships to gain leverage. While this may have been true in some cases, most women had little choice when approached by a manager. In an anonymous letter to *The Daily Chronicle*, an Indian wrote, "As soon as an overseer eyes a nice looking coolie girl, she must fall a prey to him with the assistance of a *sirdar* or driver, who plays a great figure in it...If the girl does not consent and exposes the matter, she with her whole family will be turned off the estate" (quoted in Bahadur 2014, 150). At best, such relationships were exploitative, as the managers had great power over the women, and, at worst, these women were forced into sex, either through physical threats or threats to their livelihood or family.

Relationships between British plantation officials and female laborers held a significance far beyond the two people involved. For the colonial authorities, these intimacies undermined the imperial justification of Britain's right to rule, which was based on the notion that the British were a more developed, moral, and civilized people, acting as role models for the less civilized races. For the Indians and other ethnic groups subjugated by colonization, these relationships demonstrated the hypocrisy and invasiveness of imperialism, and the *droit du seigneur* attitude that many planters adopted.

The tensions caused by such relationships were heightened by the dramatic gender disparity among indentured laborers, averaging four men to one woman. This unbalanced gender ratio meant that Indian women took on a symbolic role for men vying for power. Historian Patricia Mohammed notes that most cultures contain the idea "that the honor of men is vested in women's virtue," and, as a result, "the struggle to retain ethnic identity is viewed, not in terms of political power, but the power to control their own women, and guard and protect them from other men" (Mohammed 2002, 9). For the laborers, the few Indian women who traveled to the colonies were seen as the protectors of civilization, culture, and tradition. This was especially important in a foreign land, far from the societal institutions such as religious or governmental organizations that formed the structures of their culture.

It is not surprising, then, that one of the most common tropes to appear in indenture narratives is a relationship that forms between a British man in power—a plantation owner, an overseer, or an officer for the British government, and a female laborer. For instance, Edgar Mittelholzer's classic Caribbean novel *Corentyne Thunder* (1970) focuses on not one but two Indo-Caribbean women, half-sisters, who bear children to British planters, and the exploitative nature of these relationships.[1] The frequency of this trope indicates not only the prevalence of this occurrence, but also the central role that colonized women played in contestations for power.

There are only two known novels about Caribbean indenture written while the system was still functioning, and both depict a relationship between a British planter and a female Indian laborer. Edward Jenkins, a British barrister, published *Lutchmee and Dilloo* in 1877 in order to draw attention to the challenges that the Indian laborers faced. It tells the story of a young Indian couple who indenture in British Guiana and form a friendship with a Scottish overseer. A.R.F. Webber, a Guyanese journalist and politician of mixed race, published *Those that Be in Bondage* in 1917 to protest the unfair treatment of both the laborers and the plantation managers. This novel focuses on a young overseer in British Guiana who falls in love with a female Indian laborer. These texts do not appear often in the canon of Caribbean literature and are generally viewed as limited in their artistic merit, but they offer important insights into late nineteenth- to early twentieth-century views on gender, ethnicity, imperialism, and indenture. In particular, both authors depict a relationship between a

---

[1] See also Deepchand Beeharry's *That Others Might Live* (1976), Sharlows *The Promise* (1995), David Dabydeen: *The Counting House* (1996), and Ron Ramdin's *Rama's Voyage* (2004) for other examples.

British man and an Indian woman to suggest that, if handled correctly, an imperial relationship between Britain and India would be mutually beneficial to both nations.

In this chapter, I explore the ways that hierarchies of race, labor, and gender bolstered the British Empire, as well as the seductiveness of such hierarchies to the colonizers and colonized alike. In moments of geopolitical upheaval, many are drawn to the sense of order and structure offered by such categorizations of people, especially those at the top or near the top of the hierarchy. Jenkins, writing in the late nineteenth century, expressed anxiety about the rising might of the United States and the potential dissolution of the British Empire. In some ways, the second half of the nineteenth century was the height of British Imperialism, with its increasing control over India and portions of Africa. Yet, Jenkins argued (accurately, as it turned out) that the rumbles of discontent in Ireland and the tensions with Russia and Germany presaged the fragmentation of the Empire, and both his fiction and nonfiction defend colonialism in order to forestall such a fate. Webber wrote *Those That Be in Bondage* at a tense moment in the history of British Guiana, a decade after the deadly Ruimveldt Riots, in which a workers' uprising developed into an armed confrontation with colonial authorities, and shortly before, or possibly during, the chaos of World War I.[2] Facing the potential destruction of the British Empire and the decline of the plantation system, both Jenkins and Webber seek a sense of stability, an order in the world around them, in the classification of human populations.

Both *Lutchmee and Dilloo* and *Those That Be in Bondage* show the British and other Europeans as the height of civilization in Caribbean society, the Indian and Chinese as cultured but unsophisticated, and those of African descent as barbaric and ignorant. Tied to this is a teleological view of labor within the novels. Wage labor, as represented by the European managers, is depicted as the ultimate indicator of societal progress, while the Indians and Chinese migrants labor under indenture as a step toward self-determination. Those of African descent, while no longer enslaved, are depicted primarily completing mindless tasks or brute labor. Threaded through these hierarchies is the issue of gender: one can judge a culture, these authors suggest, by the way they treat their women. The European men generally act as models of chivalry, especially in comparison with the

---

[2] While the novel was published in 1917, Selwyn Cudjoe suggests that it was written in 1913 or 1914 (Cudjoe 2009, 16).

more violent and discourteous male characters of Indian and African descent. Further, the female laborers in these novels play a vital role in the justifications for empire, as either victims in need of rescue or scapegoats for the ills of the system.

My exploration of these themes builds on the work of postcolonial theorists who examine the connections between intimate relationships and issues of nation, race, and empire. In *Carnal Knowledge*, anthropologist Ann Laura Stoler shows that colonial officials regulated sexual relationships and child-rearing in Indonesia in order to prevent mingling between the colonizers and the colonized and maintain racial distinctions. She notes that "connections between parenting and colonial power, between nursing mothers and cultural boundaries, between servants and sentiments, and between illicit sex, orphans, and race emerge as central concerns of state and at the heart of colonial politics" (Stoler 2002, 8). Similarly, in *The Intimacies of Four Continents*, literary theorist Lisa Lowe suggests that contracts of labor and marriage, usually seen as private agreements between individuals, became signifiers of humanity and freedom for Europeans justifying the indenture system in the nineteenth century (Lowe 2015, 27). These critics establish that the distinction between the private world of personal relationships and the public world of societal conflict is not as distinct as we might imagine.

Lutchmee and Dilloo and *Those That Be in Bondage* demonstrate the justification of indenture and the gendered views of labor that Lowe points to. Both Edward Jenkins and A.R.F. Webber wrote their novels to draw attention to the suffering of indentured laborers, yet neither of these texts directly challenges the indenture system or criticizes the European planters. They highlight unfair aspects of the system, such as the lack of legal recourse available to the laborers, but argue that overall, the system benefits the Indian laborers. In addition, both novels offer a hierarchical view of race, labor, and gender, with British land-owning men presented as the height of civilization.

These novels also point to an aspect of indenture that Lowe does not explore: the metaphoric significance of the laboring woman. In both novels, the British man is handsome, strong, honorable, and kind, representing the best of British gentility, while the Indian woman is lovely, virtuous, and vulnerable. The man raises the woman out of the degradation and harsh life of field labor, and into a world of civilization and refinement. Furthermore, this gentleman rescues the Indian woman from a brutal male Indian, who in turn dies a violent death as a result of his savage behavior. This represents the primary justification of colonization: Britain would protect its helpless colonies and civilize them, eradicating their barbaric tendencies.

The similarities in these two novels are striking, given the differences in the authors' ethnicities, nationality, and views on empire. Edward Jenkins was a British barrister who staunchly supported the British Empire. Though he lived most of his adult life in London, he was born in India and grew up in Canada. The son of a Presbyterian minister, he was most likely exposed to the rhetoric of British supremacy and the civilizing benefits of colonialism, which may have then filtered into his political views and his writings. A.R.F. Webber, a native of the Caribbean, was of mixed African and European descent and in later years advocated for Guyanese independence. Yet, *Those That Be in Bondage* supports the indenture system and imperialism. This suggests that, as a middle-class man of mixed race, he felt caught between his relatively high status in the colonial society and his solidarity with the working people and desire for Guyanese autonomy. That two men writing from such different subject positions would promote the benefits of colonialism and indenture for both Britain and India indicates the pervasiveness of imperial ideology and the tensions between race and class in colonial Guiana.

Although there is extensive historical research on the British imperial system of indenture in the Caribbean, there is little critical attention to literature dealing with indentured labor. *Lutchmee and Dilloo* and *Those That Be in Bondage* in particular remain obscure. The criticism that does exist on these two novels tends to minimize the larger issues at stake in the relationship between the British man and the Indian woman. In his biography of A.R.F. Webber, Selwyn Cudjoe acknowledges that in *Those That Be in Bondage*, "both the East and West are depicted in stereotypical terms" (Cudjoe 2009, 19). However, he ignores the problematic aspect of a romance in which an English overseer must make "a stupendous leap in yielding his heart" to an Indian laborer (Webber 1988, 35). In his introduction to *Lutchmee and Dilloo*, David Dabydeen suggests that the friendship between the Scottish overseer and the Indian woman, by leading her to defy her husband, has sparked "a nascent feminism, a nascent defiance of patriarchal structures" (Dabydeen 2003, 18). Instead, as discussed in more detail later in this chapter, I argue that she is simply transferring her loyalty from her Indian husband to her European savior. The lack of critical attention to such thorny issues within these texts suggests that we have not completely eradicated the hierarchies of empire.

LUTCHMEE AND DILLOO: "WAS SHE NOT A PRETTY ANIMAL?"

While the novels discussed in this chapter focus primarily on the relationship between Indian immigrants and British colonizers, they take place in the Caribbean, emphasizing the complex network of British capitalist imperialism. The Caribbean, in a sense, is the birthplace of British Imperialism, as Britain colonized the Caribbean in the period between 1583 and 1783, termed the "First British Empire." Colonies were attempted as early as 1604 in Guiana, St. Lucia, Grenada, St. Kitts, Barbados, and Nevis. Though they initially failed, these sites became Britain's most lucrative and important early colonies. They produced sugar, among other products, which was in turn traded to Britain's colonies and other nations around the globe to great profit.

Sugar production required a massive, controlled labor population. Spanish colonialism had nearly wiped out the indigenous populations of the Caribbean, such as the Taíno and the Caribs, and so the British turned to slaves from Africa. In 1672, the Royal African Company was founded to provide slaves to the Americas, beginning two centuries of brutal slave trade. After slavery was abolished, Britain brought labor from India to the Caribbean in order to work the plantations. Many critics of indenture argued that the laborers were essentially treated as slaves, confined to the plantation, forced to endure long days of backbreaking work, and disciplined with beatings and whippings. Joseph Beaumont, who served as chief justice of British Guiana, titled his 1871 account of indentured labor, *The New Slavery* (1871).

In 1869, William Des Voeux, a stipendiary magistrate in British Guiana, wrote a letter to Lord Granville, the secretary of state for the Colonies, detailing the abuses of indentured laborers that he had witnessed. In response, a commission was set up to inquire into the state of the immigrants in the colonies. The Aborigines Protection Services and the Anti-Slavery Society asked Edward Jenkins, a barrister, author, and politician, to travel to Guiana to examine the system of indentured labor. His report, *The Coolie, His Rights and Wrongs*, published in 1871, concludes that the indenture system was beneficial to all involved parties, but he details a number of abuses to the system that needed to be remedied. These include false promises made to recruit the laborers and a justice system that heavily favored the planters. When his report failed to spur reform, he felt he had not drawn enough attention to the issues, and so he attempted to individualize the suffering of the laborers with a fictional account.

The resulting novel, *Lutchmee and Dilloo* (1877), focuses on a young Indian couple who travel to British Guiana as indentured laborers, and the many injustices that they face. It can be seen as a novel of purpose, a fictional text written to motivate social reform. Jenkins may have been inspired by anti-slavery novels such as Harriet Beecher Stowe's 1852 *Uncle Tom's Cabin*, which similarly sought to draw attention to the sufferings of a people, and similarly fostered stereotypes of those people in the process. *Lutchmee and Dilloo* is written in third-person omniscient, switching between the perspectives of the Indian laborers, the British plantation managers, and the servants of African descent. This suggests that Jenkins is striving for a sense of objectivity in order to make his case more palatable, particularly to British readers.

In their respective novels, Jenkins and Webber repeat the discourse of imperialism, overtly in Jenkins' case and perhaps inadvertently in Webber's. Britain's primary rationalization for the conquest of other nations was the civilization and improvement of the colonized people. In India, missionaries would replace the superstitious, ignorant beliefs of Hindus, Buddhists, and Muslims with the rational enlightenment of Christianity. The British would build schools to teach Indians literacy, history, and morals. Technology such as trains and telegraphs would sweep the Indians into the forward march of civilization, and the Indian people would learn to be industrious, pious, and moral. In the Caribbean, there was not much of a native population to "civilize" by the nineteenth century, as the Caribs and Taíno had been decimated by the violence and disease that accompanied European colonization of the fifteenth and sixteenth centuries. However, colonial officials deployed the same arguments toward the enslaved Africans, and then indentured laborers, that they imported to the colonies to work the plantations.

In reality, British Imperialism had a devastating effect on the Indian economy and social structure. Ranajit Guha notes that the Permanent Settlement Act of 1793, generally seen as the initiation of imperial policy in India, endeavored to shape Bengal into an imitation of England without attempting to understand the local culture or traditions. He argues that, "while being grafted to India by the most advanced capitalist power of that age, it became instrumental in building a neo-feudal organisation of landed property and in the absorption and reproduction of pre-capitalist elements in a colonial regime" (Guha 1963, 6). Ironically, then, Permanent

Settlement, which was intended to promote a capitalist agricultural system similar to that of England, actually encouraged a feudal system, installing local leaders as landlords and tax collectors, and imposing heavy taxes. As a result, many farmers were forced off lands that their families had cultivated for generations. Walton Look Lai writes that the landlord system and the heavy taxation

> succeeded in bringing to an end the underlying communalism that lay at the heart of traditional village life, despite its internal occupational and caste stratifications. In its place was erected a system which was a mix of feudal landlord-tenant relations and an uneven system of commercial agriculture, growing crops for the market beyond the horizons of the village structure, and indeed for the British metropolis. (Look Lai 1993, 23)

The British also imposed tariffs on exported Indian crafts and flooded Indian markets with British made, mass-produced goods, which put local artisans out of work. Serious crop failures exacerbated the poverty cause by the restructuring of agriculture and elimination of local crafts. It is estimated that 15 million Indians died in the famines of the nineteenth century. Even colonial officials acknowledged the degree of this misfortune. Lord William Bentinck, who served as governor-general of India, stated, "The bones of the cotton-weavers are bleaching the plains of India" (quoted in Look Lai 1993, 23).

These restructurings also led to large numbers of landless peasants, a situation that British colonialism both created and took advantage of. In his article, "Beyond the Push and Pull Model," Lomarsh Roopnarine suggests that colonialism was a major reason for the high numbers of laborers emigrating as indentured laborers. Building on Immanuel Wallerstein's idea that the world economy is held together by one capitalist system, he writes: "The process of capital accumulation is supported by a labor surplus drawn from the less progressive to the most flourishing areas of the world" (Roopnarine 2003, 102). He argues that the colonial planting system in the Caribbean created a need for such labor, and that the upheaval caused by British imperialism in India created a surplus of laborers willing to travel to the Caribbean. Displacement was most severe in the provinces of Bihar, Uttar Pradesh, Bengal, and Madras, and these are the areas where most indentured laborers came from.

Edward Jenkins was certainly concerned with the mistreatment of Indian laborers, as demonstrated by his report on his visit to British

Guiana, *The Coolie, His Rights and Wrongs* (1871). In it, he describes the many abuses of the indenture system, which he argued were based largely on economic incentives. He noted that the bounty attached to the number of laborers brought to the Caribbean colonies led recruiters to use false descriptions and the doctors inspecting the migrants to allow as many through as possible. Within the colonies themselves, most of the government officials were either planters or socially connected to planters, and thus heavily influenced by planters' interests. He pointed to injustices within the legal system; laborers who committed infractions of the contract were sent to jail, whereas planters who broke the contract were fined, if punished at all. Finally, he noted that the system was rigged to prevent laborers from becoming free men after their indenture, which was ostensibly the goal of the system.[3]

However, Jenkins does not acknowledge the brutality of the slave system that preceded indenture, the destruction of India's economy, or the inherent inequities of indentured labor. In spite of his concerns, he concludes that the system generally benefitted the laborers, and, with proper reforms and oversight, would be mutually advantageous to both India and Britain. He wrote, "Taking a fair review of the whole system, *it is one which, spite of its disabilities, its difficulties, its present evils, is full of promise, and in my belief, can be made, with care and skill and honest endeavour, not only an organisation of labour as successful as any hitherto attempted, but one leading to almost colossal benefits*" (*The Coolie* 1871a, 301, emphasis original).

He did, though, want to improve certain aspects of the system, and he was disappointed that his report did not spur greater action. To draw further attention to the injustices he had described, Jenkins wrote *Lutchmee and Dilloo* "to throw the problem of the Coolie labour in our Colonies into a concrete and picturesque form" (Jenkins 2003, 29). The novel does not seem to have gained much of a readership, though. The 1877 printing was the only edition, until it was reprinted in 2003 with an introduction

---

[3] *The Coolie* was published less than a decade after the abolition of slavery in the United States. In his preface to the American edition of the book, Jenkins notes that his observations would prove useful should the southern states consider adopting a similar system, and argues that "we can no more disregard each other's movements, each other's successes, or each other's blunders, than we can the motions of the earth or the laws of gravitation" (*The Coolie* 1871a, vi). While the United States did not adopt a system of labor immigration, there are certainly parallels between British Imperial indenture and the repressive policies of apprenticeship and sharecropping that followed the abolition of slavery in the United States.

by David Dabydeen. This suggests that there was not much of a British market for indenture narratives at the time, but today, Caribbean citizens of Indian and Chinese descent who are curious about their heritage are invested in literature that depicts indenture migration.

Lutchmee and Dilloo is much more sympathetic than the few texts written previously about indentured laborers in the Caribbean. For example, J.D. Pearson's *New Overseer's Manual* (1890) justifies indenture by describing a series of Indian "characters" in stereotypical terms and suggesting that the Indians who succeed in British Guiana are those who work hard, give up their ties to their homeland, and conform to the expectations of their European managers. J.D. McKay's *Under the Southern Cross* (1914), billed as a novel, is really a missionary tract, depicting a Brahmin who, through hard work and exposure to Christianity, becomes a convert and learns to despise his own culture.

By contrast, *Lutchmee and Dilloo* effectively highlights the suffering of the laborers, and Jenkins delves into their perspective, creating developed characters. However, Jenkins also uses the relationships between the characters as an analogue to the relationship between Britain and its colonies and a justification for colonization and indenture. He suggests that Britain's role was that of the honorable, masculine hero, saving the innocent, defenseless India from her own violent, barbaric tendencies. Craig, a Scottish overseer, befriends Lutchmee, a young Indian woman, and through him she comes to recognize the glory of British civilization.

Jenkins' defense of Britain's imperial relationship with India is unsurprising, as he was a firm proponent of empire, and both India and Guiana were highly profitable colonies. Furthermore, recent violence in both regions made the threat of revolt a real one, and Jenkins may have been attempting to prevent further violence by promoting a romantic view of imperialism. During the Indian Rebellion of 1857, members of the Indian army mutinied against the British, which led to the Government of India Act of 1858, in which the British government assumed the task of directly administering India. In 1872, Indian indentured laborers from the Devonshire Castle Plantation on the Essequibo Coast of British Guiana went on strike to protest their conditions. This led to a violent confrontation between laborers and police, in which five laborers died. Imperial officials were thus very aware that tensions could erupt into violence in any of their colonies. *Lutchmee and Dilloo* can be seen as a response to these tensions and an appeal to both groups, as the interactions between the characters offer an idealized version of the colonized-colonizer relationship.

The characters' metaphoric roles can be seen as early as the opening scene of the novel, which introduces the three major Indian characters. Lutchmee, a young Indian woman, reclines on a grassy bank in an unnamed area of India. She is pretty and graceful, and she fits European notions of beauty, with a "light-brown oval face" and "delicately-chiselled nostrils" (Jenkins 2003, 31). She does not realize that Hunoomaun, the villain of the story, watches her with mischief in his heart. He is "a tall, powerfully-built man, of extreme darkness of skin, with a shaggy head of hair and moustache that added their bristly terrors to a face naturally ugly and deeply pitted with small-pox" (Jenkins 2003, 32). His dark skin is closely linked with ugliness, aggression, and the corruption of disease. This is immediately borne out by his behavior—he tries to seduce Lutchmee, and when she runs away, he chases and attacks her. Lutchmee is rescued by her husband, Dilloo, who is "for a Hindoo, of unusually fine development" (Jenkins 2003, 33). These three characters thus represent the best and the worst of the Indian people, in keeping with colonial discourse. Lutchmee and Dilloo are European in appearance, and in temperament are open, innocent, and childlike, the finest examples of their people. They are threatened by Hunoomaun, who is dark-skinned, cunning, and malicious, always looking to take advantage of others.

Hunoomaun takes revenge on Dilloo by stealing his livestock and money, and Dilloo is forced to indenture in British Guiana, with Lutchmee following soon after. During Lutchmee's voyage, Jenkins reflects on the flaws in the system and the way that each official deflects responsibility. As the immigration agent-general examines the ship and its passengers, he and the captain discuss the unhealthy aspect of many of the laborers. The captain responds "But what can I do? I must bring 'em, you know" (Jenkins 2003, 55). Jenkins reflects that everyone involved in the system responded in the same way, shifting the blame onto others: "The cunning Indian recruiters...the colonial agents...The highly-paid officials of the Indian Government...The British Government, and the Colonial Government would each have shrugged their shoulders, and said 'What can we do?'" (Jenkins 2003, 55). Here Jenkins demonstrates that people tend to ignore the suffering of fellow humans when there are economic incentives to do so.

Yet, Jenkins is far more critical of Indians in this description of the indenture system. He calls the recruiters "cunning" and notes that the Indian officials are "highly-paid," suggesting that they are silent in exchange for good salaries, but makes no such attacks on the British. Later in the novel, he explicitly lays the majority of the blame on the Indian recruiters: "The root of the injustice had been struck in India in the exaggerated representations made by the native recruiters to induce the Indians to migrate" (Jenkins 2003, 165).[4] This supports the notion that the British were saving Indians from themselves, and also shows Jenkins' awareness of his audience. As with abolitionist slave narratives, his text is written not to the sufferers but to those in power—in this case, British men and women—and so he avoids criticism that might make his readers defensive.

Upon arriving in British Guiana, Lutchmee finds Dilloo a deeply changed man, "graver, and more stern in manner," with "a novel habit of reserve" (Jenkins 2003, 89). Prior to Lutchmee's arrival, he was unjustly imprisoned, which made him lose faith in the British system of justice and darkened his disposition. While she is there, he is again unfairly imprisoned, this time for not working five days in one week, though in reality the law stated that a laborer had to complete five tasks in a week rather than five days of work.[5] As a result of these and other mistreatments, Dilloo becomes hardened, vowing revenge on Drummond, the white owner of the estate where Lutchmee and Dilloo are bound, and Marston, the magistrate who orders Dilloo to jail.

Jenkins suggests that Dilloo's hatred is understandable but misplaced, as Drummond and Marston are depicted as flawed but not cruel men. Marston is a somewhat cowardly and narrow-minded official who slowly awakens to the injustices of the system as the novel progresses. Drummond, on the other hand, was once a good man, but his morals and sense of justice have been loosened by his power on the plantation. He has sexual relationships with his workers, but does not force himself on them. When Drummond attempts to seduce Lutchmee and she rejects him, he lets her go: "In the pursuit of his whims, the remains of generosity and justice in his nature had always hitherto restrained him from any forcible assertion of his wishes. Nor did he meditate revenge. He was good-tempered, easygoing, morally indolent" (Jenkins 2003, 76). Jenkins indicates that

---

[4] See also *The Coolie*: "Exaggerated statements in print, or made by the recruiters, mislead the ignorant Coolies, and lay the basis for that permanent sense of wrong, which makes for a resentful labourer, with the danger of corresponding harshness and oppression in enforcing another view of the contract" (1871a, 165). Jenkins advises, "The action of these recruiters, therefore, needs careful watching on the part of the Indian government" (1871a, 165).

[5] See *The Coolie*. Jenkins notes that the law states that laborers need only complete five tasks per week, whereas many managers forced their laborers to work five days even if they had already completed five tasks.

Marston and Drummond are essentially worthwhile men who have been corrupted by the flawed nature of the indenture system.

It is also worth noting that Jenkins does not depict any nonbonded field laborers in the scenes in British Guiana. Though formerly enslaved people often joined together and worked in gangs, moving from plantation to plantation and offering their services in a form of collective bargaining, this kind of labor is notably absent from the text. The planters had justified the need for indentured labor by arguing that there was a severe labor shortage, but as Madhavi Kale writes, "The alleged 'labor shortage'...reflected colonial proprietors' determination to continue to use imperial discursive, material and human resources to protect privileges they had long enjoyed in colonial labor relations, and in imperial trade" (Kale 1992, 90). Planters used indentured labor as a means of maintaining a tight hold on the labor force and providing competition for the formerly enslaved laborers. Jenkins is careful to uphold the view of a labor shortage, depicting only Indian and Chinese laborers. The Afro-Guyanese characters who appear in the text, with the exception of the obeah man who lives in the woods, are all house servants and express no discontent with their roles.

Though Jenkins gives his Indian characters a degree of humanity, he is not so generous with the characters of other ethnicities, particularly those of African descent. Sarcophagus, servant to the Marstons, is described as an ignorant ape: "If you tossed him a bundle of words, he used them as a gorilla would use a bundle of sticks. He unaccountably mixed and twisted them up together, he tore them to shreds between his teeth" (Jenkins 2003, 133–134), and the obeah man who appears at the end of the novel is described as having "baboon-like features" and "lips like those of a hippopotamus" (Jenkins 2003, 353). Chin-a-foo, the only Chinese character in the novel, fares a bit better, but only a bit. His gambling house is described as "hell," and his appearance conforms closely with stereotypes of the Chinese as cunning, inscrutable, and grotesque: "The leery slits he used as eyes were only opened sufficiently to let in the knowledge which their owner wanted, and to give no clue to the observer of the emotions or thoughts of the spirit—if there were a spirit—within...The blue shaven head...was in harmony...with the grotesqueness of his countenance" (Jenkins 2003, 106–107). These characters thus clearly delineate the hierarchy of race that pervades the novel, with Europeans depicted as the most civilized race, followed by Indians, Chinese, and Africans.

In keeping with this racial hierarchy, Hunoomaun is the real villain of the story, even though Drummond and Marston are responsible for the treatment the laborers receive. Coincidentally, Hunoomaun too signs a contract of indenture and is assigned to Drummond's estate. His cunning manipulation of others helps him achieve a position of power on the plantation, which he uses to torment Lutchmee and Dilloo. The tension culminates when Lutchmee, who is several months pregnant, is sent to work in the fields while Dilloo is in jail; the work is too much for her and she has a miscarriage. The baby's death can be seen as the end of the couple's hope for the future, but also the destruction of any sense of rootedness or belonging. After Lutchmee's miscarriage, Dilloo turns bitter and violent, rejecting any notion of building a home in Guiana or reaching a peace with the colonial management.

Just as the villain of the story is not Drummond but Hunoomaun, the hero of the story is not Dilloo, who is slowly corrupted by the evils of the system, but Craig, a young Scottish overseer with high principles. He is described as fine in both body and spirit, an Aryan ideal: "An inch over six feet in height, with broad shoulders, strong frame, bold regular features, of blonde complexion, Craig would have been marked by any one seeing the overseers together, to be as superior to the rest in both tone and manner as he was in appearance" (Jenkins 2003, 84–85). He gives Drummond some trouble because of his strong principles; over and over Drummond berates him for taking the side of the laborers, including in court. Drummond argues that the white population needs to stick together and show a united front, or else the laborers will sense weakness and revolt. Jenkins indicates that this is not the case; the laborers respect and admire Craig, and it is only his intervention that prevents violent outbreaks at various points. If only all British acted like Craig, Jenkins suggests, the system would work as it should, and all involved races would benefit.

This is particularly striking in Craig's treatment of Lutchmee, as he saves her in both figurative and literal ways. When Craig is stabbed during a riot, Drummond assigns Lutchmee to care for him in the hospital. Lutchmee is released from the backbreaking labor of the fields, and by interacting with Craig she is exposed to new ideas of refinement and civilization. As he recovers, they chat, and their conversation opens her mind: "It brought into her life fresh human elements, feelings she had never experienced before: ideas—novel, sweet piquant." This time is described as "very holy" and "halcyon" to her (Jenkins 2003, 155). In the racially and gender-encoded imperial ideal of the colonizer-colonized relationship, she comes to feel "a strange, half-god worship for him" (128). The use of religious terminology such as "holy" and "worship" emphasizes Craig's role as Lutchmee's savior as well as British Imperialism's role in bringing Christianity to the colonized people.

This sense of awakening begins to drive a wedge between Lutchmee and Dilloo. Lutchmee feels a sense of resentment toward her husband for the first time when she remembers her obligation to return to him once Craig has healed. In his introduction to the novel, David Dabydeen suggests that this is the budding of "a nascent feminism, a nascent defiance of patriarchal structures" (18). Far from being a defiance of patriarchy as Dabydeen suggests, I would argue that this is enforcing *white* patriarchy; she is simply shifting her allegiance from Dilloo to the proper receptacle, the godlike white overseer.

Though other characters suspect a sexual relationship between Lutchmee and Craig, Craig is a consummate gentleman. The characters who doubt Craig's motives, such as Drummond, Chester, the creole overseer, and eventually Dilloo, do so because of their own lack of honor, Jenkins suggests, rather than a lack of honor in Craig. He does not entertain any notions of such a relationship with Lutchmee, prevented first by his racist dismissal of her worth, and then by his purity of heart: "the repugnance of race...forbad the budding of any affectionate esteem in his heart, but he felt arising within him a strong sense of gratitude for her attentions; and...a sort of pleased admiration for her pretty features, lissome figure, and graceful ways" (Jenkins 2003, 130).

This indication of Craig's growing awareness of Lutchmee's attractions is followed quickly by a reminder that she is no equal to him: "Was she not a pretty animal?" (Jenkins 2003, 130). The text is filled with such metaphors, comparing Lutchmee to an animal or a child. For instance, Lutchmee is aware that Craig "regarded her rather as he regarded his dog and his horse, as a part of his establishment" (Jenkins 2003, 113). Again and again Jenkins emphasizes that Craig's feelings toward Lutchmee are no more than those of an owner toward a dog or a father toward a child. This is meant to be a sign of his pure intentions and protective instincts, but it serves to dehumanize Lutchmee and reinforce the view of Indian women as property seen in Phillips' narrative earlier.

Jenkins' emphasis on Craig's purity of mind can be seen as a response to concerns that arose in Britain and India over reports of British men developing sexual relationships with women laborers. Ashrufa Faruqee notes that the rigid hierarchical structure on the plantation "permitted plantation superiors to sexually exploit 'coolie' women, who held the lowest position within the plantation structure" (Faruqee 1996, 72). While later commissions, such as the McNeill-Lal Report of 1914, attempted to deny such relationships existed, the 1871 Royal Commission, parts of which Jenkins witnessed, recognized that they were common and suggested that they contributed to the general laxity of the indentured population (Faruqee 1996, 73). Jenkins does acknowledge that these relationships existed, as when he shows Drummond attempting to seduce Lutchmee. However, the text does not depict any such connections, and, as noted earlier, Jenkins is quick to point out that Drummond does not force himself on women. The reality was quite different: Joseph Beaumont, chief justice of British Guiana, wrote in 1871 that it was common for overseers and managers to engage in "illicit sexual relations" with Indian women and that it was usually a result of a "forcible abuse of power" (Beaumont 1871, 74–75).

Rather than dwelling on the unpleasantness of such relations, Jenkins suggests that Craig's paternalistic view toward Lutchmee is the solution to many of the ills of the system. In *The Coolie*, Jenkins argues that the employer should think of the laborers as his children, so that he will feel more tenderness toward them: "This immigration relation [between an employer and laborer] should not only be looked as one of pure contract...No legal adjustments can make it a happy one unless there is conjoined with them, on the side of the employer, a spirit of generosity and of half-*parental* kindness" (*The Coolie* 1871a, 122–123, emphasis mine). Thus, Craig demonstrates the ideal relationship between an employer and laborer.

Craig's protectiveness toward Lutchmee is expressed when he saves her from her husband as the tensions between the laborers and the planters reach their height. The workers, led by Dilloo, prepare to revolt under the cover of the Indian festival of Tadja, but the planters learn of their plan and buy up all the guns in town. This fictional event turned out to be tragically prescient: seven years after *Lutchmee and Dilloo* was published, there was a massacre of laborers in San Fernando during the observance of Hosay, a Muslim holiday.[6] Jenkins' narrative thus accurately depicts the potential violence laborers might confront, although in reality they faced this bloodshed simply for celebrating a religious holiday.

---

[6] Due to unrest, colonial officials in San Fernando had banned processions from entering the town. In defiance of this, on the day of Hosay, a procession of unarmed laborers marched toward the town, carrying *tadjas*, models of the tombs of the brothers of the prophet Mohammed. Police ordered the Indians, most of whom did not speak English, to disperse, and when they did not, fired into the crowd. Accounts vary, but between 9 and 22 Indians were killed and about 100 were injured.

Thwarted from revolting, Dilloo does not lose his desire for revenge, but instead shifts his focus to his individual enemies. When Dilloo sees Marston in the crowd during the festival, he attempts to stab him, but Craig intervenes, with Lutchmee's assistance. Jeremy Poynting sees this as an example of the complexity of Lutchmee's character: "She has strong moral values and at one point displays a risky independence from her husband by preventing him from murdering the hated local magistrate" ("East Indian Women" 1986a, 140). Lutchmee is certainly a more developed character than most Indian women in literature about the West Indies from this time period, including Webber's *Those That Be in Bondage*. Rather than an act of true independence, though, Lutchmee assisting Craig can be seen as another example of her swapping loyalties from an Indian man to a British one; instead of being faithful to and protecting her husband, she is now faithful to and protects Craig, and by default, Marston. Dilloo is overwhelmed with rage at this perceived betrayal, and Craig recognizes that it is not safe to send Lutchmee home, so he takes her with him to the plantation house.

This reflects the justification of many of the policies that the British implemented in India, and indeed, a major justification for imperialism itself. Colonial officials abolished practices that they considered barbaric, such as *sati*, the act of a widow committing suicide by throwing herself on the funeral pyre of her husband. In an oft-cited quote, Gayatri Spivak writes, "The abolition of this rite by the British has been generally understood as a case of 'White men are saving brown women from brown men'" (Spivak 1999, 93). This justification is evident in the dynamic between Craig, Lutchmee, Hunoomaun, and Dilloo. Craig exposes Lutchmee to ideas of refinement and civilization, protects her from Hunoomaun, and even saves her from her own husband, who wants to kill her. Lutchmee represents the innocent, exotic beauty of India, while Hunoomaun and even Dilloo represent its uncivilized, animalistic, self-destructive side. Writ large, this can be seen as a metaphor for the nations involved in the system of indenture; Britain acts as protector and savior, rescuing India from herself.

The symbolic role of the women within the novel is further emphasized by the sense of a hierarchy in how each race treats its women. The male Afro-Guyanese characters are depicted as amoral and deceitful in their relations: Simon Petey maintains an intimate relationship with a rich widow, Susan Sankey, with whom he has a child, while simultaneously promising Rosalind Dallas that he will marry her. By contrast, Lutchmee and Dilloo are described as having an honest, genuine, and pure love, at least initially. At first he protects her from harm and treats her with respect, but this changes over the course of the novel. Dilloo's cruelty to Lutchmee suggests that while the Indian men are not as barbaric as the Afro-Guyanese men, they are capable of viciousness toward women. Finally, we are presented with the idealized relationship between Craig and Isabel, the magistrate's daughter. Craig is excessively polite and respectful toward Isabel, refusing to give in to his feelings for her until she has indicated that she loves him. To emphasize the noble quality of their relationship and Craig's chivalrous treatment of Isabel, Craig saves Isabel from danger in a chapter titled "Knight and Lady." Their relationship is depicted as the ideal connection between a man and a woman, giving the Europeans the justification to claim moral superiority.

Since Dilloo is unsuccessful in his attempt to kill Marston, he must turn his anger to Hunoomaun. At the end of the festival, the two engage in a fight to the death. Dilloo triumphs and Hunoomaun falls dead, but Dilloo is fatally wounded in the process. Dilloo's degradation and eventual death effectively evoke sympathy for the workers, and Jenkins repeatedly rails against their mistreatment. He castigates the European ruling class for ignoring the suffering of the working class: "Blacks, Madeirans, Coolies, all swarming in tens of thousands, what were they? Why they were machines to make money for the people of Demerara—to provide cheap sugar to the world in general, and plenty of profit to speculating Britons in particular" (Jenkins 2003, 287–288). Here he perhaps inadvertently echoes Marx's critique that in a capitalist mode of production, the worker must sell his own labor power, and thus becomes a commodity himself, "the most wretched of commodities" (Marx 1986, 35). In keeping with Marx's view, the mistreatment that Dilloo faces as a laborer gradually divorces him from his own humanity, turning him violent and enraged, and it is only in his death that he is redeemed.

In spite of this critique, though, Jenkins cannot counsel revolt, and so Dilloo must fail as a revolutionary and die for his attempts. His death is presented as a tragic fate, but there is an imperial logic to it: Hunoomaun has died for his evil behavior, as has Dilloo for giving in to rage and hatred and conspiring against the white men. Drummond, Marston, and the other British officials remain in their positions of power, while Lutchmee, the purest and most innocent of the Indian characters, presumably will be cared for by these men. The novel concludes this way for at least two reasons; Jenkins' audience, as previously noted, is the British upper class, and so Jenkins cannot kill off the British upper-class characters in his novel. In addition, Jenkins' own political beliefs would have prevented him from condoning revolution. As Poynting suggests, "Jenkins, as a political reformist, has no concept of the just revolt. He can identify with Dilloo the sufferer, but not Dilloo the underground leader" ("John Edward Jenkins" 1986b, 216).

Yet, there is an inconsistency between Jenkins' stated ideology and the events of his novel. Dilloo turns violent against Craig, Marston, and even Lutchmee, but he is driven to do so by all of the injustices that he has faced at the hands of the Europeans. Jenkins' most dramatic indictment of the system comes as Dilloo contemplates his hatred for Lutchmee: "An artificial system of indenture, with the laws that defined and regulated it, had succeeded in moulding out of a manly, tender, generous, and loving character, a hard, unnatural and ferocious savage" (Jenkins 2003, 331). Though a staunch supporter of empire and British superiority, Jenkins' language suggests that indenture has had the opposite of its intended effect: rather than civilizing a barbarian race, it has taken a noble man and turned him savage. Jenkins argues that the system is worth saving, but the events of the novel suggest that the whole system is corrupt, and corrupts all those involved. This indictment is not limited to the laborers: as Jeremy Poynting notes, "As a manager, the true logic of the novel suggests, Craig could well become another Drummond" ("John Edward Jenkins" 1986b, 217–218).

This inconsistency can be attributed to Jenkins' anxiety about the fragmenting of the British Empire. In *The Colonial Question* (1871b), a collection of three essays, Jenkins advocates the consolidation of all of Britain's colonies into a federation as the solution to the growing threat of "imperial dissolution" (*The Colonial Question* 1871b, 3). He describes the relationship between Britain and her colonies as one of "mutual dependency" and "mutual support" (*The Colonial Question* 1871b, 53). He also points out that giving colonies independence did not mean they would not then be colonized by another nation, and he raises the specter of American dominance by quoting an American diplomat: "*The United States is watching, and I guess she'll pick up everything you let drop*" (*The Colonial Question* 1871b, 20, emphasis original). *Lutchmee and Dilloo* is meant to address these concerns by touting the benefits and superiority of the British Empire. Yet the novel reveals more than Jenkins perhaps intended, as can be seen in the parallels between *Lutchmee and Dilloo* and another of Jenkins' novels.

Ginx's Baby (1871c), Jenkins' most famous work, is a satirical novel about a baby born into poverty who becomes a rallying cry for a variety of religious and political organizations, but is quickly cast off by each. As in *Lutchmee and Dilloo*, there is a single sterling example of British aristocracy—in this case, a man who is actually named Sir Charles Sterling. Sterling is presented as the ideal British gentleman: kind, intelligent, and ardent. He is clearly meant to be the voice of reason in Jenkins' text, calling attention to the baby's unhealthy state and using him to draw attention to the mistreatment of the poor. Yet Sterling, like the religious and civil institutions that Jenkins disparages, does little to solve the problems in front of him. He gets caught up in larger debates about social inequality, debates that rage on for years while the unnamed baby grows up largely neglected. Like Dilloo, Ginx's baby turns immoral, surviving by begging and stealing, and after several desperate years, he throws himself off a bridge. Without intending to, Jenkins creates similar portraits in Craig and Sterling. Both are British gentlemen who are meant to be ideals of civilization, but both are implicated in the tide of abuses that results from the capitalistic imperialism intrinsically tied to British civilization. In spite of Craig's kind intentions, Lutchmee and Dilloo remain merely "machines to make money."

Those That Be in Bondage: "A Stupendous Leap"

Unlike Edward Jenkins, A.R.F. Webber lived his whole life in the Caribbean. Born in Tobago in 1880, he moved to British Guiana when he was nineteen and spent the rest of his life there. Webber was largely self-educated, ending his formal training after middle school. He worked in several different fields, as a clerk in a business office, an advertiser for a newspaper, a journalist, an editor, a poet, a novelist, and a politician. He was a member of what was called the colored class, persons of mixed African and European heritage. As such, he would have been at the center of the race and class tensions that shaped the colony's hierarchical social structure. In the highly stratified society of colonial Guiana, race distinctions played crucial roles, and his mixed-race and middle-class parents placed him in a position of tension between the poorer, laboring class, made up mostly of Africans, Chinese, and Indians, and the wealthy, land-owning class of Europeans.

Webber had ties to both the planters and the working class. His brother, George, and uncle-in-law, Edward Percival Ross, worked as overseers on a plantation belonging to the Davsons, a prominent English family that settled in Guiana, and there are hints that Webber himself may have worked as an overseer for a brief time.[7] In his early years, he worked as the secretary for the British Guiana Sugar Planters' Association and publicity secretary for the Georgetown Chamber of Commerce, which represented the planters' interests. Around the same time, he also worked in the advertising department of the *Daily Argosy* newspaper, and later as a freelance journalist, which gave him a broader understanding of Guyanese society and an awareness of the suffering of the working class. In later years, he became a politician and a staunch anti-colonial activist, advocating for Guyanese independence and the rights of the working class. Yet the travelogues of his visits to London suggest that he maintained a certain awed and romantic view toward imperial power.

Perhaps because of these clashing experiences, Webber's political views shifted fairly dramatically over time. In his biography of Webber, Selwyn Cudjoe describes this change:

> At the beginning of his career in Guyana, Webber may have been conservative or even indifferent to the political situation that surrounded him... Webber first worked in the cause of the planters but later began to espouse liberal causes and identify with issues that concerned working people. At the end of his career, he identified with the ideas of Fabian socialism. (Cudjoe 2009, 7)

This can be seen in his advocacy in later years for the African, Chinese, and Indian people who worked on plantations and in other oppressive conditions. Additionally, in 1926, when the British sought to return Guiana to a Crown Colony, Webber and his colleagues responded by forming the Popular Party. The first political party in the West Indies, the Popular Party fought for self-government, women's suffrage, and the protection and promotion of trade unions. When Guyana finally achieved independence on May 26, 1966, it was in part because of the hard work of Webber and the party he helped found.

Yet Webber's changes did not progress in a linear trajectory, and elements of his conservatism remained throughout his career. Traces of racial hierarchies and an idealization of empire continue to appear in his later

---

[7] In *Caribbean Visionary*, Selwyn Cudjoe reports that he spoke to a cousin of Webber who suggested but would not confirm that Webber worked as an overseer.

writings. Growing up with some amount of privilege due to the middle-class standing of his family and his mixed heritage, he was caught between the poorer laboring class of Africans, Indians, and Chinese, and the powerful European governing and planting class, aware of the suffering of the former but unwilling to give up his connections to the latter.

This tension can be seen in *Those That Be in Bondage*, published in 1917 (years before Webber became active in politics), and set in British Guiana, Trinidad, and Tobago. In the 40 years after *Lutchmee and Dilloo* was published, some aspects of the indenture system had changed, though not always in favor of the laborer. On the one hand, the 1891 British Guiana Immigration Ordinance specified that the employer was obliged to provide suitable housing, regular rations, and appropriate wages, and five-year reindenture contracts, often used in unscrupulous ways to maintain control over laborers, were discouraged. However, laborers were no longer given free passage back to India at the end of their indenture. This was a major blow to their mobility, as few laborers had saved enough money to pay all or even a portion of the return passage. Webber wrote *Those That Be in Bondage* to draw attention to the ongoing exploitation of the indentured Indians, as well as the unfair treatment of the "coloured" middle class, yet the novel focuses on two generations of a European planting family. He expresses sympathy for the sufferings of the lower classes and fights against some elements of racial prejudice, but he does not challenge indenture, colonialism, or even the notion that some races are more civilized than others. This demonstrates the pervasiveness of racist colonial ideology: Webber replicates the very power structures that he struggles against. Rather than challenging stereotypes, he often maintains them in order to differentiate the middle, "coloured" class from those races and classes lower down in the hierarchy.[8]

Like Jenkins, Webber recognizes many of the flaws of the indenture system, but expresses enthusiasm for its benefits to the colony and immigrants alike. Almost 20 years after writing *Those That Be in Bondage*, Webber wrote a detailed history of British Guiana entitled *Centenary History and Handbook of British Guiana* (1931). In this text, he emphasizes again and again how necessary immigration was to save the economy of British Guiana. He notes that the population of British Guiana was

---

[8] In "Colonial Trauma/Postcolonial Recovery?" David Lloyd notes that decolonized states struggling for nationalism often reproduce paradigms of oppression and violence (2000). See also Frantz Fanon's *Wretched of the Earth* (2004), among others.

often decreasing, and he saw ongoing immigration as a solution to this problem. He writes that the history of the 1840s and 1850s "is the history of immigration," and that "1845 saw the re-opening *at last* of Indian immigration" (Webber 1931, 214, emphasis mine). Furthermore, he suggests that laborers gained by this system as well. Though indentured immigration ended in 1917, in 1919 a delegation was sent to convince the Indian government to send more migrants, and Webber writes that the "unbiased report" of G.F. Keatinge, a member of the Indian Civil Service, "established the wonderful benefits that were and could be derived by the immigrants" (Webber 1931, 348).

Those That Be in Bondage is a largely unknown but important work: it is the first novel about East Indians in the Caribbean written by a Caribbean novelist, and one of the first novels on any topic by a Caribbean author. Like *Lutchmee and Dilloo*, it is far more sympathetic to the East Indians than other works that came before. Webber is critical of aspects of the system, showing the limited control that the laborers had over their own lives. In addition, the two main Indian characters are intelligent, honorable, and strong-willed, unlike the passive Indian characters of earlier texts. Yet, the Indian characters are painted as racial stereotypes and have little voice in the text, and Webber, like Jenkins, does not counsel revolt. At times, Webber even seems to support the colonial mission and the indenture system, and he focuses more on the injustices that the managing class faced than the suffering of the laborers. This focus is most likely a result of his personal connections to the managerial class. Since his brother and uncle-in-law both worked as overseers, he would have been familiar with their experiences and more attuned to the challenges the managers faced.

Like *Lutchmee and Dilloo*, the novel is written in third-person omniscient, but it follows the lives of the planting class, rather than dividing the story between the overseers and the laborers. The novel has two parts, with the theme of bondage running through both. In the first part, which takes place on Plantation Never Out in Tobago, the bondage is more literal. It focuses on Edwin Hamilton, a young Englishman working as an overseer for his brother-in-law, who is the owner of the plantation, and Bibi Singh, a young Indian woman who is a bonded laborer on the plantation. Edwin and Bibi fall in love, marry, and have a baby, but die tragically shortly after the baby is born. In the second half of the novel, the bondage is metaphoric. This portion of the story follows the orphaned child Marjorie and her cousin Harold as they grapple with the constrictions of the Catholic Church and society's prejudices. My analysis focuses primarily on the first half of the novel, which deals directly with indentured labor.

The similarities between this section of the novel and *Lutchmee and Dilloo* are striking. Like Craig, Edwin Hamilton is a handsome and honorable British man. Bibi, the female Indian laborer who catches Edwin's attention, is young, beautiful, and vulnerable. Though John Walton, the owner of Plantation Never Out, and his wife Marion are responsible for many of the troubles that Bibi experiences, they are shown as well-meaning, if somewhat narrow-minded. The true villain of the story, as in *Lutchmee and Dilloo*, is an Indian man, the violent and cunning Karim, whose lust for Bibi leads to Edwin and Bibi's death. Webber, like Jenkins, seems to suggest that Britain's role in India is to protect her from herself. Even though Webber struggled against racism, there is still a clear hierarchy of race within the novel, with the European planting class shown to be the height of civilization.

Yet, there are significant differences between *Lutchmee and Dilloo* and *Those That Be in Bondage*. While the former takes place primarily on the plantation, depicting the lives of both the laborers and the managers, the latter focuses on the European planters and their children, their experiences in the natural world of Tobago, and the society of British Guiana. The Caribbean plays a much more central role in the narrative, indicating Webber's pride in the land of his birth. The relationship between Edwin, the British man, and Bibi, the Indian woman, can still be seen as a metaphor for relations between Britain and India, but added to this dynamic is their child, a girl named Marjorie. Marjorie, who combines British, African, and Indian ancestry, can be seen as representing the Caribbean, and Webber uses Marjorie to suggest that the Caribbean is a blending of the best of East and West. This is a radical move, positioning not only the British and the Africans, but also Indians, who are often elided in the history of the Caribbean, as critical to Caribbean identity. Cultural theorist Stuart Hall, among others, calls for this kind of recognition of cultural hybridity in the Caribbean. In his article "Negotiating Caribbean Identities," he argues that, for Caribbean people today, the key to creating a sense of identity lies in acknowledging the histories of the marginalized and "in using the enormously rich and complex cultural heritages to which history has made them heir" (Hall 1995, 8). In a sense, Webber performs this acknowledgment in the character of Marjorie, who is a mix of several ethnicities.

Though there is a clear hierarchy of race in the story, Webber also blurs the boundaries of race much more than Jenkins. This suggests that, while Webber did not entirely reject notions of racial superiority, he did struggle with them. In *Lutchmee and Dilloo*, with the exception of one creole overseer, the characters fall clearly into categories that are fixed along ethnic and national lines: English and Scottish, Indian, Chinese, and Afro-Guyanese. In *Those That Be in Bondage*, the major characters, including those of the planting class, are of mixed ancestry, which challenges colonial rhetoric around racial purity and acknowledges the frequency of interracial unions. This hybridity is also depicted as a boon, rather than a source of embarrassment: Webber indicates that the women of mixed blood are often the most beautiful.

While Jenkins was anxious about the potential dissolution of the British Empire and believed that indentured immigration was one way to strengthen the empire, Webber expresses anxiety about the potential collapse of the sugar industry and the destruction of the economy of the colony. Webber wrote *Those That Be in Bondage* shortly before indentured migration was banned and was perhaps attempting to bolster the crumbling system, and with it, the labor force. His treatment of indentured labor, like that of Jenkins, suggests that if managed correctly, indentured labor would benefit all those involved. This can be seen most clearly in the relationship between Edwin and Bibi. Edwin, like Craig, is an honorable British man who lifts Bibi out of the poverty and degradation of bonded labor. He, too, is a new arrival to the plantation system, having grown up in England. "Reared far from colonial influences," he is less prone to the racism that his sister and brother-in-law feel toward the laborers who work on their plantation, and having been "bred in the atmosphere of an English public school, he had absorbed to a hypersensitive degree its spirit of fairplay" (Webber 1988, 6). Both authors suggest that the plantation system corrupts those involved: Edwin, a recent transplant from the morally pure world of England, is more ethical and fair-minded than those of the other overseers and even his own family members.

A major difference between Edwin and Craig is that Edwin is of mixed European and African descent, challenging notions of racial purity. Marion, his sister, is described as having hair "of that sheen of raven so rarely met in pure-blooded Europeans, yet often found in colonial families—a sure index of some negro-blooded ancestor" (Webber 1988, 18). The descriptor "sheen of raven" has a highly positive connotation, indicating that Marion's beauty comes in part from her African ancestry, while the phrase "so rarely seen in pure-blooded Europeans," suggests that Marion is not the only member of the planting class with mixed blood. Yet, Marion and Edwin are still classified as European, and Webber depicts them as the height of beauty and nobility, so these characters do not radically defy views of racial superiority.

Like Lutchmee, Bibi has highly Europeanized features and is described as superior to most of her race: "Her bold luminous eyes and Caucasian features had brought many men to her feet...the soft clear tint of her skin proclaimed her parentage to be far beyond that of the average East Indian immigrant" (Webber 1988, 25). In fact, Edwin later learns that Bibi is a kind of Indian royalty, descended from a hill chief. In spite of Bibi's superior appearance and pedigree, Edwin feels great inner conflict in accepting that he loves her. He is aware of her beauty and refinement, but equally conscious that "she was bare-toed and worked like Ruth in the fields" (Webber 1988, 28). When he first considers marrying her, he dismisses the idea immediately with the thought that "he was not quite prepared to make a fool of himself" (Webber 1988, 28).

It is clear that Bibi is only a viable mate for Edwin because of her highclass status. Edwin contemplates that "there was not really so much disparity in their social positions if she could take up her rightful place at the court of her grandfather" (Webber 1988, 42). This reflects historian David Cannadine's argument that social hierarchies were just as integral to the British Empire as racial hierarchies. He notes that the British applied the conventions of their own society to the nations they colonized: royalty and members of the aristocracy in colonized societies were afforded more respect than peasants (2001, 9). The importance of Bibi's heritage is emphasized again later in the novel. Edwin is said to be descended from Napoleon, and so their daughter Marjorie is described as uniting "in her own veins the blood of the old Indian chief and that of the mighty Genius who had stood astride the world and rattled his scabbarded sabre in the presence of the Earth's greatest" (Webber 1988, 73). Though Webber challenges race and class distinctions in some ways, he emphasizes Bibi's superiority to the other laborers in order to make her an acceptable love interest for Edwin; an average laborer could not be so.

The story of Singh, Bibi's father, suggests that Webber saw colonialism as beneficial, at least in India. As a young man, Singh attended a Mission School, where he did so well that he seemed destined for a "University career" (Webber 1988, 38). He would have been a wealthy landowner had he not married the daughter of a hill chief and spent all of his wealth running from the chief's persecutions. Singh tells Edwin that "nothing but the fear of the English Raj had saved his life from the fierce resentment of the Chief" (Webber 1988, 38), suggesting that British law and order protected the more civilized, Westernized Indians like Singh from the barbaric violence of Indians like the Hill Chief. Singh's education at the Mission School and his chance at a university education are treated as valuable opportunities, and out of gratitude for his education, Singh gives his daughter the anglicized name of Ursula (though she is called Bibi). While this emphasis on the benefits of imperialism was not an uncommon view at the time, other early twentieth century Caribbean authors depict the damages of colonialism and indenture. As noted earlier, Edgar Mittelholzer's 1941 novel *Corentyne Thunder* depicts British planters exploiting their Indian laborers rather than treating them with paternalistic kindness.

Just as the antagonist in *Lutchmee and Dilloo* is not Drummond the plantation owner or Marston the magistrate, in *Those That Be in Bondage*, the villain is not John Walton, but Karim, an Indian laborer and revolutionary. John and his wife Marion are depicted as flawed but well-meaning, while Karim is spiteful and violent, spreading lies about Bibi and Edwin and fomenting rebellion in response to Bibi's rejection of him. His defects extend beyond these acts: Karim is "hot-headed and educated above his station," suggesting that it is dangerous to educate the working class. Equally damning, "he indulged some of the fancies of East Indian socialism" (Webber 1988, 26). Over time, Webber became more sympathetic toward socialism,[9] but at the time of writing *Those*, he was much more connected to the commercial class in British Guiana and a firm supporter of capitalism. In this novel, he seems to view socialism as a weed, spreading threateningly among the workers.

Webber's treatment of Karim reflects a great deal of ambivalence toward the Indian immigrants. His harshest stereotypes and deepest sympathies are evoked when he describes Karim, often in the same moment. For example, Webber employs a common stereotype about Indians, noting that the lies Karim makes up about Edwin and Bibi are characteristic of his race: "Those who know the East Indian character will readily realize how

---

[9] After visiting London in 1926, he expressed the belief that socialism was not relevant in British Guiana, but necessary in London: "In Urban England, industrialized to the fingertips, the strong crushing the weak, and the poor gripped in unspeakable misery, the plant must flourish" (quoted in Cudjoe 2009, 74).

prone they are to romance every conceivable subject" (Webber 1988, 27). Immediately after this statement, the tone shifts, and Webber uses this moment to draw attention to the suffering of the East Indians: "But when it is considered that he is the child of centuries of tyranny and oppression: when it is remembered that lying and chicanery are perhaps the only weapons available to the defenseless and the bitterly oppressed; we may perhaps spare a tear for the failing of his race" (Webber 1988, 27).

However, this sympathy is mixed with condescension, and since it is attached to the description of a man who has just attempted to assault a woman and then spread the rumor that she is the consort of an overseer, it is difficult to see much genuine compassion for the Indians here.

In fact, we see little of any of the Indian characters, and what we do see is through Edwin's eyes. Webber does draw attention to some of the concerns the laborers faced, such as the lack of control that they had over their own destiny. When John Walton, owner of the plantation, orders Singh and Bibi to leave seemingly on a whim, they must leave, though no reason is given and they have done nothing wrong. In addition, Webber uses Karim's bad behavior toward his workers to note that the drivers on the estate often took advantage of the laborers: "to prey upon the labourers under them is the perquisite [sic] of the 'driver.' All must pay tribute for favours past or to come: the men must pay with silver, or service, and the women in pain and person" (Webber 1988, 29). Other than these indications, though, there is little sense of the laborers' lives or the suffering they experienced.

The lack of a sense of the laborers' interiority is compounded by the passivity of Bibi's character. Bibi, like Lutchmee, cannot save herself, but must be lifted by Edwin out of poverty and abuse. She has little voice, as the only words she speaks in the text are filtered through Edwin's consciousness. For example, he considers their early interactions and reflects that "she had given little more than a coy 'Salaam'" (Webber 1988, 37). Similarly, when Edwin decides to marry Bibi, there is no question of her answer, only the obstacles he must overcome to marry a "bare-toed" immigrant (Webber 1988, 28). After announcing his attention to Singh, Edwin calls Bibi to him, and she quickly accedes. Her feelings are similar to the half-god worship that Lutchmee feels for Craig: "She had long secretly loved 'the Sahib Hamilton'" (Webber 1988, 37). The figurative language of the novel supports this image of Edwin as godlike. As Edwin gazes at Bibi with growing love, she sits "at his table, shading her eyes from the rays of the rude lamp which was all the ornament boasted by

Edwin's room" (Webber 1988, 34). She must shield herself from the brightness of the lamp and the blazing love that it represents.

In some respects, Webber had a more realistic view of relations between managers and female laborers than Jenkins, or was simply more willing to show this reality. Unlike Craig, Edwin's feelings toward Bibi are decidedly unchaste, and his lust for her is one of the major forces that propels him toward marriage. In other respects, though, Webber's depictions do not accurately represent the experience of the female migrant. Bibi is overwhelmed by various offers of marriage and sex, but Webber emphasizes that she had the option to decline each one: "No matter what may be written to the contrary of the sexual abuses under the present system of Emigration from India to the British Colonies, the fact remains that a woman, under any circumstances can remain mistress of herself" (Webber 1988, 25). This is contradicted, not only by the reports of commissioners investigating the treatment of laborers, but by the events of the novel itself. Edwin marries Bibi in part to shelter her from anyone "who dared to suborn the graceful young woman sitting in his presence, into an unwelcome or repulsive embrace" (Webber 1988, 34). It may be that Webber was trying to protect the planter class, the immigration system, and the reputation of British Guiana as a civilized society. It could also be that, because sexual assault was a taboo subject (as it still is to some extent today), Webber truly believed that there were no such forced relations.

In the culminating scene of this section, there is a tension between the laborers' legitimate reasons to revolt and the misguided way in which they do so. Webber shows some sympathy for the workers, indicating that they have suffered abuses such as the unfair transfer of Singh and Bibi, the cruelty and corruption of the drivers, and the sexual exploitation of the women. On the other hand, Karim, their leader is shown to be a malicious, jealous man stirring rebellion for his own selfish purposes. This section also suggests that the immigrants are easily deceived and manipulated, as they readily believe Karim's rumors and riot as a result. Jenkins shows sympathy toward Dilloo's cause but can not condone his revolt. By contrast, Webber shows a violent clash erupt between the immigrants and the police, but he focuses on the racism that leads to this violence, rather than the systemic oppressions of indenture and colonialism. The police are mobilized, he writes, "Because one heart had cooed to its mate, and that mate was bare-toed: her skin was not ivory, and she bound up the sheaves in the field" (Webber 1988, 44).

Once the uprising is addressed and Edwin and Bibi are married, they live a brief but happy life together. While the civilizing influence of the British is a common theme in colonial literature, Edwin and Bibi's relationship demonstrates another frequent trope, the depiction of the colonized people as mysterious, and alluring in their other-ness. Edwin sees Bibi's cultural differences as delightfully exotic and strives to keep her unchanged by Western culture: "Though Bibi showed wonderful aptitude for Western ideas, Edwin, however, resolutely set his face against any westernizing of her dress" (Webber 1988, 59). She thus becomes a static representative of her culture, trapped in amber at the moment of her migration.

Additionally, Webber seems to preclude the possibility of a true intermingling of culture in their marriage. Edwin makes their house as close to an Indian home as possible, and "thus was ensured unto him his wife as a never-ending source of delight; never once had he felt that indescribable feeling of disappointment in seeing anything like *gaucherie* in any effort to ape the manners and customs of her western sisters" (Webber 1988, 59, emphasis original). While Webber ascribes value to Indian culture, that value lies only in its charming novelty, the mysterious orientalism that it holds for her British husband. There is no sense that Edwin might learn something from her culture, or be changed in any way by their interactions. Similarly, Bibi is shown as incapable of learning anything valuable from Western ideas; if she were to try, she would only be "aping," and the result would be disappointing and grotesque.

This interethnic marriage is ultimately unsustainable and ends in tragedy, due once again to Karim's villainy. Edwin comes home to find Karim standing over Bibi's bed holding a cutlass and is killed in the violent struggle that follows. The shock of this is too much for Bibi and she dies, leaving their daughter, Marjorie, an orphan.

Karim's trial, like much of his treatment in the novel, contains echoes of imperial discourse and reflects a striking ambivalence toward the Indian population. Webber contrasts the viewing crowds, "a dense surging mass of every hue," including "gaudy" Indian women, with the "huge marble statue of Victoria...Empress of India, looking down benign and calm on the struggling mass" (Webber 1988, 64). Queen Victoria looms above her subjects, a chaotic mass of people desperately in need of her benevolent leadership and the salvation she offers. The defense lawyer, an Indian barrister, is described as taking "no notice of questions of fact" (Webber

1988, 64), instead focusing on the detail that Edwin could have chosen a wife from his own social circles, whereas Karim would have had a difficult time finding a wife due to the extreme shortage of female immigrants. The lawyer has also coached Karim to misrepresent the story, and when Karim takes the stand, he claims that he deeply loved Bibi and had no intention of harming her, and that he only killed Edwin in self-defense. In this way, both characters feed into the stereotype of Indians as cunning liars. In his closing statements, the defense lawyer speaks of the injustices that Indians faced in British Guiana, "brought across two oceans to be shot down, or hanged; their liberty impaired and their wives stolen" (Webber 1988, 66). This is one of the clearest indictments of the system, but it is difficult to give it much weight, as it comes in the defense of the villain of the story, a defense that is largely made up of lies.

Webber's critique of the indentured labor system is not a call to overthrow the system. He draws attention to the sexual predation of women and the undue control that planters had over the workers, but he does not show the lives of the workers in any detail, and the one true revolutionary among the Indian workers is the villain of the novel, suggesting a low regard for labor movements. Webber's main critiques of the system are the gender imbalance and the treatment of overseers. He argues that the country does not prosper because the sugar industry does not prosper, and that the sugar industry does not prosper because the overseers create no ties. They either leave their position or fall into self-destructive behavior: "no home life, no social element, no anything—save gin and coolie women. No wonder that these young men are so frequently to be found strewn along the byways of the country" (Webber 1988, 182). This section of the novel ends with Eloise Funston, the one European woman in whom Edwin had shown interest, learning of Edwin's death and finally accepting an offer of marriage from another man. If social norms were looser and allowed overseers to interact with upper-class European women, the novel suggests, Edwin and Eloise might have married and prevented the "ghastly tragedy" of Edwin and Bibi's death (Webber 1988, 68). The true outrage of the indenture system, it seems, is the denigration of the overseers.

The remainder of the novel deals with the next generation of the Waltons. Marion, Edwin's sister, adopts Marjorie, and the family moves to Tobago. Years later, Marjorie and Harold, her cousin, fall in love, but they face various obstacles to a happy life together. Though Bibi and the other Indian characters are largely depicted as passive objects, Bibi's daughter Marjorie is not a stereotype, and a large portion of this section is devoted to her story. Marjorie is the true heroine of the novel, and more than any other character in the book, she is fully developed: impetuous, intelligent, and kindhearted. While Edwin and Bibi can be seen as symbols of Britain and India, their child, Marjorie, represents the Caribbean. Like the population of this region, she combines different ancestries: Marjorie's mother is Indian, and her father is of British and African descent. Born and raised in the Caribbean, she knows and loves its history, taking Harold on excursions to various notable spots in Tobago, including the cave that she believes is the setting of *Robinson Crusoe*.

In addition, Marjorie is depicted as combining the best of East and West, though what she gains from each culture fits the colonial stereotypes that appear earlier in the novel. She inherits her sensual beauty from her mother's side of the family: "At fourteen Marjorie had developed with all the precocity of the tropics and her Indian blood" (Webber 1988, 73). Through her aunt, she is exposed to Western culture and civilization, and quotes Keats and Robert Louis Stevenson. Bibi and Singh remain mysterious, but Marjorie is knowable because she is, intellectually at least, British.[10] Jenkins suggests that both India and Britain would prosper if the system of indenture and colonization continued with some modifications. Webber also indicates that colonization has been beneficial to both Britain and its colonies, but adds that the child of this relationship, Marjorie/the Caribbean, combines the best of both worlds.

Significantly, the novel ends when Harold and Marjorie, after a series of misfortunes, decide to move to London. There they will be free from the church, who persecute Harold for his decision to leave the priesthood in order to marry Marjorie. Marjorie, who has been writing for the London newspapers, will gain the worldwide recognition that she craves. In an act of reverse colonization, Marjorie states that she and Harold "shall...make a little Tobago Colony in London...I can close my eyes and see the world before me" (Webber 1988, 235–236). London is depicted as the source of true freedom, the place where they will achieve their dreams. Wilson Harris points out that this is especially striking given the timing: "It seems incongruous that Harold and Marjorie contemplated departure for England in 1913...that no inkling possessed them of the end of an age and the impending outbreak of the Great War" (Harris 1990, 149). I suggest that the novel contains this image of London because Webber maintains a view of the metropole as the height of power and civilization. Later in life,

[10] Though Marjorie is depicted as having some African ancestry, there is little indication of what she has gained from it. This, in conjunction with the limited space given to Afro-Caribbean characters in the novel, might indicate that Webber views Africans' contributions to Caribbean culture as limited.

he advocated for the independence of the colonies, but here he mourns the impending end of the empire and all that it represents.[11]

Webber's greatest concern within this novel is to address injustices within the colonial structure, such as the prejudice faced by those of mixed race. Many of his European characters are multiracial, acknowledging the prevalence of interracial relations in colonial society and pointing to the arbitrary nature of the prejudice against the children of such unions: "today they all pass for white, and none are the worse or the wiser for it" (Webber 1988, 18). Yet, he seems to accept passing for white as an acceptable goal, and objects only to the fact that those who look white are not treated as white. He thus advocates a more progressive view of race, but one still limited by a sense of a racial hierarchy.

This racial hierarchy is closely connected to a hierarchy of labor and is underscored by how visible each ethnicity is within the story. The few characters of African descent in the novel appear only briefly, as servants delighted to help their European masters. A "bare-footed black girl…her face all wreathed in smiles" brings milk to Marjorie (Webber 1988, 100), and an African man named Old Cudjoe guides Harold and Marjorie on their explorations through a cave. When the two later visit Cudjoe's home, he is deeply honored by their visit: "If Angels had descended on the habitation of the old African…he could not have been more overwhelmed" (Webber 1988, 116). Webber treats this old man with respect, as do Harold and Marjorie, yet he is still in a position of extreme subservience.[12] The characters of mixed race play an equally minor role in the novel.

---

[11] This ambivalence can also be seen in his journalism, especially *An Innocent's Pilgrimage*, in which he describes his impressions of London. Though he is critical of Britain, he shows a certain awe for its history: "This is the London which inspired the arrogance that cost the Empire the American colonies; the London which freed the slaves; the London which has been guilty of every sin under the sun; and has been in the van of every cause of righteousness. What mighty traditions, what fatal errors lay enshrouded in its folds" (quoted in Cudjoe 2009, 72).

[12] This dismissal of Africans is echoed in his nonfiction works. In his historical account, *Centenary History and Handbook of British Guiana*, Webber feeds in to the stereotype that Africans were childlike and lazy: "There was…no effort made to engender self-reliance and industry in the Negro. He was still a child, to be induced to labour by free gifts" (Webber 1931, 197). In an article for *The Daily Chronicle*, he writes that it is a mistake "to confuse the higher standard of civilization and culture of the West Indies with that of the African dependencies…where you have millions of illiterate people, practically naked savages, you cannot compare them with the clothed people of British Guiana" (quoted in Cudjoe 2009, 100). He thus replicates racist and inaccurate views of Africa in order to place British Guiana higher on the hierarchy of civilized cultures.

Murray, the creole overseer, makes a brief appearance to advise Edwin, but is otherwise absent from the text. The Indian laborers, in particular Bibi, Singh, and Karim, are more central to the text, but they are only shown as field laborers, and they appear primarily as plot devices. The third-person narrator does not attempt to explore their thoughts or feelings as he does with the European characters, and we only see the Indian characters as they interact with the Europeans, not with each other. The European planters occupy the positions of power, both within the plantation, and within the novel itself. As with Jenkins, this may be an issue of audience. Webber's foreword suggests that his story is aimed at Europe; he describes his novel as a ship, and he hopes that she will weather the storms she experiences "while sailing to the West" (Webber 1988).[13]

It is worth noting that this perspective is not universal in texts from this time period. H.G. de Lisser, a Jamaican journalist and author who lived around the same time as Webber, published *Jane's Career* in 1914. This novel, a coming-of-age story about a young peasant woman who moves from the countryside to Kingston, is one of the first published novels by a West Indian author, and one of the first to depict a peasant as the main character. Jane, the main character, works first as a domestic servant and then as a factory worker in a bottling plant, compelled by her innate sense of self-worth to leave positions where she is treated unfairly. De Lisser challenges notions of racial superiority, showing characters of lighter complexions affecting superiority over Jane and other poor, dark-skinned workers as a justification for treating them with cruelty and selfishness (de Lisser 1972).

Aside from the mistreatment of the overseers and the prejudice against those of mixed race, Webber's major critique of the indenture system is the disproportionate number of males who emigrate. Each major conflict in *Those That Be in Bondage* revolves around women; either the lack of available women causes tensions between men or a man falls in love with a woman from a different class, which leads to his downfall. When describing Edwin's limited options for marriage, Webber pauses to expound on the issues created by the gender imbalance: "The problems of sex on a sugar estate are the problems of that immigration system on which the very existence of the sugar industry,

---

[13] Vishnudat Singh points out that the second half of the novel, which spends a great deal of time following Harold and Marjorie on their explorations of the Tobago coast, has the travelogue quality of works by British authors who visited the Caribbean, like Anthony Trollope. Singh concludes, "He wants to explain Guyana to those who stay at home, the clearest indication that the novel is addressed to metropolitan readers" (Singh 1986, 49).

and consequently the whole industrial life of the colony, may be said to be at stake" (Webber 1988, 7). He goes on to describe the violent feelings that are aroused by this disproportion, citing as proof the numbers of wife slayers who are hanged every year and the women whose noses or hands have been chopped off by a jealous husband.[14]

British colonizers often used the gender imbalance as a scapegoat, arguing that it was the root of many of the problems of the system. Ashrufa Faruqee highlights a contradiction in the imperial rhetoric around women: "The colonial state believed that women were causing the problems on the estate, yet it also maintained that women were needed to solve these same problems" (Faruqee 1996, 62). The lack of women, they suggested, led to jealousy among the men, which turned into violence. Without women, the men lost the softening benefit of civilization, and became amoral and vicious. In addition, British authorities blamed the class of women who did immigrate for the degradation of the workers' morals and lifestyle; it was commonly reported that only prostitutes and other low-class women could be persuaded to travel under indenture. In the Des Voeux hearings, the commissioners conclude, "There is among the Coolie population in India no class of respectable single women. The proportion of females was accordingly made up 'in the bazaars' and the results were, few children and many diseases" (British Guiana 1870, 53). No doubt the disproportionate number of men to women did lead to tensions and unhappiness, but the focus on this issue draws attention away from the more systemic ways that laborers suffered: the brutal labor they were forced to perform, the terrible living conditions they endured, the rigging of the system to protect the planters, and the lack of control of their own lives.

Yet many critics today still focus on the gender imbalance as the cause of the immigrants' unhappiness and violence. Wilson Harris writes of the unequal gender ratio and its role in the events of *Those That Be in Bondage*, "Such disproportion--though it had begun to ease--still remained a disfiguring feature in British Guiana in the early twentieth century. No wonder Karim the rebel was blindly jealous of the overseer Edwin Hamilton" (Harris 1990, 149). This perspective is supported in the text, as Webber

---

[14] Though the gender disparity appears in *Lutchmee and Dilloo*—there are only two female Indian characters in the entire text—it is much less central to the plot. This suggests that Jenkins saw other issues, such as the government and legal system's partiality to the planters, as more responsible for the suffering of the workers.

suggests that Karim's jealousy is the main motivation for his hatred of Edwin. Both Harris and Webber brush aside the other reasons that Karim might have had for hating Edwin, such as the position of power he holds based solely on his race and family connection to John Walton.

In his treatment of the female characters within his novel, Webber supports the argument that both the absence and the presence of women have disastrous effects on the men of the colony. As noted earlier, Edwin finds solace in Bibi in part because of the lack of social and marriage options available to overseers, which then leads to the tragic death of both. Had either Edwin or Karim had more suitable options for a mate, the book suggests, all of the tragedy that follows could have been avoided. In the second half of the novel, Harold has become a famous and successful preacher for the Catholic Church, but he succumbs to the temptation of a sexual relationship with Marjorie. He then feels compelled to leave the priesthood, which makes his life difficult for years to come. There is also the minor but noteworthy story of the couple that manages the plantation where Harold works as an overseer. The manager's wife is a stark contrast to Bibi, a caricature of the unwomanly woman, "spare and angular in look, manner and speech. Her husband she ruled with a rod of iron...so far as the social element or feminine softness was concerned, she might as well have stayed away" (Webber 1988, 183). Her presence is even worse than her absence; not only does she not play the role of hostess, as Webber expects women to do, she has control over the estate's finances to ruinous result. As seen through these examples, women become scapegoats in Webber's text, responsible for most of the problems that the male characters endure, effectively exonerating colonialism and indenture.

Lingering Hierarchies: *Sugar's Sweet Allure* and *Bound for Trinidad*

The British Empire was effective at promoting the notion that indenture was beneficial, that imperialism promoted progress, and that some ethnic groups held inherent superiority over others. So effective, in fact, that we continue to see these convictions in contemporary literature, including *Sugar's Sweet Allure* (2013), and *Bound for Trinidad, An Historical Novel* (2004). *Sugar's Sweet Allure*, a novel by Guyanese-born author Khalil Rahman Ali, follows a young Indian man named Mustafa Ali, who indentures in British Guiana in 1843. In some respects, this novel differs from *Lutchmee and Dilloo* and *Those That Be in Bondage*: it does not feature a relationship between a female Indian laborer and a British man; it promotes religious pluralism; and the Indian, Chinese, African, and Amerindian characters are depicted as offering different but equally valuable contributions to Caribbean society. In key ways, though, the text conforms to the patterns laid out by the earlier indenture novels. There is still an element of racial hierarchy; indenture, on the whole, is depicted as beneficial for the laborers; and the British bear little responsibility for what suffering the migrants do experience.

There are certainly hints within the novel that the British are not perfectly behaved, but these moments are quickly brushed aside. Ali acknowledges that in the initial stage of indenture, migrants were physically abused and not provided with enough provisions, but suggests that most of the problems within the system had been resolved by 1843. This is contradicted by historical evidence: William Des Voeux's letter detailing the mistreatment of laborers was not written until 1869. Additionally, when Mustafa, on behalf of the plantation owner, seeks to resolve a conflict with Miss Betty, a formerly enslaved person, she replies that she is not frightened of the plantation owner: "what is your Massa Bass planning to do?…Beat me like he did when I was a young girl and refused to have sex with him?" (Ali 2013, 203). Yet, there is no further discussion of Miss Betty's accusation beyond its mention in this brief bit of dialogue, minimizing the seriousness of the abuse.

Aside from these moments, the overwhelming impression of the British characters is one of paternalistic kindness and superior cultivation. The laborers praise "the doctors and nurses for the treatment and medication they received" (Ali 2013, 80), are "impressed with the calm efficiency by which the Captain and his crew organized themselves with precision" (Ali 2013, 88), and, when invited to tea with the plantation owner, find themselves "aping" the "air of supreme British decorum" of the master (Ali 2013, 200). This last description echoes Edwin's concern that Bibi would "ape" the qualities of British women, and similarly views this form of imitation as an impossible and animalistic attempt at refinement. In a similar example of mimesis, a female laborer named Neesha describes Mustafa by saying, "He has never said a bad word to me, and is always polite. Sometimes I think he is more of an Englishman than an Indian" (Ali 2013, 182). That this is the highest praise she can offer is indicative of the regard with which these characters seem to hold their colonizers.

In stark contrast with the sophistication of the British, the home nations of the laborers are described as backward and violent. Neesha and Mustafa, now married, consider returning to India, but Neesha worries about the "great hardships being suffered by people back in the villages" (Ali 2013, 271). Similarly, Joshua, a formerly enslaved person, is awed by the train that he, Mustafa, and Neesha take across the country, saying, "in Africa there was nothing like this. Only jungles and small villages" (Ali 2013, 258). British Guiana is depicted as a paradise of sorts, a place of technological sophistication and solidarity, where the people of Indian, Chinese, and African descent work together to build a new and great nation. The implication is that Britain brought civilization to British Guiana and all of the laborers are better off for their forced or coerced migration.

In this vein, the novel offers a fairly rosy image of indenture, and the problems that Mustafa and his fellow laborers face are due primarily to the machinations of the labor recruiters in India and the gender imbalance of the migrants. Mustafa is convinced to indenture by an unscrupulous man named Sundar Das, who is "of very dark complexion" (Ali 2013, 54). In addition to using deceitful practices, Sundar Das assaults one of the women he has recruited, placing him in line with Hunoomaun and Karim. Once the migrants have arrived at the plantation, Ragubir, an experienced laborer, responds to the rumors that the Indians who preceded them were mistreated: "Much of what you say is true. But the people who came here were told lies by the recruiting agents in India" (Ali 2013, 128). Ali, like Jenkins, thus absolves the British of blame and holds the recruiters responsible for the suffering of the laborers. Finally, Ali, like Webber, accepts the argument that the scarcity of women was the cause of the high rate of domestic abuse. At one point in the story, a female laborer is chopped to death by her machete-wielding husband. The omniscient narrator reports that these incidents were due to the "very small proportion of women" who indentured, which was "a principal reason for husbands to take such drastic action against their wives for any behavior they felt was adulterous" (Ali 2013, 164).

We see similarly lingering symptoms of empire in Helen Atteck's novel, *Bound for Trinidad*. Set primarily in 1862, this text tells the story of a young Chinese woman named Cricket, who is kidnapped and forced to indenture upon a Trinidadian plantation. Atteck challenges colonial dogma in some important respects. The characters in this novel show none of the awe for the British as those in *Sugar's Sweet Allure*: when Cricket first sees the colonial officials, she describes them as "giant, overstuffed dolls" and wonders, "Who are those barbarians?" (Atteck 2004, 16). Cricket is hurt when the governor of Trinidad snubs his Chinese hosts at a party, drawing attention to the race consciousness of colonial officials, and she develops a sense of solidarity with the female migrants from India, hinting that she does not share such prejudices. The text even explicitly identifies the hierarchies of labor on the plantation: "The owner and overseer were white. The houseworkers were brown. The foremen were black. The field workers were Indian, and now Chinese" (Atteck 2004, 21).

Yet, the novel does little to challenge those hierarchies. Like Jenkins and Ali, Atteck lays most of the blame on the villainous native recruiters who force Cricket and the other migrants to indenture. The harshness of indenture itself is minimized: we see little of the actual labor, and the main characters remain on the plantation only briefly. Cricket and Lui, her husband, are taken under the wing of a wealthy businessman named Chan, who buys out their indenture and adopts them into his family. Cricket, like Mustafa, finds herself grateful that she was forced to indenture: "She had enjoyed the new-found freedom here in Trinidad. Her former life just seemed like a bad dream" (Atteck 2004, 113). While some migrants may have gained relative success and freedom with indenture or celebrated their departure from their home nation, the testimonials and interviews from Chap. 2 indicate that this was the exception rather than the norm. That Ali and Atteck both choose to focus on such "success stories" suggests an unwillingness to acknowledge the brutality of the indenture system.

Additionally, the two main characters of African descent in *Bound for Trinidad* are fairly one-dimensional and almost indistinguishable from each other. Stella, Chan's cook, is described as "a plump, middle-aged woman" who "greeted them with a broad grin" (Atteck 2004, 96). Imelda, the cook and housekeeper of Chan's estate is "rather portly and of indeterminate age. Her black face broke into a broad grin when she was introduced" (Atteck 2004, 121). These descriptions are not only nearly identical; they also position both women within the stereotype of the happy black servant, akin to Old Cudjoe in *Those That Be in Bondage*. Furthermore, Chan soon asks Cricket to manage his household, though Stella has been working for him for years, indicating that Stella is not suitable to rise above the rank of servant and into a managerial position.

While Lui is visiting Chan's estate, he reflects, "A few months ago he was just an estate laborer and now he was enjoying the leisure activities of an estate owner" (Atteck 2004, 130). The migrants' goal, Atteck indicates, should not have been to end the system of indenture or imperialism, but to rise through the ranks of capitalism until wealthy enough to imitate the lifestyle of the European colonizers. A similar moment occurs in the final scene of *Sugar's Sweet Allure*, at the wedding of Mustafa and Neesha's son. The plantation owner gives a speech, telling the gathered crowd, "You are all British, as are my family and I" (Ali 2013, 302). Through their hard work and integrity, Mustafa, his family, and his friends have earned the greatest honor of all: they are considered as British as the colonizers themselves. While Ali and Atteck effectively defy some of the ideologies of empire, it seems that others prove more stubborn. The next chapter further explores the pervasiveness of colonial rhetoric in contemporary narratives of Caribbean indenture.

Bibliography

Ali, Khalil Rahman. 2013. *Sugar's Sweet Allure*. Hertfordshire: Hansib Publications.
Atteck, Helen. 2004. *Bound for Trinidad – An Historical Novel*. St. Catharines, Ontario: Wanata Enterprises.
Bahadur, Gaiutra. 2014. *Coolie Woman: The Odyssey of Indenture*. Chicago: University of Chicago Press.
Beaumont, Joseph. 1871. *The New Slavery: An Account of the Indian and Chinese Immigrants in British Guiana*. London: W. Ridgway.
British Guiana. 1870. *Evidence and Proceedings: Commission of Enquiry into the Treatment of Immigrants*. Ed. William E. Frere, Chairman. Georgetown, Demerara: "The Colonist" Newspaper.
Cannadine, David. 2001. *Ornamentalism: How the British Saw Their Empire*. Oxford: Oxford University Press.
Cudjoe, Selwyn R. 2009. *Caribbean Visionary: A. R. F. Webber and the Making of the Guyanese Nation*. Jackson: University Press of Mississippi.
Dabydeen, David. 2003. Introduction. In *Lutchmee and Dilloo: A Study of West Indian Life*, ed. David Dabydeen. Oxford: Macmillan Education.
de Lisser, Herbert G. 1972. *Jane's Career: A Story of Jamaica*. London: Heinemann.
Fanon, Frantz. 2004. *Wretched of the Earth*. New York: Grove Press.
Faruqee, Ashrufa. 1996. Conceiving the Coolie Woman: Indentured Labour, Indian Women and Colonial Discourse. *South Asia Research* 16 (1): 61–76.
Guha, Ranajit. 1963. *A Rule of Property for Bengal; An Essay on the Idea of Permanent Settlement*. Paris: Mouton.
Hall, Stuart. 1995. Negotiating Caribbean Identities. *New Left Review* 209: 3–14.
Harris, Wilson. 1990. A Note on A. R. F. Webber's Those That Be in Bondage. *Callaloo* 13 (1): 147–149.

Jenkins, Edward. 1871a. *The Coolie, His Rights and Wrongs*. New York: George Routledge and Sons.
———. 1871b. *The Colonial Question: Being Essays on Imperial Federalism*. Montreal: Dawson Brothers.
———. 1871c. *Ginx's Baby: His Birth and Other Misfortunes*. London: Strahan & Co.
———. 2003. *Lutchmee and Dilloo: A Study of West Indian Life*. Edited by David Dabydeen. Oxford: Macmillan Education.
Kale, Madhavi. 1992. *Casting Labor: Empire and Indentured Migration from India to the British Caribbean, 1837–1845*. PhD Diss., University of Pennsylvania.
Lloyd, David. 2000. Colonial Trauma/Postcolonial Recovery? *interventions* 2 (2): 212–228.
Look Lai, Walton. 1993. *Indentured Labor, Caribbean Sugar*. Baltimore, MD: The Johns Hopkins University Press.
Lowe, Lisa. 2015. *The Intimacies of Four Continents*. Durham: Duke University Press.
Marx, Karl. 1986. *Karl Marx: A Reader*. Edited by Jon Elster. Cambridge: Press Syndicate of the University of Cambridge.
McKay, J.D. 1914. *Under the Southern Cross: A Tale of Love and Missions*. W.F. and H.M.S. (Eastern Division).
Mittelhölzer, Edgar. 1970. *Corentyne Thunder*. London: Heinemann.
Mohammed, Patricia. 2002. *Gender Negotiations Among Indians in Trinidad, 1917–1947*. New York: Palgrave.
Pearson, J.D., ed. 1890. *New Overseer's Manual: or the Reasons Why of Julius Jugler*. Georgetown: Argosy.
Phillips, Leslie H.C. 1961. Single Men in Barracks: Some Memories of Sugar Plantation Life. *Timehri* 40: 23–24.
Poynting, Jeremy. 1986a. East Indian Women in the Caribbean: Experience, Image and Voice. *Journal of South Asian Literature* 21 (1): 133–180.
———. 1986b. John Edward Jenkins and the Imperial Conscience. *The Journal of Commonwealth Literature* 21 (1): 211–221.
Roopnarine, Lomarsh. 2003. East Indian Indentured Emigration to the Caribbean: Beyond the Push and Pull Model. *Caribbean Studies* 31 (2): 97–134.
Singh, Vishnudat. 1986. From Indentured Labourer to Anglo-Indian Immigrant: A Study of A.R.F. Webber's Those That Be in Bondage. *Caribbean Quarterly* 32 (1/2): 47–54.
Spivak, Gayatri Chakravorty. 1999. *A Critique of Postcolonial Reason: Toward a History of the Vanishing Present*. Cambridge, MA: Harvard University Press.

Stoler, Ann Laura. 2002. *Carnal Knowledge and Imperial Power: Race and the Intimate in Colonial Rule*. Berkeley: University of California.

Webber, A.R.F. 1931. *Centenary History and Handbook of British Guiana*. Georgetown, British Guiana: "The Argosy" Company.

Webber, A.R. 1988. *Those That Be in Bondage: A Tale of Indian Indentures and Sunlit Western Waters*. Wellesley: Calaloux Publications.

CHAPTER 4

Tangled Up: Gendered Metaphors of Nation in Contemporary Indo-Caribbean Narratives

INTRODUCTION: PATRIARCHAL NATIONALISM

As described in Chap. 2, a young, widowed woman named Maharani migrated from India to Trinidad under indenture in 1916 in order to escape a life of subservience to her in-laws. In an interview, Maharani conveys the endless, grueling labor on the estate: "e have to chap/e have to cut cane an ting/tote/carry on top de truck/five truck have to full/…/ all kinda wuk"[1] (Maharani 1985, 83). She faced repressive gender roles, as well, as when her manager pressured her into a partnership with a man named Ramgolam, telling her, "Maharani you want de man" (Maharani 1985, 84). Her recounting of her life experiences demonstrates the ways that female migrants were triply vulnerable due to their gender, ethnicity, and class. Yet, Maharani resisted these repressive gender roles, announcing to the manager who pushed her to partner with Ramgolam, "i no want nobody" (Maharani 1985, 85), and even trying rum, generally considered the province of men.

The lived experiences of women like Maharani are often flattened into stereotypical accounts in indenture narratives, either to champion

[1] Noor Kumar Mahabir conducted one of the interviews with Maharani and then published it with several other testimonies in the book *The Still Cry* (1985). He does not change the wording of the interviews, but arranges them in verse, with no punctuation or capitalization.

imperialism, as seen in the previous chapter, or to challenge imperialism, as this chapter demonstrates. As I note in Chap. 2, the literature of indenture often depicts a relationship developing between a British man in power and a female Indian laborer. The frequency with which this trope appears denotes its symbolic significance: the characters represent their home nations, and the relationship between them serves as an analogy for Britain's colonization of India. Authors like Edward Jenkins, who wrote his novel *Lutchmee and Dilloo* (1877) after touring plantations in the Caribbean, used this relationship to justify indenture and the colonial system that depended on it. *Lutchmee and Dilloo* depicts a noble British man rescuing a poverty-stricken Indian woman by offering her respectable employment and introducing her to Christianity and other refined ideas. Britain, Jenkins implies, would likewise protect India from her own barbaric tendencies and expose her to civilization and Christianity.

Contemporary Caribbean authors employ a similar relationship in their indenture narratives, but do so to demonstrate the devastating impact of colonialism. If the British men in power in the earlier texts were meant to show that Britain was the protector and savior of India, the behavior of similar characters in later texts suggests that Britain used its civilizing mission as a justification to exploit India. Both David Dabydeen's *The Counting House* (Dabydeen 2005) and Sharlow's *The Promise* (1995) depict a British man who takes advantage of an Indian woman, sexually abusing her and giving little in return. There is no sense that he is saving her, and there is no Indian male villain who threatens her or the white men. The indenture system is depicted as exploitative, growing out of colonialism and helping to bolster it, and the relationship between the British man and the Indian woman is representative of this abuse. Yet, while *The Counting House* and *The Promise* confront the racist interventions of imperialism and indenture, they maintain the more conventional views of gender that were concretized under these systems and that persist in the Caribbean today, erasing the experience of women like Maharani. This chapter will consider the ways that Dabydeen and Sharlow[2] restructure the metaphor of the relationship between an Indian woman and a British man in order to challenge the cultural hierarchy of imperialism, yet fail to dismantle the patriarchal view of nationalism that underlies this metaphor.

---

[2] Sharlow Mohammed writes under the name Sharlow, or, at times, Sharlowe.

As a counterpoint to these novels, this chapter also explores Patricia Powell's *The Pagoda* (Powell 1998), which addresses Chinese migration to Jamaica and includes a similar relationship between a British man in power and a female migrant. By contrast with *The Counting House* and *The Promise*, the characters in *The Pagoda* defy stereotypes, and there is little sense they represent their nation, offering an alternative to the allegorical relationships depicted in *The Counting House* and *The Promise*.

The differences between the novels of Jenkins and Webber and those of Dabydeen and Sharlow are emblematic of the changes that occurred in the years between their publications. The system of indenture, which began in 1838, went through some temporary halts, due primarily to the objections of the laborers' home countries. As abuses became public, indentured labor became increasingly controversial in Britain and its colonies. The debate was fueled by the economic arguments of the powerful plantocracy, the human rights concerns raised by abolitionists, increasing protest from the home countries of the laborers, and the ever-present fear of revolt.[3] In 1917, the British outlawed indentured labor, and the system came to a halt for good. In the years after indenture, laborers sought better opportunities for their children and generally prioritized education as a way out of hard labor and into managerial or merchant positions. Second- and third-generation immigrants like Sam Selvon, Shiva Naipaul, and V.S. Naipaul explored the post-indenture experiences of Indians in the Caribbean through writing.[4]

Contemporary Indo-Caribbean authors such as Dabydeen and Sharlow instead reach back, turning to the lives of their ancestors in order to better understand the conditions that brought them to the Caribbean. These authors, writing after the anti-colonial liberation movements of the mid-twentieth century and a century after Edward Jenkins and A.R.F. Webber, reflect on the same time period but with a dramatically dissimilar viewpoint, due to their different subject positions, the many changes that had taken place in the Caribbean, and the political climate during which these novels were written. Both novels focus on the early stages of the indenture

---

[3] The Haitian Revolution of 1791 to 1804, in which enslaved Africans successfully overthrew their French masters and founded a republic, had shaken planters' sense of security. Revolts of indentured laborers, such as the Rose Hall Disturbances of 1913, in which 300 laborers in Berbice, British Guiana, rioted over unfair treatment and police killed 14 Indians suggested that outbreaks of violence were not a thing of the past.

[4] For instance, Selvon's *A Brighter Sun* (1953) follows a young man's efforts to understand his role as a new husband and father in Trinidad during the turbulent years of World War II.

period to draw attention to the shifting role of the British Empire in the mid-nineteenth century and the connections indenture created between Britain, India, and the Caribbean, as well as the ongoing effect of those connections on the Caribbean.

The depictions of indenture in *The Counting House* and *The Promise* address many of the exploitative aspects of colonialism that are ignored in early texts. While the British argued that they offered Indians education and civilization, in reality most Indians gained little; at best, they shifted from one form of poverty to another and, at worst, lost their means of subsistence. These novels also highlight the connection between the disruption of traditional life caused by colonialism and the number of people who were willing to emigrate as bound laborers. Many of those people might otherwise have been unwilling to sign contracts of indenture or leave India but did so because they saw no other choice for survival.

Yet, these novels perpetuate the stereotypical and damaging views of Indo-Caribbean women that developed under indenture. Both *The Counting House* and *The Promise* feature a female Indian protagonist, and, in some ways, these women laborers are depicted as strong and independent, as when Rohini, the female protagonist of *The Counting House*, sets in motion a plot to convince her husband to indenture with her. Ultimately, though, these characters are incomplete representations. Literary scholar Sharmila Sen argues that the character of Rohini perpetuates the stereotype of the vulnerable, promiscuous Indo-Caribbean woman and that the novel, "while ostensibly attempting to give a voice to Rohini, finds itself unable to articulate that experience" (Sen 2005, 194–195). Similarly, Mariam Pirbhai suggests that Sharlow fails to develop the character of his protagonist Rati, as she appears as little more than a stereotype of the devout Hindu woman: "Though Rati is set up as the ostensible heroine of the indenture narrative, her heroism is couched in Hindu patriarchal discourse, for she is typecast as a spiritually chaste devotee to father, husband, and Brahma" (Pirbhai 2009, 144). These are valid and important critiques, yet there are more systemic silencings of Indo-Caribbean females in these texts.

The metaphoric role that each woman plays diminishes the sense of her as an individual caught in the brutal system of colonialism and indenture, and minimizes the small and large acts of independence that real female laborers took. In *The Promise* in particular, the female protagonist is clearly meant to represent India, as she is described as an ideal of Indian womanhood, and her abuse at the hands of a British manager is symbolic of the rape of her homeland by the British colonizers. This maintains the view of women as the bearers of culture who must be protected and controlled, and whose virtue must be fought over. The use of rape as symbol also minimizes the impact of sexual abuse, suggesting that it is only meaningful when it is indicative of the subjugation of a whole people. It is certainly true that *The Counting House* and *The Promise* expose the brutality of indenture, the destructiveness of imperialism, and the dangers of neocolonialism. Yet, a close examination of these texts demonstrates that they also maintain the traditional patriarchal views of women that Indian migrants brought with them to the Caribbean and that were exacerbated by indenture and imperialism.

The Counting House: The Eroding Power of Capital

The Counting House follows a young Indian couple, Rohini and Vidia, who indenture on a plantation in British Guiana in order to escape the suffocating provincialism of village life, only to find themselves trapped within the crushing system of plantation labor. In the preface of the novel, David Dabydeen states that the inspiration for the novel came from artifacts discovered on the remains of Plantation Albion in Guyana. These evocative objects included "a cow-skin purse, a child's tooth, an ivory button, a drawing of the Hindu God, Rama, haloed by seven stars, a set of iron needles, some kumari seeds, and an empty tin marked 'Huntley's Dominion Biscuits', its cover depicting a scene of the Battle of Waterloo" (Dabydeen 2005, 9). Plantation Albion was owned by John Gladstone, the first planter to petition the British government for Indian laborers, and so the novel is set at a moment of upheaval—the inception of Indian migration to the Caribbean. Dabydeen also includes a quote from Gladstone in the preface: "No account of the coolie experience can ever be complete, for they are but the scraps of history" (Dabydeen 2005, 9).

The Counting House is clearly meant as a response to this quote, an attempt to write the experience of the Indian migrants in order to rescue them from the scrap heap of history. That the novel is based on the few remaining objects that act as a testimony to the lives of these laborers, by comparison to the volumes of records kept by the British colonizers, points to the difficulty of such an endeavor. In a twist of irony, the objects were discovered in the counting house of Plantation Albion, symbolizing the way that these laborers were counted as part of Gladstone's wealth.

The novel has received mixed critical reception. Charles P. Sarvan suggests that the story lacks empathy: "This text treats degraded lives degradingly. The depiction of poverty is contemptuous; the character, mind and efforts of the workers cruelly ridiculed" (Sarvan 1997, 635). On the other hand, Gail Low acknowledges that the novel "frustrates expectations of a redemptive and cathartic delivery" (Low 2007, 205), but sees this as a realistic depiction and a deliberate critique: "What happens to the characters in the novel corresponds to the real life experience of indentured labourers, swept up in the anonymous statistics of capitalism's remorseless expansions across the globe" (Low 2007, 213).

As suggested in this quotation, Dabydeen's novel highlights the close connections between wealth and imperialism. Dabydeen, like many critics of imperialism, brushes aside the moral justifications for colonization, drawing attention instead to the economic motivations: "The British Empire was…a feudal structure with robber barons and serfs" (Dabydeen 2011, 23). *The Counting House* seeks to expose this dynamic, pointing to the ways that planters exploited their laborers in order to maximize profits. Further, Dabydeen indicates the pervasiveness of sexual relations within this system of exploitation. As Foucault notes, sexuality appears as "an especially dense transfer point for relations of power" (Foucault 1978, 103), and, in this novel, having access to money and sex is both a signifier of power and a means to increase it. This is true both for those in power and those who seek to gain it; power does not flow in one direction only.

One way that Dabydeen seeks to upend the power dynamics of colonialism is through the structure of the novel, which is split into three sections. Each section focuses on a different character: Rohini, a female indentured laborer; Kampta, an Indian laborer who is not bound by indenture; and Miriam, a formerly enslaved woman. In this way, Dabydeen gives voices to various members of repressed groups and captures the diversity of experience of the laborers who worked the land. Further, Dabydeen creates a solidarity between the characters of African and Indian descent, a solidarity that is often invisible to the characters themselves. Though they often treat each other as competition, the reader recognizes that the workers are all suffering under the same oppressive system.

The novel is also written in fragmented chronology, shifting between Vidia and Rohini's experiences on the plantation and their lives in India before they indentured. This blurring of the timeline ties together Britain's colonial presence in India and in British Guiana, emphasizing the ways that Britain's destabilization of traditional Indian life led to a mobile workforce for their plantations in other colonies. Gail Low notes that Vidia and Rohini use Creole expressions and slang while they are still in India, which "has the effect of making the world of the village community echo the world of Plantation Albion, as if the latter has corrupted—against apparent causal logic—even the temporal space of the former" (Low 2007, 215). This disjointed chronology also helps convey the disruption in the lives of the laborers, which are permanently altered by their migration to British Guiana.

Some authors, such as Edward Jenkins, depict precolonial India in Edenic terms. In *Lutchmee and Dilloo*, India is a primitive paradise where the young couple leads a life of childlike simplicity, threatened only by the evil of other Indians. This romantic view supports the vision of India as an exotic, uncivilized land in comparison to the well-structured world of industrial England. Dabydeen, however, highlights the pervasive poverty and rigid caste system of India prior to colonialism, reminding the readers that imperialism is not the only oppressive societal system. At the beginning of the novel, Rohini and her mother live in grinding poverty, cherishing the few valuable possessions that act as "their insurance against starvation: the silver anklet belonging to her mother, two brass lotas, an enamel plate painted with maharajas on elephants" (Dabydeen 2005, 28). The enamel plate acts as a constant reminder of the imbalance of wealth: while Rohini and her mother barely scrape together enough food to survive, maharajas ride on elephants, literally and figuratively raised above the peasants.

Dabydeen's critical view of India is particularly striking when compared with Sharlow's *The Promise*. Like Jenkins, Sharlow describes India in idyllic terms, though for a very different purpose. While Jenkins emphasizes the simple, uncivilized nature of the colonized people, *The Promise* depicts India as idyllic to indicate that this utopia was destroyed by colonialism. This suggests nostalgia for a home that never really existed. By contrast, Dabydeen certainly depicts the damages of colonialism, but shows that the exploitation of the poor in India did not begin with British imperialism.[5]

The opening scenes of *The Counting House* focus on a cross-caste love story, as Vidia, who comes from a comparatively wealthy family, falls in love with Rohini and insists on marrying her. This seems to offer a hope

---

[5] In an interview, Dabydeen said, "I reject any notion of home that is idyllic…India was a desperate and, in some ways, turmoiled place. We were…enslaved in the caste system and the women were enslaved in the sati system" (Dabydeen 2011, 134).

of nation-building across class and caste lines. However, this symbolic hope does not last long. Rohini is unhappy, chaffing under the restrictions and demands of her mother-in-law and frustrated with Vidia's dependence on his parents. She is drawn to the seductive tales told by a labor recruiter: "'British people them come and clear away all we mud and bamboo huts and put up things like this,' he said proudly, showing them a drawing of the Governor's residence—a massive building surrounded by colonnades, its arches enriched with white marble and coloured stone" (Dabydeen 2005, 46). Of course, the governor's mansion is no more accessible to Rohini than the palaces of the maharajas depicted on her enamel plate, but she is swayed by the image of wealth and grandeur.

This section of the novel also points to the ways that Britain's policies in India increased the number of laborers willing to indenture. The novel takes place shortly after the Indian Rebellion of 1857. Angered by British restructuring of Indian society and the annexation and heavy taxation of Indian land, sepoys within the British army, later joined by civilians, revolted and killed British soldiers as well as civilians. The British army responded with a brutal crackdown, summarily executing great numbers of Indians who they claimed were involved in the revolt. Viewing the rebellion as an Islamic movement, the British targeted Muslims, although Hindus took part in the violence as well. After the rebellion, there was a rise in those signing up for indenture, perhaps hoping to escape retribution for the rebellion. In *The Counting House*, the recruiter takes advantage of this chaos, frightening the villagers by describing the violent rebellion and warning of the British army's retribution.

At certain points in the novel, Rohini does make bold decisions, working against cultural restrictions and gendered expectations in order to improve her life. She secretly poisons the family's cow so that when it dies, the villagers will believe the family is cursed and the family will have to move. It is worth noting, though, that she takes these actions so that Vidia will indenture with her, rather than choosing to indenture alone. The McNeil-Lal Report of 1915 indicates that two-thirds of the women who indentured were single,[6] and the interview described earlier offers a specific example of this: Maharani explains that she indentured by herself to

---

[6] The report states that, "The women who come out consist as to one-third of married women who accompany their husbands, the remainder being mostly widows and women who have run away from their husbands or been put away from them" (Great Britain 1915, 313).

escape the mistreatment of her in-laws. Female characters like Rohini, who indenture with their husbands, tend to obscure the real women who traveled alone under indenture.

This lack of representation of single female migrants is not unique to *The Counting House*. The main characters in indenture narratives tend to be males traveling alone or a male and female couple.[7] This suggests that images of labor remain highly gendered: men are viewed as laborers and women as wives, even though in many traditional cultures, women perform the majority of the hard labor. Chandra Mohanty notes that in developing societies, it is usually women who perform agricultural and factory work, yet women are often defined as "housewives" as opposed to "workers." She writes, "The effects of this definition of labor is not only that it makes women's labor and its costs invisible, but that it undercuts women's agency by defining them as victims of a process of pauperization or of 'tradition' or 'patriarchy,' rather than as agents capable of making their own choices" (Mohanty 2003, 151). Though Rohini is frustrated with Vidia's weak-willed behavior, she cannot conceive of indenturing without him. This casts her clearly in the role of "wife," limiting her agency and placing her in a recognizable, "safe" category for women. The character of Rohini offers an incomplete representation of women's experience of indenture in another respect: we only see her completing relatively light tasks, such as cleaning and cooking, whereas the majority of female laborers worked in the fields alongside the men.

There is one aspect of gender relations that *The Counting House* treats with complexity. While authors like Jenkins and Webber focus only on the violence that resulted from the gender disparity of indentured laborers, Dabydeen highlights some of the ways that female laborers gained independence. Rohini earns wages for the first time in her life, which makes her less reliant upon Vidia, and she has options should she wish to pursue a partnership with another man. Reports indicate that many indentured women sought a measure of protection or financial stability by changing mates or pursuing more than one relationship at a time, suggesting a fluid view of partnership. Sarah Morton, a Canadian missionary, recalls a conversation with an Indian woman who stated, "When the last [immigrant]

---

[7] See Edward Jenkins' *Lutchmee and Dilloo*, David Dabydeen's *The Counting House*, Sharlow's *The Promise*, and Amitav Ghosh's *Ibis* trilogy, among others. The novels that do depict women traveling alone tend to be written by women—see Peggy Mohan's *Jahajin* (2007), for instance.

ship came in I took a papa. I will keep him as long as he treats me well. If he does not treat me well I shall send him off at once; that's the right way, is it not?" (quoted in Niranjana 2006, 65). At the same time, Rohini reflects on the limited nature of her options: "What could she gain by them, these uncouth coolies who would throw a few coppers her way and expect to devour her in return" (Dabydeen 2005, 66–67). Rohini's potential mates might offer her a bit more financial security, but they would still view her as a possession, a delicacy to be consumed. As an Indian laborer and a female, she is still doubly vulnerable.

The novel also uses the intimate relationships between the characters to reflect on the troubling dynamics of class and ethnicity under indenture. For example, Vidia had never been abusive toward Rohini, but that shifts once they are in British Guiana. He feels a sense of inadequacy on the plantation, due in part to his inability to impregnate Rohini, and he expends his frustration upon her. After Rohini confesses that she killed his family's cow, he beats her, and it is clear that underlying his aggression is his desire to reassert his masculinity. Vidia accuses Rohini of sleeping with other men, believing that her enjoyment of sex must mean that she is experimenting elsewhere: "Niggerman digging in your belly for gold that belong to me" (Dabydeen 2005, 87). He equates her sexuality with wealth that is by rights his, and he seems to have accepted the stereotype of African males as hypersexual and feel threatened by them. His reactions demonstrate the ways that struggles between men of different ethnic groups often play out in attempts to control women.

Vidia's sense of inadequacy stems from another, deeper source, as well. Laboring on Plantation Albion puts Vidia in close proximity to the wealth of the British colonizers, and he becomes aware of his relative poverty in a way that he never had been in India. He covets Gladstone's money and power, and seems to accept the racialized hierarchy that is so central to imperialism:

> To be something you had to be like Gladstone. Gladstone was the science that invented the machines, and the world run by machines like the steam turbines and boilers which made molasses, sugar and rum from a simple plant. A coolie could stay pagan and chew on the plant, or he could learn the science of the machine. To be a Gladstone-coolie was the first stage in becoming Gladstone himself. (Dabydeen 2005, 126)

Vidia accepts the barbaric/civilized binary of imperialism and determines to be on the "civilized" side, in the hopes that he will somehow become

British himself. Homi Bhabha points to the impossibility of this mimicry, noting that even the most Anglicized colonial subject will be *"almost the same but not white"* (Bhabha 2012, 128, emphasis original). While Bhabha sees this difference as a site of potential subversion, Dabydeen focuses more on the way that such mimicry disintegrates the colonial subject's sense of self. Vidia's constant comparison of himself to Gladstone increases his belief in his own inferiority, which in turn increases his violence toward Rohini.

These moments in the novel effectively analyze the complex psychology that leads to domestic abuse and critique the imperial system that led to an increase in violence against women. Yet, the degradation and abuse of women is pervasive in the text and rarely challenged by the characters themselves. The indenture recruiter in India uses graphic and violent language to incite the villagers to assault Muslim women: "Mouth or pokey-hole or arse-hole, or puncture she belly and bore new hole, it is all one to me" (Dabydeen 2005, 48). The men of the village are quick to obey, raping and then killing a Muslim woman named Rashida. The only character to condemn this behavior is Rohini's mother, Finee, but her objection is undermined when she steals Rashida's belongings while Rashida is being raped.

Dabydeen argues that he is drawing attention to what he terms "the pornography of empire," indicating that "at the heart of empire…is callousness to the female" (Dabydeen 2011, 153). However, within the novel, the "callousness to the female" is just as pervasive in India before the arrival of the colonizers. In Rohini and Vidia's village, a man named Kumar harasses a young girl: "You with bow-leg as if egg hatching in your panty…When period pain catch you…and your Ma stuff you with cloth, then we really see how crooked you does walk" (Dabydeen 2005, 35). Additionally, the degradation of women comes primarily from the Indian and African characters. On Gladstone's estate, the Indians taunt Miriam, an Afro-Caribbean woman: "Is true nigger pokey-hair hard like wire broom and scratch up your face when you go down to suck? I hear you got to close your eyes when you go down in case the hairs juk them out and blind you" (Dabydeen 2005, 78). These moments are more likely to perpetuate than challenge the demeaning treatment of women.

Even Rohini's response to her abuse seems to support the misogyny that she faces. She is pleased that Vidia beats her because it shows that "he had his own will, even though it was not as big and important as Gladstone's who was in charge of more than a wife, but nine-ten hundred coolies"

(Dabydeen 2005, 70). Rohini has internalized the notion that a real man must control his wife, with violence if necessary. Further, Rohini, like Vidia, sees Gladstone as the ultimate model of manhood and wants Vidia to take any steps he can to become like him. Both Rohini and Vidia have accepted the idea that the British are superior to them, although they do not see themselves as culturally inferior so much as lacking the colonizers' wealth and power.

Gaiutra Bahadur, Marina Carter, Shaheeda Hosein, and other historians have documented the ways that Indo-Caribbean women resisted or undermined traditional gender roles. Women laborers developed small businesses such as selling food or charcoal, they held positions of authority as *sirdars*[8] and leaders of rebellions, and they worked within the colonial administration to fight for their rights. For example, Bahadur tells the story of a woman named Baby, who repeatedly petitioned the courts in British Guiana, and eventually the colonial officials in London, alleging patterns of assault, trespassing, and harassment by male laborers and colonial police alike (Bahadur 2014, 94). Yet indenture narratives such as *The Counting House* rarely depict these moments of resistance. In India, Rohini takes bold action to convince Vidia to indenture, but once they reach the estate, she falls into stereotypical roles: abused woman, adulterous wife.

Although Rohini is faithful to Vidia at the time of his accusations, she does eventually develop a sexual relationship with Gladstone. Ironically, it is Vidia's abuse that first brings Rohini to Gladstone's attention. Moved by her bruises, he offers to let Rohini stay in the house. Initially, he seems to be playing the role of the white male savior, protector of colonized women. Colonial officials often described their role as a paternal one, seeing themselves as acting *in loco parentis*[9] for the laborers. Gladstone seems to fit this model, showing concern for Rohini's well-being and threatening to punish Vidia for his behavior. This concern quickly shifts into sexual exploitation, suggesting that the intentions of the colonizers were rarely pure. Gladstone already has a similar relationship with Miriam, his servant, further challenging the view of British plantation owners as models of honorable behavior.

Far from acting paternalistically, Gladstone often treats his laborers with brutal force, using methods of discipline that were common under

---

[8] Drivers on the estates.
[9] Latin for "in place of a parent"; see Walter Rodney on Immigration Agent General James Crosby's approach to his duties (Rodney 1981, 151).

slavery. Kampta, an Indian laborer, is caught stealing from him and sentenced to 14 whiplashes every Sunday for three months. Gladstone turns this into a public spectacle; he has Kampta whipped in his garden and watches from the balcony of his house. He even summons the newly landed coolie laborers to watch as a deterrent against misbehaving.

In addition, while Vidia is abusive at times, he is not a villain like Hunoomaun from *Lutchmee and Dilloo*, or Karim from *Those That Be in Bondage*. When Gladstone asks Rohini to stay in the Great House overnight to help with visitors, Vidia insists that she take their only blanket. He dreams of taking a day off with her, picnicking by the river, and walking through the market to examine the goods that they will one day be able to afford. Rohini's relationship with Gladstone pulls Rohini away from her husband, but this is depicted as harmful to both Vidia and Rohini, rather than a step toward her salvation.

Although Rohini is initially awed by Gladstone, she quickly comes to resent his degrading treatment of her. He gains sexual favors in exchange for throwaway gifts that cost him nothing, such as the biscuit tin mentioned in the prologue. As she cleans Gladstone's house, Rohini imagines herself standing up to him: "You think you can fill my mouth with your confectionery and do nastiness inside me and afterwards give me empty glass jar and tin-can...You think you can dig me up, put something inside me secretly, then bury me again so that no one can catch you and bring shame on your name?" (Dabydeen 2005, 111). The image of a sugary treat in Rohini's mouth contrasts sharply with the dark, secret, and shameful thing inside her, which represents the sexual relationship that cannot be openly acknowledged, and also, perhaps, the pregnancy that will eventually destroy Rohini and Vidia. Rohini's description of being dug up and buried again also echoes the money that Vidia buries in the yard for safekeeping, again drawing a parallel between women's sexuality and financial wealth.

In *Lutchmee and Dilloo*, Craig introduces Lutchmee to a world of refined ideas and advanced culture, but there is no such development in *The Counting House*. Rohini longs for Gladstone's wealth and power, but shows little interest in his education or ideas. When Rohini realizes she is pregnant with Gladstone's baby, she imagines her child as Gladstone's heir, "reveling even as it burdened her with pain, swelling her body to the roundness of the globe which one day it would inherit" (Dabydeen 2005, 133). In this image of the future, Rohini seems to brush aside her earlier awareness that her relationship with Gladstone is an unacknowledged one, and that he, much less the rest of society, is unlikely to treat Rohini's child as a legitimate heir.

That it is Gladstone who impregnates Rohini confirms Vidia's sense of inadequacy and plays into a deeper fear held by many migrants, the dissolution of their culture. Ramabai Espinet notes that Indian migrants tended to reproduce traditional gender roles as a way of maintaining ethnic purity and that a particularly important aspect of this was "the ownership of woman and her reproductive capacity—the only means by which the powerful male can perpetuate himself" (Espinet 1993, 43). Rohini's pregnancy thus reflects the fears of many diasporic Indian communities, that if women are not controlled, they will consort with men of other ethnicities and bring destruction upon the community. In *The Counting House*, that destruction is literal: Miriam, jealous of Rohini's baby, tricks her into having an abortion, and when Rohini realizes what has happened, she goes mad with grief. Vidia plans to return to India but dies on the voyage, and so their indenture ends in tragedy.

The rivalry between Miriam and Rohini also reflects the tensions that colonizers deliberately stoked between members of different ethnic groups. Colonizers tended to play races against each other, bringing Indians to the plantations as a weapon against formerly enslaved Africans, to prevent them from organizing for better pay and conditions. Planters also did their best to keep laborers of different ethnicities from interacting, worried that they might find solidarity and resist imperial power. Historian Walter Rodney writes, "Planters took advantage of the possibilities of manipulating existing racial separation or tension between African and Indians. The notion that races should help police each other was at the center of the racially divisive policy of the colonial state" (Rodney 1981, 187). This came in the form of physical separation—creating different living areas for laborers of different ethnic backgrounds and forbidding them from interacting with each other, but also in rhetoric. The colonial stereotypes of Africans as lazy and barbaric and Indians as stingy and passive, demonstrated in *Lutchmee and Dilloo*, were insidious, and often led to further tensions between groups. Miriam's behavior demonstrates the results of this racial rivalry.

Rodney acknowledges that there was a sense of rivalry between the African and Indian laborers but points to forms of solidarity that existed between them: "Ex-slaves were among those who testified that the first Indian arrivals were treated in precisely the same manner as Africans under slavery" (Rodney 1981, 32). In addition, he argues that there was a greater blending of their cultures than is often recognized. He notes that Indians born on the estate would pass through the Creole gang as their first socializing experience, and he indicates that the Indian culture influenced the formerly enslaved population as well. Afro-Guyanese often participated in the Muslim Tadjah ceremony, a fixture of Guyanese culture.

This solidarity is reflected in some of the interactions between the Indian and African characters in *The Counting House*; though they do not rise up together to fight their mutual foe, that potential exists in their small acts of compassion and unity. Rohini and Miriam are exploited by Gladstone in the same way, engaged in a sexual relationship with him in order to gain some small measure of material improvement. There is initially a sense of deep friendship, almost a sisterly relationship, between Miriam and Rohini. Miriam shows the younger woman how to make curls in her hair "like the whiteladies in the photographs" (Dabydeen 2005, 67), tends to her bruises after Vidia beats her, and empathizes with her desire for a baby. This makes it all the more painful when Miriam decides that she must abort Rohini's baby in order to survive, which in turn leads to the destruction of all of the main characters other than herself. There is also solidarity between Kampta, an unbound Indian laborer, and the African characters. After he is whipped, none of the Indian workers dare to help him, but a gang of African workers "cut him loose, laid him in a makeshift stretcher and took him to their village," where Miriam dresses his wounds and cares for him until he recovers (Dabydeen 2005, 77).

Kampta's presence in the novel challenges colonial power and rhetoric in multiple ways. As an unbound laborer, he can work or not, as he chooses, which demonstrates that the planters' control over their workers was not absolute. His unbound status also illustrates that different forms of labor existed on the plantations, undermining the planters' argument that without coerced labor, the plantation system would collapse. Kampta also flouts colonial authority, stealing from Gladstone and training Miriam's younger brothers to do the same. In addition to his connections with Miriam and her brothers, Kampta sometimes lives with the Amerindian tribes, and thus builds connections across ethnic groups.

Gladstone, too, is treated with complexity. Though he is not depicted as a noble British man rescuing a vulnerable Indian woman, he is also not a villain. Dabydeen depicts him as a lonely, middle-aged man, and Miriam's descriptions of him as a lover hardly inspire fear or respect: "rising and falling and fanning me with his flab, and he so excited he fart and dribble" (Dabydeen 2005, 117). Both Miriam and Rohini have some measure of power over him, indicating that the laborers were not completely subservient to their masters. Rohini gains some leverage over Gladstone when she becomes pregnant with his child, and at one point when Gladstone's sexual aggressions become too much for Miriam, she knocks him off, "leaving him sprawling at the foot of the couch, utterly terrified by what else she might do" (Dabydeen 2005, 98). Even Kampta, planning to kill Gladstone, begins to doubt his mission: "What Gladstone do to him to deserve death? He didn't ask to born whiteman, just as Kampta didn't ask to born a base coolie" (Dabydeen 2005, 122).

In fact, Gladstone is strangely absent from the text. Interestingly, the real John Gladstone never lived in the Caribbean. Though he did own plantations in British Guiana, he lived most of his life in Liverpool, England, managing his estates and the laborers who worked them from afar. In *The Counting House*, Dabydeen shifts this narrative, creating a more direct connection between the plantation owner and the laborers, making his abuse of power all the more evident.[10] Yet in the novel, the character of Gladstone is still something of a ghostly presence. He appears primarily as refracted by other characters' view of him, as when Rohini imagines a conversation in which she convinces him to give up Miriam.

During Gladstone's cruelest act in the novel, prosecuting Kampta for theft, he adopts the role of British colonizer as if it is a mask he puts on and takes off. In court, he switches from his curt plantation speech to official-sounding English, declaring Kampta to be "'of an incorrigible and unrepentant nature'" (Dabydeen 2005, 74). Hearing this, the villagers are terrified, "wondering whether Kampta had not committed even greater crimes" (Dabydeen 2005, 74). The court scene is one of the only times in the text that we hear Gladstone speak. Dabydeen thus reverses the silence that colonial archives impose on the subaltern. While British officials kept extensive records on the judicial and legislative proceedings in the colonies, these documents narrated events through the lens of imperial ideology and rarely recorded the voices of the colonized. In this novel, we only hear Gladstone speak in court, as if he exists solely in the archives, whereas the rest of the novel is devoted to the voices of the laborers. As a result,

---

[10] "In so doing," Abigail Ward argues, "Dabydeen demonstrates a deliberate irreverence towards—almost vandalisation of—received history, seemingly in part born of the insubstantial portrayal of Indian indentured people in representations of this past" (Ward 2011, 90).

the laborers appear as fully developed, living human beings, while the colonial officials seem to be constructions of empire.

Gladstone's description of Kampta in this scene is worth quoting at length, as it effectively captures the British colonial prejudices toward the Indian laborers:

> Through birth and rearing in the colony he has taken on nigger values to add to his Madrasi instincts for troublesomeness; he is indolent, thievish and cunning, and seeks the company of lewd and faithless Creole women in preference to the sobriety of a settled relationship. He has no sense of the rights of ownership and in stealing from his fellow coolies—a crime to which he is habituated—he creates a web of accusation and counter-accusation among them, which is detrimental to the welfare of the Plantation. The loss of his property causes acute distress to a coolie. It will provoke the most docile of them to the kind of barbarism that breaks out in India randomly and for no apparent reason other than the conditioning of centuries which no English effort can reverse. (Dabydeen 2005, 75)

Well versed in colonial rhetoric, Gladstone employs stereotypes of both Indians and Africans, describing the former as amoral and inherently barbaric and the latter as sexual and heathen. He also appeals to fears of the races interacting with each other, suggesting that they will bring out the worst in each other. By playing on these fears, Gladstone inspires the court to impose a harsh punishment on Kampta, which buttresses Gladstone's control over his workers.

Although characters like Kampta and Gladstone generally function as individuals, rather than as representatives of their nation, there are moments within the novel when the relationships take on the feel of allegory. This is especially true in the treatment of sexual relations between Gladstone and the women in his employ. Kampta jeers at Miriam, "'So everytime you lie with Gladstone, is England you lying with? When he heave on top of you is a whole country, great and heavy, pressing down on you so you can't escape?'" (Dabydeen 2005, 117). He draws an explicit connection between the coercive nature of her sexual relationship with Gladstone and the suffocating weight of imperial power. This parallels the moment when Rohini compares her swelling belly to the "roundness of the globe which one day [her baby] would inherit" (Dabydeen 2005, 133), seeing Gladstone as a representative of England's power.

The novel ends tragically. Miriam predicts the fate of each of the characters: Rohini will live out her life as either the whore of the plantation, or as a nun, embodying the virgin/whore dichotomy; Vidia will die on the return trip to India and his body will be thrown into the sea; Kampta will seek refuge from the Amerindian tribes and be killed—his body will float down the river. Miriam will be left alone, crying out in mourning, and only Gladstone will be left to comfort her. Dabydeen describes this last chapter as "one loud creole outburst...where she curses the world and then ends up by cursing herself" (Dabydeen 2011, 155). Though she has saved her position on the plantation by aborting Rohini's baby, it is an empty, lonely victory, emphasizing the importance of the solidarity that she sacrificed.

The tragic conclusion suggests that the villain in the story is not Gladstone, but the systematic abuse of vulnerable populations that accompanies divisions of wealth and hierarchies of labor. Rohini lives hand to mouth under the caste system, but her exploitation increases once she becomes an indentured laborer under British Imperialism. Although Vidia and Rohini gain some measure of financial stability on the plantation, their relationship and eventually their lives are destroyed by the power that Gladstone holds over them, the ethnic rivalry fostered by colonial officials, and the sexual exploitation of female laborers.

The desolation entwined in the plot of *The Counting House*, as well as that of *The Promise*, as will be seen later, fits the pattern of the anti-national romance, as described by literary critic Doris Sommer. Sommer argues that novels by nineteenth-century Latin American authors like José Mármol, who wrote during periods of burgeoning nationalism and political conflict, offered hope for the binding of the nation through a heterosexual love story between members of different racial, class, or religious groups. By contrast, later authors like Gabriel García Márquez and Isabel Allende, critical of the corrupt, authoritarian regimes that took power after colonialism, write against these national romances, offering fractured, tragic, or stultified romance stories instead (Sommer 1991). Dabydeen and Sharlow write at the same historical moment and from a similar geopolitical position as Márquez and Allende; in the Caribbean, as in Latin America, the full impact of colonialism in the Caribbean is coming to be understood and nationalistic projects may seem naïve.[11]

Initially, both *The Counting House* and *The Promise* seem to follow the pattern of a nationalist romance, in which a young couple overcomes

---

[11] Dabydeen has expressed dismay at the current state of politics in the Caribbean, describing Guyana as "a dangerous pit, fitter for the habitation of the unscrupulous, immoral, and criminal" (Dabydeen 1993, 28).

obstacles in order to be together. Yet when they travel to the Caribbean, their relationship is destroyed by the cruelties of plantation life. Additionally, death is pervasive on the estates. The male protagonists in both novels die, suggesting that these authors see Indian masculinity as a threat to colonial power. In *The Counting House*, as in *Lutchmee and Dilloo*, Rohini's baby dies in the womb, suggesting a cynical view of nationalism, a rejection of Victorian ideals of family, and a lack of hope for the future. The anti-romance, anti-nationalism storyline of these novels indicates a frustration with national projects similar to that of twentieth-century Latin American authors.

The tragic events of the novel can also be seen as a response to the turmoil Dabydeen witnessed in Guyana. Guyana was still a British colony throughout his childhood, and political tensions were erupting between Afro-Guyanese and Indo-Guyanese nationalist groups. In 1964, Dabydeen's family moved from New Amsterdam back to his family village of Brighton to escape race riots. Interviews with Dabydeen reveal that he was strongly influenced by the upheaval he witnessed growing up, the incomplete process of decolonization of the 1950s and 1960s,[12] and the financial exploitation of neocolonialism.[13] Further, *The Counting House* was published shortly after the election of Cheddi Jagan, a member of the left-wing People's Progressive Party, which was supported primarily by Guyanese of Indian descent. Jagan's win was viewed as a sign of hope by many in the Indo-Guyanese community, but international observers reported that the elections were marred by violence, intimidation, and attempted fraud. The disintegration of interpersonal relationships in *The Counting House* can thus be seen as an indictment of the colonialism that so effectively turned ethnic groups against each other that resentments lingered decades later.

The relationship between the Indian and British characters in *The Counting House* serves a different purpose than in *Lutchmee and Dilloo*, or

---

[12] In one interview, Dabydeen attacks the involvement of Western powers in decolonization: "The CIA and the British government 'fixed' Guyana's history. They fixed it historically and then when they left, they fixed who would be in positions of power. As a result of their political corruption, we all had to flee" (Dabydeen 2011, 133).

[13] Dabydeen has drawn attention to the abuse of natural resources in underdeveloped nations: "Economically, of course, the fact is that we still bleed the Third World. There's more money coming into the West from debt repayments than there's going out in terms of new loans. It's like mugging a beggar...it's very unsubtle; it's just the banks grabbing chunks of rainforest, and chunks of people's hard-earned foreign exports" (Dabydeen 2011, 129).

Those That Be in Bondage. It is not as clearly allegorical—while Jenkins seeks to justify colonialism by demonstrating that noble British men can save beautiful young Indian women from poverty and barbarism, Dabydeen complicates this relationship and offers a much more devastating view of colonialism. In a cycle of domination, Gladstone uses his Indian laborers to gain wealth, which he then employs to maintain his power over them. He expresses vaguely protective feelings toward Rohini, but has few qualms about exploiting her labor and her sexuality, and seems indifferent to the wreckage that his behavior causes. Britain, Dabydeen suggests, was equally callous and careless about its colonization of India and Guyana.

In this view of imperialism, colonizers are not malevolent or evil so much as indifferent, so far removed by wealth and power from the colonized that they cannot see the suffering that they are causing. In an interview, Dabydeen said of the eighteenth-century satirical British painter William Hogarth, "One of the major themes in [his] works is the way that materialism affects ethical, moral, imaginative sensibilities...the cash nexus replaces human relationships" (Dabydeen 2011, 166). This is the cruelty at the heart of *The Counting House*; the ties between Rohini, Vidia, Gladstone, Miriam, and Kampta are eroded by the power of capital.

Yet, Dabydeen does not effectively challenge what he terms "the pornography of empire." The degradation of his female characters dehumanizes them, and the ubiquitous descriptions of violence against women normalizes such behavior. The character of Rohini in particular serves to maintain, rather than confront, the stereotypes of Indo-Caribbean women as passive objects whose sexuality must be controlled in order to protect Indian culture.

THE PROMISE: SEXUAL ASSAULT AS COLONIAL CONQUEST

The Promise similarly focuses on the corrupting quality of capital, and similarly supports the problematic view of woman as nation. Like *The Counting House*, this novel describes the experiences of a young indentured couple, Rati and Guha, but it is set in Trinidad, another major center of the British indenture system. Trinidad's history with colonialism, the plantation system, slavery, and indenture is similar to that of British Guiana, although its current economy is stronger than that of Guyana, due in part to tourism and exports of natural gas and oil.

Sharlow Mohammed, who wrote *The Promise* under the name Sharlow, was born in 1949 in Longdenville, a rural township in Trinidad. Though he converted to Christianity, his 1992 novel *The Elect* attacks the Christian evangelical movement that spread through the Caribbean in the 1970s. The ties between the power-hungry, immoral, and hypocritical pastor of the novel and the United States Christian church suggest that Sharlow sees the American influence in the Caribbean as a destructive one. *The Promise* depicts British colonists in a similar way, as tyrannical hypocrites who profit from the back-breaking labor of the Indians and take sexual advantage of the Indian women. The events of the novel bring to light the abuses of colonial power, but also serve as a metaphor for current-day politics and symbolize the ongoing exploitation of the Caribbean.

Both *The Counting House* and *The Promise* use a relationship between a British man in power and a young Indian woman as a metaphoric criticism of imperialism, but there are important differences between the novels. While Dabydeen examines various forms of economic oppression of the poor, Sharlow focuses specifically on colonialism and its damaging effects. Dabydeen's goal seems to be to give voice to the laborers, to make their lives real. Sharlow's purpose is to challenge imperial stereotypes of India as barbaric and uncivilized and to draw attention to the cruelty and destruction of colonialism. In addition, Dabydeen's Indian characters seem to accept the imperial view of their inferiority. On the other hand, Sharlow highlights the fierce will of his Indian characters and the richness of their culture, which perhaps does more to fight against the psychological damage of colonialism. While the potential for solidarity between the races is eventually wasted in Dabydeen's text, in Sharlow's novel, the friendship that develops between the female Indian characters and an African woman named Miss Mary is one of the few rays of hope.

The Promise, which was self-published, has received little critical attention. In the only review of the novel, Frank Birbalsingh writes, "*The Promise* can be said to do for Indian indentureship what novels by Phillips and D'Aguiar do for African slavery: present basic facts of Caribbean history in all their human complexity...these novels show us what works of history can never do: the complex and varied reaction of individual human beings both to historical circumstances and to one another" (Birbalsingh n.d.). Mariam Pirbhai briefly discusses *The Promise* in *Mythologies of Migration*, noting that it "provides a scathing indictment of colonial practices and the internal forms of displacement they produced for the local Indian civilian" (Pirbhai 2009, 6). The novel does indeed bring to light many aspects of colonialism and indenture that are otherwise ignored, such as the frequency of sexual violence against female laborers. This directly challenges the colonial view of the planters as benevolent, paternal figures interested only in exposing the Indians to civilization and Christianity.

However, aspects of the text are so polemical as to become exaggerated—the depictions of India before colonization are idealistic and the British characters become caricatures of evil rather than complex human beings capable of great cruelty. This simplification simply reverses the civilized-barbaric binary of colonization, rather than recognizing the hazards of such a binary. In a similarly problematic move, the use of rape as a literary trope suggests that women, the bearers of tradition and culture, must be protected, and minimizes women's individual experiences of violent oppression.

The Promise begins as a love story set in the town of Gaya in the early nineteenth century, when British military rule was replacing company rule in India. In these early chapters, the novel strives to counter the negative stereotypes of India as a backward, poverty-ridden, caste-bound society. Rati, the main character of the novel, is kind, virtuous, and stunningly beautiful, and as the daughter of a Brahmin, she is well educated. Her love interest, Guha, is a member of the Chandal, or untouchable caste, but this does not prevent them from marrying.

Unlike Dabydeen's descriptions of Rohini's village in India, Sharlow's descriptions of Gaya before colonialism are romanticized, suggesting nostalgia for an idyllic time that most likely never existed. Rati and Mura, Rati's friend, repeatedly tell Guha that caste is unimportant in their town, and Rati's father, a Brahmin, easily overlooks Guha's caste. While scholars such as Divya Vaid and J. Albert Rorabacher have noted that the caste system in India was more flexible than is often perceived and that it was, to some extent, a construct of British colonialism (Vaid 2014; Rorabacher 2016), historian Jawaid Alam argues that in the early twentieth century "caste and religious solidarities were…pronounced and rigid in Bihar," the state in which Gaya is located (Alam 2005, 18). Idealizing India before colonialism may help combat negative imperial stereotypes, but it also brushes aside the negative aspects of India in the nineteenth century, such as the widespread poverty and the oppressive caste system.

The text itself contradicts the idea that caste does not matter in Gaya. When Guha first tells Rati that he is untouchable, she looks "again at his intelligent face, his noble bearing," (Sharlow 1995, 8) suggesting that she expects those of low caste to be stupid and humble. The background of the characters in the novel confirms this bias. The two heroes are essentially Brahmin; Rati is born a Brahmin and educated as a Brahmin in the village's Hindu temple. Guha, though untouchable, was born into a Brahmin family and for all purposes is high caste. In reality, the majority of Indians who indentured were of low caste.[14] Sharlow has said that he wrote *The Promise* out of "the need to return the pride and dignity of the East Indian, defamed through the system of indentureship" (Sharlow n.d.). That he chooses to do so by focusing on two characters from high-caste families indicates that the stigma of low caste remains.

The novel suggests that the love story between Rati and Guha would have ended with the two happily married, were it not for the interference of colonialism. As noted in the previous chapter, British colonizers disrupted traditional village life and replaced it with "a mix of feudal landlord-tenant relations and an uneven system of commercial agriculture, growing crops for the market beyond the horizons of the village structure, and indeed for the British metropolis" (Look Lai 1993, 23). The British installed local landlords and imposed severe taxes, which drove many Indians off their land. This is represented in the novel when British officials give near-complete control over Gaya to Raja Ram, a local landowner, in exchange for enforcing their high taxes. He floods the textile market with cheap, mass-produced products from England: "The folks gazed with a kind of bizarre curiosity at the plimsoles, the gross-looking leather shoes; at the awkward and inferior textile materials" (Sharlow 1995, 22). This reflects the destruction of the Indian textile industry, which had once been a major source of employment, by British protectionist policies. The situation in Gaya becomes more and more dire: those who cannot pay the taxes lose their land, while Raja Ram and other wealthy landowners gain more and more property.

Through these events, as well as the character of Judge Jennings, Sharlow directly challenges the justification of colonialism as a civilizing mission. Jennings and the other British officials show little respect for Indian culture: on a tour of Gaya, "Jennings was contemptuous of their school and hospital, of their language and dress, and even of their eating

---

[14] There were indeed some Brahmin who traveled to the Caribbean as indentured laborers, but they were in the minority. For Hindus, crossing the ocean, or the *kali pani*, erased caste, and so high-caste Hindus were reluctant to do so, whereas low caste Hindus, who had little to lose, and were more likely to be struggling to survive, were much more willing to indenture themselves.

habits" (Sharlow 1995, 19). The only time he appears happy is when the Indians present him with gifts of food and jewelry. Jennings represents British colonialism at its worst—he is dismissive of the culture of the colonized and seeks only to gain wealth from his interactions with them, rather than engaging with their culture or offering anything in return.

The text also illuminates an important aspect of colonization that is not explored in earlier texts about indentured labor: the connection between imperialism and the increase in emigration. Both Edward Jenkins and A.R.F. Webber depict Indians emigrating to British Guiana in order to seek better opportunities. Sharlow, on the other hand, focuses on the disruption of Indian life by colonialism as a major cause for emigration. Though Raja Ram's cruel behavior drives Rati and Guha to indenture as a means of escaping India, Sharlow makes it clear that he gained his power through the British colonial authorities.

Earlier texts like *Lutchmee and Dilloo* acknowledge that recruiters were often misleading, but do not go so far as to suggest that laborers were taken against their will. However, on board the ship, Rati and Guha hear many tales of coercive recruitment: "Some men told how they were kidnapped, forced at gun point. Others were duped into drunkenness, and when they realized themselves again, were already imprisoned inside the depot" (Sharlow 1995, 42). This was a fairly common practice, encouraged by the bounty that recruiters received for each laborer they brought in. Walton Look Lai writes, "Cases of illegal detention or kidnapping or other coercion were frequent enough to warrant the attention of the authorities in India" (Look Lai 1993, 28).

The novel employs a split narrative technique, switching between the story of Rati and Guha, and that of John Paul, a young British man who becomes the owner of the plantation where Rati and Guha are bound. Birbalsingh suggests that this structure "enables us to see the human dimensions of the indenture experience in greater fullness, not just as a conflict between victims and victimisers, but as an experience in which either side felt justified in what they did" (Birbalsingh n.d.). While the parallel storylines do broaden the scope of the narrative, John Paul, his father Thomas Fox, and the other British characters tend to appear as one-dimensional villains rather than well-developed, complex humans. In this way, Sharlow simply reverses the Manichean binary that he seeks to challenge. British imperialists depicted colonization as a beneficent undertaking in which the civilized East brought morality and culture to the barbaric West. By flipping this view to suggest that all evil originated with the colonizers, Sharlow indirectly supports the categorization of cultures that imperialism rested upon and ignores the complexity of both Indian and British society. Ironically, Sharlow's view of precolonial India bears a resemblance to the idyllic paradise of the opening scenes of *Lutchmee and Dilloo*, further demonstrating the problematic nature of these images.

The exaggerated nature of the British characters does serve a purpose: their cruelty indicates that the plantation system corrupts those in positions of power. Abolitionists similarly argued that slavery destroyed the morals of slave owners, and Sharlow draws clear links between slavery and indenture. Thomas Fox, John Paul's father, is shaped by his experiences as a slave owner in Jamaica. He convinces his mistress Anne to send their son to Trinidad by telling her, "Were you to become Queen of England, you would not command the authority...nay half the authority of the West Indian planter...Do you know what it is to own scores, hundreds of slaves, to have absolute power over their lives?" (Sharlow 1995, 53). In other words, the way to become a real man is to own other men; masculine strength depends on making others weak. We have already seen how this experience has corrupted Thomas Fox, so that he treats others like objects and believes he is entitled to whomever he wants, and as the novel develops, we see the plantation system corrupt John Paul in the same way.

Sharlow suggests that even the colonizers were aware that their moral rationales were a cover for the economic benefits of imperialism. Thomas Fox argues that indenture is beneficial to both England and the Indians: "'For his labour, [the coolie] shall earn the benefits of our superior civilization...England has at the moment, the capacity to manufacture the entire world'" (Sharlow 1995, 48), drawing a clear link between "civilizing" the laborers and increasing England's economic power. Sharlow suggests that notions of moral and intellectual superiority can be highly seductive, especially to a man like John Paul, who is struggling to prove his worth to his father. John Paul begins to feel that his role as colonizer is "to civilize the barbarian, the primitive worshippers of idols" (Sharlow 1995, 58). This is a dramatically different image of British men than those that appear in earlier texts. John Paul and Fox may tell themselves that they are noble and altruistic, but it is clearly a way of rationalizing their cruel and self-interested behavior and, by extension, colonialism.

This hypocrisy becomes even clearer once these men encounter Rati on John Paul's plantation, and her sexuality becomes a source of contention. John Paul attempts to build intimacy with Rati, ordering her to attend lessons with him on the tenets of Christianity. It is clear that this is a ploy—he does not attempt to convert any of the other laborers, only the woman he finds seductively attractive. Emmanuel Chase, John Paul's manager, makes no attempt to hide his feelings. He dehumanizes the laborers, and the women in particular, as when he asks John Paul if he has taken a liking to "coolie flesh." Coming across half-naked Rati as she bathes in a stream, Chase thinks, "This was a splendid beast" (Sharlow 1995, 94). Chase's view of Rati is not so different from that of Craig, the Scottish hero of *Lutchmee and Dilloo*, who compares his affection for Lutchmee to the affection he would have for his dog. While Jenkins intends to show that Craig's feelings toward Lutchmee are protective and paternalistic, in the end, both characters deny the humanity of the Indians.

As noted in the previous chapter, female indentured laborers were in a doubly vulnerable position, at risk of abuse because of their colonized status and because of their gender. This is demonstrated in *The Promise*, as Chase rapes Rati repeatedly and threatens to kill her husband if she reports his assaults. It is important to recognize that Sharlow's depictions of assault against women laborers is a rare and crucial acknowledgment of a reality of plantation life, one that does not appear in earlier texts. In addition, Rati is a powerful female figure in many ways, using various forms of resistance to fight back against colonial power and survive her brutal treatment; she remains defiant toward Chase and John Paul in spite of the ongoing sexual assault, she stands up to the police, and she eventually becomes an entrepreneur, running her own store.

Yet, Chase's assault of Rati acts as a metaphor for Britain's conquest of India, a move that supports the view of women's sexuality as a trophy in broader struggles for power. Toward the end of the novel, Sharlow makes the comparison overt: "The rape of the sub-continent was in full swing… Realizing that imperialism must be supported by the concept of a superior civilization, the British now held that all things Indian were contemptible. As in the previous system of slavery, Christianity was employed as the forerunner, paving the way for a college of organized schemes and outright lies" (Sharlow 1995, 161). John Paul's attempts to convert Rati as a means of gaining power over her are echoed in Sharlow's descriptions of Christianity as a tool of imperialism, while Chase's behavior matches the "rape of the sub-continent."

As in *The Counting House*, the men in the novel view Rati as an object to be won, a possession whose acquisition serves as a symbol of masculine power. When John Paul learns that Chase has raped Rati, he is indignant, not because of the assault itself but because Chase has had sexual intercourse with Rati and he has not. He feels "utterly defeated. Once again, he saw how Chase was the complete master...The Indian woman was his reward" (Sharlow 1995, 100). Like Chase, he sees Rati not as a human but as a prize that he has earned.

This mindset could be seen as a criticism of the colonizers, except that it is not unique to the British: nearly every male in the text sees Rati in this way. In the early chapters, Raja Ram tries to assault Rati, and an indenture recruiter separates Rati from Guha in an attempt to force himself upon her. Even Bodil, a fellow laborer and Rati's friend insists that he deserves pleasure with her: "'You think it easy for Bodil to live and to see Rati's beauty every day, ay, and not to have desire for one single day?'" (Sharlow 1995, 196). Such repetition reinforces the notion that men cannot control their urges, thus absolving them of blame when they commit rape, and suggests that if a woman is beautiful enough, she becomes subject to the needs of the men around her. It is striking that even the women in the novel seem to hold this mindset. At a celebration to mark the end of the harvest season, Indrani urges a weary and heart-sore Rati to dance for the men: "'Here there are so many men, miserable without women. Proper *dharma*[15] is to make our hard-working men happy'" (Sharlow 1995, 117). This further normalizes the view that women's needs and desires are subordinate to those of men.

As in earlier texts like *Lutchmee and Dilloo*, the British man in power takes the Indian woman away from her husband, but, instead of doing so to protect her, he tears apart a loving, devoted couple for his own desires. Guha and Rati attempt to run away from the plantations, but Chase discovers them and Guha is killed. If we see their romance as a representation of Indian nationalism, the destruction of their marriage acts as a metaphor for Britain's resistance to Indian statehood. Guha's loss leaves Rati adrift, disconnected from her homeland. She gives up all hope of returning to Gaya, and the symbolic hope of Indian nationhood offered by their union has been destroyed, as well.

Separated from her loved ones, Rati is forced to create new family ties and find support in less traditional ways. The tragedy leads to one positive development—the forming of a proto-feminist bond between Indrani and Rati, based on a recognition of their shared oppression. These bonds can be seen as a challenge to the preeminence of the male-female erotic relationship. The friendship between these two women is the central relationship of

---

[15] Moral duty.

The Promise, more so than that of Guha and Rati. Sharlow thus emphasizes the importance of nontraditional forms of family in the survival of the laborers.

Conditions do not improve for Rati and her friends once their contract is up. They eke out a living cultivating their own land and trying to save enough money to open a shop or build a house. Life for former laborers in general is grim: "With no place to go, the Indians wandered about the countryside...By the dozens, and by the score, they became either the victims of venomous snakes, or the savage beasts of the wild" (Sharlow 1995, 129). The police arrest anyone who is found off a plantation, and the officials who are meant to protect them also oversee the laws against them. Even after their contract has ended, the laborers remain trapped within a repressive system.

Rati, Indrani, Arjun, and Bodil are able to survive because they are *jahajin*, meaning they treat each other as kin: they live in the same household, pool financial resources, and support each other emotionally. As an alternative to the Victorian ideal of a nuclear household, the text thus offers a more fluid, inclusive view of familial relationships, one that has been explored by many Caribbean historians. In *Family Love in the Diaspora*, Mary Chamberlain challenges the notion that slaves and their descendants lacked stable, loving families simply because their family structures did not conform to the Victorian image of a mother, father, and children living under one roof. Slaves brought different patterns of family from their homelands, and slavery and its aftereffects forced Afro-Caribbeans to find alternative ways to constitute families. These included common-law unions, matriarchal households, generations living together, and broad views of kinship (Chamberlain 2006).

Indentured laborers similarly extended the notion of family. Mariam Pirbhai notes that the Hindi term "jahaji bhai," or "ship brother," is unique to indentured peoples and their descendants (Pirbhai 2009, 50). It indicates the bond that is formed by those who travel across the water together under indenture, and suggests an alternative form of kinship for those who have been separated from many or all of their blood relatives. Though Sharlow does not directly use the term, the bond it represents is depicted between the four friends, especially Rati and Indrani. Their friendship plays a more important role in the novel than any of the romantic relationships: Rati's strength and virtue inspire Indrani, and Indrani's sharp wit makes Rati laugh at moments when their pain becomes almost unbearable. When Rati despairs of British power ever waning, Indrani suggests, "'Perhaps one day, the British might drop dead from eating too much sugar?'" (Sharlow 1995, 177). The connection between these women acts as both a challenge to colonial norms and as an indication of the alternative survival strategies developed by those living under the harsh conditions of plantation life.

Indrani and Rati also develop a friendship with an African woman named Miss Mary, indicating the importance of forming connections between, as well as within oppressed groups. Sharlow draws attention to the ways that the planting class tried to prevent different groups from interacting, fearing the strength that they would have if they did. Miss Mary, upon meeting the two women, learns that they speak English and notes, "'I have heard otherwise'" (Sharlow 1995, 169), pointing to the misconceptions that colonizers fostered about different ethnic groups. The friendship between the Indian women and Miss Mary also helps them recognize the similarity of their experiences and the necessity of solidarity. Miss Mary comments, "'The white man lies on the African nation, and now the Indian. If we do not fight back, the lies will become truth'" (Sharlow 1995, 177).[16]

This friendship can be seen as a response to contemporary ethnic clashes in Trinidad and Tobago. Published in 1995, *The Promise* was born out of a particularly turbulent moment in Trinidad's history. In the 1986 elections, the National Alliance for Reconstruction (NAR), a multiethnic political party founded with the intention of uniting Trinidadians of Indian and African descent, burst into power, winning 33 of 36 seats. They gradually lost support, however, due to increasing unemployment and decreasing social services, and in 1990, a militant Muslim group attempted a violent takeover of the government. This group held the prime minister and members of parliament hostage for five days, during which riots and looting broke out in the capital, Port of Spain. The hostages were eventually released, but the NAR struggled to recover from this attack. In 1991, the People's National Movement (PNM), supported primarily by Afro-Trinidadians,

---

[16] This sense of solidarity between formerly enslaved persons and the indentured Indians can also be seen in the subject matter of Sharlow's novel *When Gods Were Slaves* (1993). Written two years before *The Promise*, this novel traces the transatlantic journey of a group of Africans who were kidnapped, sold as slaves, and taken to the Caribbean to work on sugar plantations. Sharlow writes that his novels "achieve the specific perspective of returning the pride and dignity of the peoples of the continents defamed through the systems of slavery and indentureship," indicating a desire to draw connections between these forms of exploitation ("Sharlow" n.d.).

took power again. The solidarity that Sharlow promotes in *The Promise* thus calls back to the promise of solidarity offered by the NAR.

The kindness and respect with which the Indo- and Afro-Trinidadian characters treat each other contrast sharply with the intimate connections between the colonizers. John Paul's relationship with Christine Fuller, the daughter of a plantation owner, is described in terms of sadism and masochism, qualities that have developed in both of them through their experiences on the plantation. Though Sharlow is trying to indicate the extent to which the brutality of slavery and indenture corrupt those in power, there is an element of misogyny here, and a sense that Christine is inviting assault. Christine thinks of John Paul, "Oh, it was his total lack of respect, his boldness towards her body that aroused the beast inside her" (Sharlow 1995, 97). The use of "beast" here connects this passage to Chase's description of Rati as "a splendid beast"; women in this novel, Indian and British alike, are repeatedly dehumanized. In addition, Christine's longings feed into one of the most common justifications for sexual assault: that the victim "asked for it." Finally, there is a sense that a woman who is openly sexual must be depraved. Rati, who is modest, enjoys sex in a pure way, and does not seek it out, while Christine actively pursues John Paul. This aggressiveness is tied to her "strange passions" (Sharlow 1995, 97), indicating that an overtly sexual woman is also degenerate.

John Paul has become crueler and more power hungry in other ways as well. For example, he schemes ways to hold the laborers past their contracts' official expiration, which refers to the many ways that plantation owners extended the laborers' contracts. According to colonial law, managers could count the days that laborers missed work because of illness and add them to the end of the contract, and in some colonies, managers were allowed to double that time.[17] The novel indicates that the power that comes with owning the plantation and controlling the lives of so many people, as well as the wealth the plantation generates, is corrupting; it has destroyed John Paul's kindness and empathy, while Chase, once he relinquishes that power, becomes more benevolent.

None of the characters are content at the end of the novel, pointing to the pervasive damage caused by imperialism. The marriage between Christine and John Paul falls apart because he cannot forget his lust for Rati. Even though he has power over the material aspects of her life, she

---

[17] Since this was only reported to the laborers once the contract was over, laborers had no way of protesting the managers' calculations.

has emotional power over him, because he cannot contain her—he will long for her forever and never fully grasp her. It is tempting to see this as a statement about Britain's inevitably thwarted desire to possess India, body and soul. The intimacy between Rati and Indrani continues into the final scenes of the novel; they even die within six months of each other. Rati and Indrani die knowing that the system of indenture is coming to an end and their children's lives are somewhat improved, working in shops instead of fields, but Sharlow indicates that the oppression continues. One day, Savita, Rati's daughter, observes the children playing teacher by pretending to whip a post. Hierarchies of power, Sharlow suggests, do not rapidly dissolve.

The Pagoda: Defying Colonial Categories

The Pagoda, by Patricia Powell, does not deal directly with indenture, but features a protagonist, Lowe, who smuggles himself on board a ship of Chinese migrants traveling to Jamaica under indenture. Lowe is born female but presents as male, and the novel refers to Lowe using masculine pronouns, and so this chapter does the same. Like *The Counting House* and *The Promise*, *The Pagoda* explores the relationship between a white man in power and the migrant that he sexually assaults—in this case, Cecil, the captain of the ship upon which Lowe stows away, and Lowe. By contrast with *The Counting House* and *The Promise*, there is no sense that the characters in this novel represent their home nations, nor does Cecil's treatment of Lowe act as an allegory for Britain's treatment of China. Instead, the characters defy stereotypes, and their interactions with each other, while impacted by the broader dynamics of colonialism, are shaped more powerfully by the local: individual relationships, community norms, and shared experiences. *The Pagoda* thus acts as an example of fiction that condemns the abuses of colonialism and indenture without replicating the hierarchies underlying those systems.

The novel begins with Cecil's death, which stuns Lowe, who is living as a shopkeeper in Jamaica. He reflects on their first encounter decades earlier and how their lives developed in the years that followed. Lowe bore Cecil a daughter, Elizabeth, now grown and married. Cecil's death acts as a catalyst for Lowe to reevaluate his life, and he struggles to tell Elizabeth the truth: Lowe is Elizabeth's biological mother, and Cecil, not Lowe, is her father. As Lowe searches for a way to explain this to Elizabeth, he begins to shed the false identity that Cecil had developed for him and to recognize all of the ways that he and those around him push against the seemingly fixed categories of gender, ethnicity, and sexuality.

While Lowe never labors on the plantation, the suffering of those migrants who did acts as a backdrop for Lowe's own traumatic experiences. Lowe describes his time on the ship, which he shared with "stolen Chinese...thin men spare as bones...piled in like prisoners and stowed tight with the chests of tea and silk, for sale to the highest bidder in the West Indies" (Powell 1998, 17). This description demonstrates the dehumanizing treatment of the laborers, who are packed onto the ship with the tea and silk, goods to be sold across the ocean. The words "stolen" and "prisoner" also indicate the involuntary nature of this migration, which is further emphasized when the Chinese migrants gather in Lowe's shop and tell tales of being kidnapped or tricked into signing a contract (Powell 1998, 43). The British system of Indian indenture certainly included its share of corruption, ill-treatment of laborers, and dehumanization, but in some ways, the Chinese system of indenture may have been worse, as it was a system of private profiteers as opposed to a state-run system. Walton Look Lai writes that the professional recruiters relied on "all manner of fraud, trickery, and intimidation of the kind associated with the earliest indenture migrations from seventeenth-century Europe, and indeed African slavery" (Look Lai 1993, 46). Conditions for the laborers did not improve once they reached the plantations. Lowe describes "Chinese who walked off cliffs from overwork, who hung themselves with pigtails looped around tree limbs, who tied stones to their feet and jumped into rivers" (Powell 1998, 45). In this gruesome respect, the experience of the Chinese laborers was similar to that of the Indian laborers, who often committed suicide by hanging themselves or jumping into the vats of boiling cane.

Powell, like Dabydeen and Sharlow, highlights the extreme vulnerability of migrants, particularly the few women who migrated. One of the major differences between Indian and Chinese migration was the lower rate of Chinese women indenturing. Walton Look Lai writes that "for the Chinese female...emigration continued to be so rare as to be noticeable when it did occur at all" (Look Lai 1993, 47). Look Lai attributes this in part to traditional gender roles in China but also to the fact that Chinese migrants, much more so than Indian migrants, intended to return home at the end of their indenture. As a result, they did not bring family members with them. Literary scholar Kimberly Bain depicts the isolation faced by the rare female Chinese migrant in a short fictional text titled "The Journey Across Black Waters." Bain based the character of You on a real woman, the sole female in a group of 272 migrants who voyaged from China to Trinidad in 1865–1866. In the story, You and her baby are repudiated by her husband, after which You segregates herself as much as possible from the rest of the migrants. The ghostly nature of You's baby, who is heard but never seen, raises the question of whether it exists at all. Like You herself, who is described as "a tiny figure curled up in the bunk above [Cheung See]" (Bain 2013), the child seems barely present. You ultimately throws the baby into the ocean, seeming to anticipate her inability to care for her child and to view drowning as a better fate. This reflects the tenuous existence of women and children in indentured migration and also the way that vulnerable migrants learned to hide their presence as a means of protection.

Lowe remains similarly hidden on his voyage to Jamaica, first stowed away in a barrel, and then after Cecil discovers him, confined within Cecil's cabin. Both Cecil and Lowe are aware that Lowe, as the sole female on board, would be seen as available to any man who wanted sexual gratification. Later, when Lowe complains that Cecil placed him in a position as a shopkeeper without asking what he wanted, Cecil sneers in response, "'You, the only Chinee woman on the island…You know what them do with the Chinee women in British Guiana. In Cuba. In Trinidad? Bring them to whorehouse. Is that you wanted?'" (Powell 1998, 99). These passages suggest that Chinese women migrating to the Caribbean may have been even more vulnerable than Indian women, due to their extremely low numbers. Cecil's repeated assault of Lowe further highlights this vulnerability. Lowe, speaking to Cecil's memory, says, "'You forget me and you down in the belly of that ship. How you loved me as you like. Treated me as you want. Lock up in that cabin for days!'" (Powell 1998, 22).

Though Cecil abuses Lowe and then blithely dismisses that abuse, there is no sense that Cecil's attacks represent Britain's relationship with China. Cecil is presented as a complex figure, one who assaults Lowe but also nurses him back to health and sets him up as a store owner in a town in Jamaica. After Lowe gives birth to Elizabeth, Cecil builds a large house for the two, and brings a woman named Miss Sylvie to feign a marriage with Lowe and act as mother to Elizabeth. Upon Cecil's death, Lowe tells Elizabeth, "'You Uncle Cecil did love you a whole heap,'" and though Lowe struggles to admit this after the torment that Cecil caused him, he appears to believe it (Powell 1998, 66).

Instead of using this relationship to critique Britain's relationship with China, Powell reflects on the fluidity of gender and sexuality, and the ways that colonial subjects defied categorization in order to survive. Lowe is far from a stereotypical image of a submissive Chinese female. His father raised him as a boy, and so he learned to read and write and was able to explore the town in which he lived, privileges not allowed to many Chinese women of the time. After being forced into marriage, Lowe takes the dramatic step of disguising himself as a boy and smuggles onto Cecil's ship. While Lowe develops this disguise in order to escape a restrictive life in patriarchal China, he maintains it in Jamaica to gain some standing in the community.[18]

Interestingly, the members of the village who recognize or come to realize that Lowe is physically female seem indifferent to this fact, suggesting a flexible view of gender within the community itself. After learning of Lowe's disguise, Jake, who oversees Lowe's project of building a Chinese community center, begins responding to Lowe with "Yes, ma'am, Mr. Lowe" (Powell 1998, 241), simultaneously acknowledging Lowe's biological and adopted gender, and also continuing to refer to Lowe with terms of respect. This suggests that once individuals have come to know one another, labels of gender, ethnicity, and sexuality hold less meaning. Literary critic Anne-Marie Lee-Loy argues that Lowe's "unknowable" gender and sexuality identity echoes the stereotype of the "unknowable" Chinese and thus "draws attention to the question of whether or not such identities actually reveal anything meaningful about the individuals who wear them or whether, despite the labels we wear, we all remain essentially unknowable" (Lee-Loy 2010, 70).

Lowe's character, as well as the way he is treated by other characters, thus acts as a challenge to fixed notions of gender and sexuality that pervaded the rhetoric of both British Imperialism and Caribbean nationalism. As described earlier in this chapter and in greater depth in Chap. 2, the arguments of both colonial and anti-colonial texts often centered on the treatment of the colonized female and rested on views of heteronormative patriarchy. For example, colonial officials claimed that they were protecting female laborers by promoting monogamous relationships between man and wife, even when that meant forcing women to stay in abusive

---

[18] There are historical examples of women resisting categorization in this way: in nineteenth-century Cuba, Dr. Enrique Fabar practiced medicine and was briefly married to a young woman named Juana de León, until his wife discovered that he was biologically female, while Anne Bonny and Mary Read disguised themselves as men aboard a pirate ship in the early eighteenth century.

relationships. On the other hand, Indian nationalists argued that the frequency with which British men developed sexual relations with Indian women undermined Indian masculinity and the purity of Indian blood, a sentiment that is reflected in the interpersonal dynamics of *The Counting House* and *The Promise*.

By contrast with the characters of Rohini and Rati, who resist patriarchy in small ways but are primarily defined by their heteronormative roles as wives and mothers, Lowe maintains a position of relative wealth and power and engages in sexual relationships with both men and women. Presenting as male, he is protected, to some extent, from the exploitation of women. This serves not only to highlight the repressive norms that women (particularly women of color and the working class) faced in Britain's Caribbean colonies in the nineteenth century, but also to reveal the cracks in those norms. As Maria Cristina Fumagalli, Bénédicte Ledent, and Roberto del Valle Alcalá note, literary and historical examples of cross-dressing "powerfully realign the Caribbean, a region only too often associated with machismo and homophobia, with daring transgressions of colonial values, predicated upon gender binarism, patriarchy, and race and class division" (Fumagalli 2013, 2). In other words, Lowe's unwillingness to conform to expectations acts as a challenge to the dominance of imperialism and the values that it attempted to impose upon its colonial subjects.

Lowe is not the only character who sidesteps defined societal roles. Lowe, who struggles to command the servants, envies Miss Sylvie's ease in giving orders, but recognizes that "this came with the authority of near-alabaster skin. The coppery mass of hair that fell to her waist" (Powell 1998, 33). Her first husband was a "big government man with money and clout and a face to hold up and a lot of people working for him and capturing black people and still selling them" (Powell 1998, 143). Miss Sylvie thus seems to represent the height of white colonial power, yet Lowe learns that she has African ancestry and had to give up her children because they were "too brown" (Powell 1998, 143). When Lowe asks why she married a white man, she points to the jewelry that he bought her and the power that he held. "'I mean, what women have, Lowe, if it ain't what the father give them, what the husband give them?'" (Powell 1998, 146). In order to gain financial stability in the patriarchal and racist world of nineteenth-century Jamaica, Miss Sylvie hid her African ancestry. That she was able to pass for years emphasizes the unstable nature of the category of "white."

As can be seen, the relationships between the characters in *The Pagoda* lack the allegorical nature of the interactions in *The Counting House* and *The Promise*. One possible explanation for this is that Britain never formally colonized mainland China as it did India. Though Hong Kong became a British colony in 1842 and Britain exerted significant economic and political influence over China in the nineteenth and early twentieth centuries, Britain's role in the history of Chinese migration may loom less large in the Caribbean imaginary than their role in Indian migration. Highlighting this, Cecil plays a fairly minor role in the novel. His assault of Lowe on board the ship and his death are the two major incidents that set the events of plot in motion, but aside from these moments, he is fairly absent from the story.

Additionally, Powell's motivations in writing this novel seem different from those of Dabydeen and Sharlow. Rather than crafting a direct critique of imperialism, Powell focuses more on the impact of migration. She notes that the process of writing the book helped her understand her own resettlement from Jamaica to the United States: "I drew deeply on my experiences as a person of color, a foreigner who had immigrated to North America and who after many years was still not quite at home here" (Powell 2004, 54). *The Pagoda* thus dwells primarily on Lowe's relations with the villagers once he has settled in Jamaica—the mistrust they feel toward him, the tensions between those of Indian, African, and Chinese descent, and the bonds that he creates in spite of those tensions. Powell centers these interactions, rather than Lowe's relationship with Cecil or with any colonial officials, within the novel, deprioritizing Britain's role in the development of Caribbean identity. This is partly a function of the fact that Powell's novel is set in a village rather than on a plantation, but the choice of setting can be seen as a part of that deprioritization.

The Pagoda thus offers a critique of imperialism that does not foreground the colonizer-colonized relationship, characters written as individuals rather than representations of their home nation, and an acknowledgment of hierarchies of gender and ethnicity that does not perpetuate them. Powell draws attention to the repressive societal norms in both traditional Chinese society and colonial Jamaica, as the disguises that Lowe and Miss Sylvie adopt help them survive in these patriarchal and racist worlds. In addition, she highlights the abuses of the indenture system that so many Chinese migrants suffered under. Yet her focus seems to be on teasing out the ways that these oppressive systems push together or pull apart people from different identity groups and the ways that the disguises we adopt for survival under these repressive regimes often end up corroding our own sense of self.

The film *Guiana 1838: The Arrival* (2007), written and directed by Rohit Jagessar, is an additional case of a narrative in which the characters represent only their own experiences rather than a national identity. This docu-drama begins with the abolition of slavery in British Guiana, then follows the recruitment, migration, and indenture period of the first Indian laborers who were brought to the colony. While the characters, particularly the British ones, are somewhat one-dimensional, they are reduced to personality traits such as lecherousness (Bullock), viciousness (Youngblood), or nobility (Scoble) instead of standing in for Britain as a whole. Jagessar's goal in making the film is highlighted by the significant amount of time devoted to the lives of the enslaved Africans before abolition; the friendship that develops between Cabi, a formerly enslaved man, and Laxman, a rebellious laborer; and the many parallels that Jagessar draws between indenture and slavery. These aspects of the film suggest that he, like Sharlow, hoped to encourage a sense of solidarity between contemporary Indo- and Afro-Guyanese and to counter the view that Indian migrants have no claim to the suffering of forced labor.

While the film does not treat the British or Indian characters as symbolic representatives of their nation, it does little to expand our understanding of women laborers. Jagessar does draw attention to the sexual violence that female laborers faced, but that violence is underplayed, especially when compared to the brutal and drawn out depictions of the whippings the male laborers endure. For example, a man named Lalu begins to assault a female laborer before he realizes what he is doing and apologizes, while the overseer Bullock attempts to force himself onto Laxman's love interest, Urmilla, but runs away when she scratches him in the face. Urmilla herself skirts some, but not all, stereotypes of Indian women. She is courageous and fierce, scratching both of the overseers who attempt to seduce her, offering herself to Bullock in order to stop the brutal whipping of Laxman, and stealing a gun with the attention of killing Bullock. However, she does all this for love of Laxman, ultimately revealing herself to be, like Sita, a devoted partner willing to wholly sacrifice herself for her mate. Thus, while the film does not present women laborers as the bearers of Indian culture, it still supports some problematic images of Indian womanhood.

Conclusion: The Dangers of Nationalist Metaphors

Both *The Counting House* and *The Promise* turn the metaphor of a relationship between an Indian woman and a British man into a criticism of the systems of imperialism and indenture. Yet there is a danger in these metaphors, as they tend to erase the real experiences of women like Maharani, described at the beginning of this chapter. Instead, these depictions suggest that women are the bearers of culture and must be restricted to the domestic sphere. This view, a common one in many traditional societies, was concretized by the imperial indentured labor system, in which women were doubly marginalized and became a site of contestation between ethnic groups.

It is certainly true that in the last century, Indo-Caribbean and Chinese-Caribbean women have made significant gains in access to education and position of power. This is evidenced by the election of Kamla Persad-Bissessar, a woman of Indian descent, to the position of prime minister of Trinidad and Tobago in 2010. Yet there are many indications that the repressive gender roles and high rates of domestic abuse that developed under colonialism and indenture continue to play out in insidious ways in the Caribbean. To take Guyana as an example, the 2016 Human Rights Report for Guyana states that "domestic violence and violence against women, including spousal abuse, was widespread" (United States 2016, 8), while women were dramatically underrepresented in the work force.[19] Gaiutra Bahadur reports that between 2007 and 2010, on average, one woman a month was killed in Guyana by her boyfriend or husband (Bahadur 2014, 194). Further, Indo-Guyanese women show a dismaying lack of awareness of the protections available to them.[20] *The Counting House* and *The Promise* both reflect and support the troubling view of woman as representatives of Indian culture and heritage, who must be protected and controlled. In our examination of the rhetoric around labor, nation, and gender, it is critical that we recognize the dangers of such representations.

---

[19] According to this report, 44% of women in Guyana were reported to be in the workforce, compared with 83% of men. The number of women in a country's labor force indicates the prevalence of traditional gender divisions into domestic and public spheres and is often used as an indicator of women's status in a society. While this indicator can be problematic, as it continues to make domestic labor invisible, it is a fair representation of the number of women in public forms of employment.

[20] According to a report by the women's organization Red Thread, in 1999, 77.3% of Indo-Guyanese women did not know about the Domestic Violence Act that had passed in 1996, the highest percentage of any ethnic group in Guyana (Red Thread 2000).

Bibliography

Alam, Jawaid. 2005. *Government and Politics in Colonial Bihar, 1921–1937.* New Delhi: Mittal Publications.
Bahadur, Gaiutra. 2014. *Coolie Woman: The Odyssey of Indenture.* Chicago: The University of Chicago Press.
Bain, Kimberly. 2013. *The Journey Across Black Waters.* https://ghostsinthewater.wordpress.com/. Accessed 7 Mar 2018.
Bhabha, Homi. 2012. *The Location of Culture.* New York: Routledge.
Birbalsingh, Frank. (n.d.). *The Promise*: A Review by Professor Frank Birbalsingh. http://sharlow.virtualave.net/THE%20PROMISE.htm.
Chamberlain, Mary. 2006. *Family Love in the Diaspora: Migration and the Anglo-Caribbean Experience.* New Brunswick: Transaction.
Dabydeen, David. 1993. *Indo-Caribbean Resistance.* Edited by Frank Birbalsingh, 27–32. Toronto: TSAR.
———. 2005. *The Counting House.* Leeds: Peepal Tree Press.
———. 2011. Getting Back to the Idea of Art as Art: An Interview with David Dabydeen. Interview with Lars Eckstein. *Pak"s Britannica: Articles by and Interviews with David Dabydeen*, edited by Lynne Macedo, 163–172. Kingston, Jamaica: University of the West Indies.
Espinet, Ramabai. 1993. Representation and the Indo-Caribbean Woman in Trinidad and Tobago. In *Indo-Caribbean Resistance*, ed. Frank Birbalsingh, 42–61. Toronto: TSAR.
Foucault, Michel. 1978. *History of Sexuality, Volume 1: An Introduction.* New York: Vintage.
Fumagalli, Maria Cristina, et al. 2013. Introduction. In *The Cross-Dressed Caribbean: Writing, Politics, Sexualities*, 1–21. Charlottesville: University of Virginia Press.
Great Britain Parliament. 1915. Report to the Government of India on the Conditions of the Indian Emigrants in Four British Colonies and Surinam, by Mr. James McNeil and Mr. Chimman Lal. Part I. *Parliamentary Papers* 1914–1916, (Cd 7744), vol. 47.
Guiana 1838: The Arrival. Directed by Rohit Jagessar. New York: RBC Radio, 2007.
Lee-Loy, Ann-Marie. 2010. *Searching for Mr. Chin: Constructions of Nation and the Chinese in West Indian Literature.* Philadelphia: Temple University Press.
Look Lai, Walton. 1993. *Indentured Labor, Caribbean Sugar: Chinese and Indian Migrants to the British West Indies, 1838–1918.* Baltimore: The Johns Hopkins University Press.

Low, Gail. 2007. 'To Make Bountiful Our Minds in an England Starved of Gold': Reading *The Counting House*. In *No Land, No Mother: Essays on the Work of David Dabydeen*, ed. Kampta Karran and Lynne Macedo, 204–217. Leeds: Peepal Tree.

Maharani. 1985. *The Still Cry: Personal Accounts of East Indians in Trinidad and Tobago during Indentureship, 1845–1917*. Interview by Noor Kumar Mahabir. Tacarigua, Trinidad: Calaloux Publications.

Mohammed, Sharlow. 1992. *The Elect*. Leeds: Peepal Tree.

Mohan, Peggy. 2007. *Jahajin*. New Delhi: HarperCollins and The India Today Group.

Mohanty, Chandra Talpade. 2003. *Feminism without Borders: Decolonizing Theory, Practicing Solidarity*. Durham: Duke University Press.

Niranjana, Tejaswini. 2006. *Mobilizing India: Women, Music, and Migration between India and Trinidad*. Durham: Duke University Press.

Pirbhai, Mariam. 2009. *Mythologies of Migration, Vocabularies of Indenture: Novels of the South Asian Diaspora in Africa, the Caribbean, and Asia-Pacific*. Toronto: University of Toronto Press.

Powell, Patricia. 1998. *The Pagoda*. New York: Harcourt Brace & Company.

———. 2004. A Literary Landscape: From Jamaica to Boston. In *The Good City: Writers Explore 21st Century Boston*, ed. Emily Hiestand and Ande Zellman, 43–57. Boston: Beacon Press.

Red Thread. 2000. Women Researching Women. http://www.hands.org.gy/download/wom_surv.htm. Accessed 17 Aug 2013.

Rodney, Walter. 1981. *A History of the Guyanese Working People, 1881–1905*. Baltimore: The Johns Hopkins University Press.

Rorabacher, J. Albert. 2016. *Bihar and Mithila: The Historical Roots of Backwardness*. New York: Routledge.

Sarvan, Charles P. 1997. Review of *The Counting House*. *World Literature Today* 71 (3): 634–635.

Selvon, Sam. 1953. *A Brighter Sun*. New York: The Viking Press.

Sen, Sharmila. 2005. Indian Spices Across the Black Waters. In *From Betty Crocker to Feminist Food Studies: Critical Perspectives on Women and Food*, ed. Arlene Voski Avakian and Barbara Haber, 185–199. Amherst: University of Massachusetts Press.

Sharlow. 1993. *When Gods Were Slaves, Or, A Search for Truth*. Longdenville: Sharlow Mohammed.

———. 1995. *The Promise, Or, After All We've Done for You*. Longdenville: S. Mohammed.

———. (n.d.). *Knowing Our Heritage is Important*. Interview by Anthony Milne. http://sharlow.virtualave.net/THE%20PROMISE.htm.

Sommer, Doris. 1991. *Foundational Fictions: The National Romances of Latin America*. Berkeley: University of California.

United States Department of State. 2016. *Guyana 2016 Human Rights Report*. Washington, DC. https://www.state.gov/documents/organization/265804.pdf.

Vaid, Divya. 2014. Caste in Contemporary India: Flexibility and Persistence. *Annual Review of Sociology* 40: 391–410.

Ward, Abigail. 2011. *Caryl Phillips, David Dabydeen and Fred D'Aguiar: Representations of Slavery*. New York: Manchester University Press.

CHAPTER 5

Family Ties: Embodiment of Female Laborers in the Poetry of Indenture

INTRODUCTION: FROM NATIONALISM TO DISPLACEMENT

During indenture and its aftermath, plantation managers, husbands, fathers, and children all laid claim to the bodies of women laborers: to cultivate the cane fields, for sexual gratification, for reproduction, and for the production of food and clothing. To some extent, this was true of male laborers as well, whose hands cut cane and whose backs carried it in bundles, but the claim on their bodies was generally limited to the fields and the mills. Women's bodies, it seemed, were available to all and at all times, a paradigm that is brought to light and challenged in the work of Indo-Caribbean and Chinese-Caribbean poets. When writing about this time period, authors such as Mahadai Das and David Dabydeen paint images of the female laborer's body: women in these poems are wombs, hands, foreheads, and eyes. This focus draws attention to the colonizers' view of the laborers, particularly the women, as mere bodies, useful for labor and sexual gratification. It also emphasizes the physical nature of the laborers' lives, the bodily suffering that they endured. Rajkumari Singh describes "bent figures" and "emaciated bodies" (Singh 1971, 2, 10), while Lelawattee Manoo-Rahming imagines the "rotting bodies…thrown overboard" (Manoo-Rahming 2000, 4–5) on the voyage to the Caribbean.

In the poems by these authors, the descriptions of women's bodies are inescapably tied to images of land and fields. Mahadai Das tells women laborers, "Your curved back in the fields revitalized sugar./Brought forth,

© The Author(s) 2018
A. Klein, *Anglophone Literature of Caribbean Indenture*,
New Caribbean Studies,
https://doi.org/10.1007/978-3-319-99055-2_5

145

out of your womb, a new industry/Of waving paddy leaves" (Das 2010, 3–5), while in Easton Lee's poem, a female cane worker describes her conception in the cane fields: "my falla-line father/.../took my innocent mother/under the sun tying bundles/near the end of crop" (Lee 1998, 5–9). These themes—the emphasis on the body of the female laborers, and the connection between the woman's body and the land—are threaded through the vast majority of poems depicting indenture, but across time there are significant differences in the poets' treatment of these threads. These differences reflect the changing political climate in the poets' homelands and the poets' responses to those changes.

Poems written by Guyanese authors Rajkumari Singh and Mahadai Das in the 1970s, in the early, still hopeful days of Guyana's independence, describe women working the land and producing crops as a metaphor for women's fertility, their ability to give birth to a new people and a new nation. These authors celebrate Indo-Caribbean women's capacity for reproduction, indicating a belief in the fertile possibilities of the people and the country. By contrast, for David Dabydeen (Guyana), Lelawattee Manoo-Rahming (Trinidad), and Easton Lee (Jamaica), who write in the wake of violent and dictatorial postindependence movements in the Caribbean, this hopefulness has dissipated. Rather than drawing sweeping parallels between the female migrants' labor on the land and their labor in birthing a new generation, these authors narrow their focus, seeking instead to strengthen ties with individual ancestors. They reembody these women as way of grounding themselves, tying themselves to the land of their birth by tracing their genealogy.

This chapter explores how the images of female Indian and Chinese laborers in the poetry of indenture shift across periods of historical change, reflecting a change from nationalist sentiments to a sense of displacement and an attempt to address that displacement through a rebuilding of lineage. This shift is an example of the development within indenture narratives that is tracked by this book, a move away from the categories of gender binaries and national borders and toward a poetics of kinship. As described in the introduction, theoretical conceptions of the experience and impact of indenture, such as Shalini Puri's notion of dougla poetics, Brinda Mehta's emphasis on *kala pani* discourse, and Gabrielle Jamela Hosein and Lisa Outar's proposal of post-indentureship feminisms, tend to focus on the connections that descendants of the indenture population build across ethnic and geographic boundaries. While these issues underlie the works by more contemporary poets, they seek primarily to span temporal limits, evoking the poets' ancestors in order to construct a sense of belonging.

The role of gender and land in colonial and postcolonial literature is a well-trodden subject, so to speak. Postcolonial feminist theorists such as Anne McClintock have noted the frequency with which colonial literature describes colonized land as a female body to be conquered. Analyzing Henry Rider Haggard's classic imperial novel *King Solomon's Mines*, McClintock notes the overt similarities between the treasure map that leads to a diamond mine in southern Africa and the body of a colonized woman, arguing, "Haggard's map thereby hints at a hidden order underlying industrial modernity: the conquest of the sexual and labor power of colonized women" (McClintock 1995, 3). Scholars of Caribbean literature have pointed to similar patterns in the texts of this region. Denise deCaires Narain notes, "Woman...has often been represented *as* the land; either by the colonizers in their depictions of the New World as virginal territory to be penetrated and conquered, or by nationalists for whom the woman/land conflation functions as the obvious symbol of what is being fought *for*" (deCaires Narain 2004, 151, emphasis original). The poems discussed in this chapter wrestle with this tension, and the connections they draw between women's bodies and the land are occasionally problematic. Literary critics Letizia Gramaglia and Joseph Jackson point out that "by depicting a feminized and fertile landscape, [Mahadai] Das skirts close to the trap of patriarchal binaries" (Gramaglia and Jackson 2013, 130), though they suggest that Das ultimately escapes this trap by adding the dimension of nation-building to the female role of life-giver.

However, few critics have tracked the imagery of indentured women and their ties to the land in the work of poets from different generations. Doing so reveals an increasing sense of alienation for postcolonial subjects. One might expect that in the decades after the rupture of migration and the upheaval of gaining independence from imperial nations, the descendants of migrants would feel more and more settled, but the shift in tone within this poetry suggests the opposite: in a postcolonial world, a feeling of belonging often dissipates across generations. This is most likely due to the raised and then disappointed hopes that independence would bring equality and prosperity. History has shown over and over that governments forming in the wake of colonialism often repeat the patterns of oppression and autocracy modeled by imperial nations, or fracture along fault lines created under colonial rule.

This can be seen in especially stark terms in Guyana, and to a lesser extent, in Trinidad and Jamaica. Guyana experienced a tentative sense of unity after gaining independence from Britain in 1966. However, The

People's National Congress (PNC), the ruling party, became increasingly unpopular due to widespread election fraud and a sense of disenfranchisement among the Indo-Guyanese population. Forbes Burnham, prime minister of Guyana from 1964 to 1980, exhibited more and more authoritarian behavior, culminating in the government-backed assassination of political activist Walter Rodney in 1980. Trinidad, which gained its independence in 1962, had a smoother transition to independent rule, although the late 1960s and early 1970s saw a series of protests and strikes organized by the Black Power Movement. In 1970, Prime Minister Eric Williams responded by curtailing civil liberties and declaring a state of emergency. Like Trinidad, Jamaica experienced a relatively peaceful transition to independence in 1962, but in 1976, a dramatic increase in violent crime and clashes between the Jamaica Labour Party and the People's National Party led to a yearlong state of emergency, which included curtailing of civil liberties.[1] These tensions between the governments and the peoples of Guyana, Trinidad, and Jamaica help explain the sense of alienation expressed by the poets analyzed in this chapter.

Additionally, for poets writing toward the end of the twentieth century, increasing globalization has led to a fractured sense of identity. David Dabydeen, Lelawattee Manoo-Rahming, and Easton Lee all settled outside of the nation of their birth, and Dabydeen and Manoo-Rahming both expressed a sense of displacement in their new home. Dabydeen moved to England at age 18 to attend Cambridge, then settled in London, and he admits that he never truly felt at home there: "Leaving Guyana as a boy was exciting…but then proved to be lonely and hurtful, since I was never settled in England. On the one hand, England was a world of books but at the same time a world of grunting and guttural 'skinheads' daubing racist slogans on walls and threatening to assault immigrants" (Dabydeen 2016). Manoo-Rahming similarly felt out of place in her adopted homeland. She left Trinidad to settle in the Bahamas with her husband, Hammond Rahming, but "it was not until she went to the Bahamas where a paucity of Indians made her noticeable as an 'outsider,' that she was inspired to explore her inherited Hindu belief, and formally research her Indo-Caribbean cultural roots which she had taken for granted in Trinidad" (Birbalsingh 2012). While Easton Lee has not described the

[1] Historian Spencer Mawby suggests that in the lead up to independence, the British "delayed the implementation of constitutional reform, encouraged the development of authoritarian politics and neglected the economic conditions which stimulated discontent" (Mawby 2012, 3), and thus bear significant responsibility for the emergence of violent conflicts in the 1970s.

same sense of unease, he has spent a great deal of time abroad, studying drama at the Pasadena Playhouse in California and broadcasting with the BBC in London, and eventually settling in Florida. All three are thus members of the growing population of Caribbean citizens termed the "double diaspora"—descended from migrants, who then migrated themselves.

Connected to this, many nations in the Caribbean, including Guyana, adopted socialist governing practices after achieving independence. A primary goal in many of these socialist movements was land reform, in which land was either redistributed from concentrated, wealthy landowners to the working class, or developed for nationalist interests. Unfortunately, many of these projects failed due to mismanagement. For example, the PNC in Guyana aimed to develop 25,000 acres of land for agriculture by 1976 in order to boost the economy and decrease unemployment, but the plan was scrapped due to massive corruption. The failure of these land-based projects and a growing sense of cynicism toward socialism may have increased the sense of displacement for the authors mentioned here.

Neil Lazarus writes of a similar disillusionment that authors from African nations such as Ghana, Uganda, and Senegal faced in the years after achieving independence. The parallels between these nations and the nations of the Caribbean are striking: rather than achieving "unity, strength, and humanity" with independence, these African countries experienced "fragmentation, weakness, and social violence" (Lazarus 1990, 3).[2] Radical anti-colonial authors like Chinua Achebe and Kofi Awoonor began to express a deep sense of cynicism in their work and "cast around for new forms and styles of writing that would enable them to escape the hidebound implications of their intellectualism" (Lazarus 1990, 26). Lazarus gives examples of the ways that African authors of the 1970s addressed this disillusionment and sought a more effective way of maintaining a social and political engagement in their writing: Ousmane Sembéne included highly detailed descriptions of the material effects of political conflicts, while Bessie Head focused on the interconnections between gender and culture.

Caribbean authors such as Dabydeen and Manoo-Rahming, on the other hand, address their sense of alienation and disillusionment by

[2] Lazarus describes some factors that contributed to this: the expectations that independence would bring solidarity and prosperity were far too high; nationalists had little incentive to dismantle the colonial state apparatus that they had inherited; and the middle class, newly freed from the restrictions of imperialism, felt a theoretical camaraderie with the working class, but did not feel the same urgency for the radical restructuring of society.

strengthening ties with their ancestors. It is unsurprising that Caribbean authors, especially those descended from indentured laborers, would turn to such a strategy. The indenture migration is relatively recent, meaning that it remains vivid in the cultural imaginary of the descendants, but also that these authors struggle against the view that they are latecomers to the region and have contributed less to Caribbean culture than some other ethnic groups. Tracing lineage and forming connections across generations is a way of saying to themselves and others, "I belong."

A major goal of this book is to explore the parallels and divergences between the literature of Indian and Chinese indenture. Regrettably, there is little poetry of Chinese indenture, and so this chapter focuses primarily on the work of Indo-Caribbean poets. However, if we broaden our exploration to poetry that contains echoes of indenture, such as the work of Easton Lee, we can see similar patterns to those described earlier. In 1998, Lee, a Jamaican poet of Chinese descent, published "Cane Piece Blues," which addresses the experience of a female cane worker. In this poem, we see metaphoric ties drawn between the body of the female laborer and the fertility of the land, and in this poem, as in the work of Dabydeen and Manoo-Rahming, there is an ominous feel to that connection, rather than an optimistic one. This suggests that the experience of alienation and displacement is not unique to descendants of Indian migrants.

Analyzing Lelawattee Manoo-Rahming's poem "Caged Soul," Brinda Mehta writes that "women's cries for recognition echo back their invisibility and voicelessness. The unmaking of the female body complements the unmaking of Indo-Caribbean history" (Mehta 2004, 167). The poems described in this chapter seek to do the reverse: to remake the female body as a means of making visible these women's lives, as well as the history of Indian and Chinese migration. This imaging of women's physicality seeks to create a connection with the past, with the ancestors that gave birth to the Indo-Caribbean and Chinese-Caribbean people.

NATIONALISM AND THE BIRTH OF INDENTURE POETRY: RAJKUMARI SINGH

Poetry has played a particularly vital role in Caribbean anti-colonial literature. Due to the primacy of British poets such as William Wordsworth and John Keats in the colonial education system, much of early Caribbean poetry imitated or reappropriated British Romantic literary traditions. As Caribbean literature blossomed in the 1940s, 1950s, and 1960s, the work of anti-colonial poets such as Louise Bennett and Kamau Brathwaite challenged imperialism in both content and form. In addition to criticizing Britain's military and cultural interventions, these poets exploded the conventions of the Romantics by integrating into their poems Creole language, free verse, and rhythms inspired by African music. Until this point, published Caribbean poets tended to be of European or African descent, but this shifted in the 1970s and 1980s with the publication of authors like Rajkumari Singh and Mahadai Das.

The first woman of Indian descent to be published in the Caribbean, Rajkumari Singh was instrumental in developing the cultural and literary life of the Indo-Guyanese community. In addition to being a broadcaster on Radio Demerara and authoring many plays and poems, in the 1970s she founded the influential Messenger Group, a literary collective that fostered writers and artists of Indian descent. Rajkumari Singh was born in 1923 to Alice Singh, whose autobiography is explored in Chap. 2, and who was the granddaughter of an indentured laborer. Rajkumari Singh's father, Jung Bahadur Singh, had worked as a doctor on ships that brought indentured laborers to British Guiana, and so Rajkumari Singh would have been very familiar with the experiences of indentured laborers. This shaped the themes of her work, as did the fact that she faced significant physical challenges. Crippled by polio at age six, she lived in a wheelchair for the rest of her life. Her poetry focuses on the physical experiences of her ancestors as a way of processing the impact of indenture and migration on the Indo-Caribbean population, and perhaps also the impact that polio had on her own physical capabilities.

Singh's writings receive less critical attention than those of the more prolific Mahadai Das, but scholars who do write about her work tend to explore the connections between her poetry and her role in the political and cultural life of Guyana. Anita Baksh argues that while Singh publicly praised the PNC leadership, her poetry "indirectly critiqued the party's biases and avidly promoted Indo-Caribbean culture and women" (Baksh 2016, 77). Jeremy Poynting suggests that "her work emerges out of a number of creative tensions: though intensely active in public affairs her poetry speaks of a deep need for spiritual withdrawal" (Poynting 1986, 167). This desire for "spiritual withdrawal" is seen in Singh's intense focus on the figure of the *aji*, or matriarchal figure, who represents the heart of the Indo-Caribbean community.

Writing about the trope of matriarchal figures that appear in Indo-Caribbean literature, Brinda Mehta argues that "Indo-Caribbean women reclaim a sense of self through *aji* culture" and that "the Indo-Caribbean *ajis* are communal healers who are responsible, through their personal example, for providing inspirational role models of affirmation for Indo-Caribbean societies that have been victimized by colonial and racist ideologies" (Mehta 2004, 140). This emphasis on recuperation and affirmation is especially notable in Singh's 1973 essay, "I am a Coolie," in which she reclaims the term "coolie" as a way of honoring her ancestors and their hard work: "Surely you cannot forget Per-Agie our great-Coolie grandmother squatting on her haunches, blowing through the phookni to help the chuha fire blaze" (Singh 1996, 353). And of course, the *aji* is central to Singh's most famous poem, "Per Ajie" (1971), one of the first works by an Indo-Caribbean author to explore the experience of the indentured laborer. In it, the poet imagines the moment of arrival of her paternal great-grandmother to Guyana, and her subsequent experiences in the field.

Literary critics note the female-oriented nature of the poem, and the emphasis on the role of Indian women in founding the Indo-Caribbean community. Poynting suggests that "Singh pays special homage to the steadfastness of Indian women, whose virtues she saw as central to the character of the Indo-Guyanese as a people 'bred to sacrifice and to achieve'" (Poynting 1986, 167). Mehta argues that in "Per Ajie" Singh "pays tribute to these grandmothers as the original makers of Indo-Caribbean history, women whose fortitude, cultural authority and sense of pride in themselves provided stabilizing forces to combat sociocultural and political displacement" (Mehta 2004, 140).[3] Yet critics have not considered the connection between the woman laborer's body and the land, or the hopeful quality that is attached to this connection.

The poem raises an evocative question: Did the first indentured laborers traveling from India to the Caribbean know they were beginning a new chapter in the history of Indian migration, founding a diasporic community? The full title of the poem, "Per Ajie—A Tribute to the First Immigrant Woman" combined with the opening imagery, "Thy dark eyes[4]/Peering

---

[3] Allison Donnell and Sarah Lawson Welsh add, "The gendering of Per Ajie as both an erotic and exotic object in the eyes of a brutal colonial and masculine regime, and as a maternal figure of blessing and redemption...cannot be disentangled in this case from the telling of a founding Indo-Caribbean experience" (1996, 286).

[4] The poem is written in somewhat stilted English, most likely influenced by English Romantic poetry. Jeremy Poynting attributes this to Singh's desire to add a sense of significance to the Indian migrant's experience, though he concludes that it ultimately gives the poem an "archaic" quality (Poynting 1986, 167).

to penetrate/The misty haze/Veiling the coast/Of Guyana" (Singh 1971, 4–8) evoke the nervous anticipation of the first migrants upon their arrival in a strange land. The short lines and enjambment create a sense of breathlessness, further emphasizing the migrant's apprehension. Singh asks her ancestress whether she knew that she was voyaging "to land/Far-flung from home." We wonder whether this woman regretted her choice, whether she already wished to return to her home in India.

In this opening section, the woman migrant appears in glimpses of body parts, evoking the dehumanizing gaze of the British overseer watching her arrive. The woman's "bangled-ankles" (Singh 1971, 18) contrast with Victorian mores that women remained covered from neck to ankle and emphasize the stereotypical British view of Indian women as provocatively dressed. The white man's gaze devours the migrant's "exotic/Gazelle beauty" (Singh 1971, 20–21), conveying the view of Indian women as not only mysterious, but as animals—graceful, delicate, and easily startled animals. Prey. Here the truncated lines contribute to the sense of disjointedness: the poem is chopped into fragments just as the woman is dismembered under the colonizer's eyes. There is one interesting word choice in this section that reverses the gendered relations: the woman's gaze seeks "to penetrate" the coastal fog (Singh 1971, 5). As Anita Baksh writes, "The poet appropriates colonial male gazes, effectively inverting two common colonial tropes: (1) the Indian woman as the object that is being gazed upon, and (2) the land as a woman's body to be conquered" (Baksh 2016, 81). In these early stanzas, Singh both illustrates and challenges the debasing view of Indian women laborers that dominated colonial rhetoric.

There is a jarring shift in tone, however, when the poem describes the overseer sexually assaulting the female migrant. The poet frames this experience as a future possibility rather than an actual occurrence: "If later/Thy chastity/He violated" (Singh 1971, 25–27). This may be a function of the hypothetical nature of the poem; the whole piece is framed as the poet imagining her ancestor's experiences. It's also likely that Singh acknowledged the prevalence of assault on the estates but struggles with the extreme discomfort of imagining her ancestors suffering through such an experience. If left as a hypothetical, there is hope that one's great-grandmothers escaped such a fate. This is confirmed in the lines that follow, which absolve the victim of blame, but also dismiss the incident: "'Tis nought/'Tis no shame/To thee" (Singh 1971, 28–30). The message that the assault should not be a source of shame for the survivor is a vital one, but to state "'Tis nought" minimizes the trauma of the experience, brushing it aside as meaningless.

The last two sections of the poem focus on the woman's cultivation of the land, which acts as a metaphor for her own fertility. Singh writes, "Two blades you caused/To grow where first/'Twas/But only one" (Singh 1971, 60–63). This refers not only to the actual planting and harvesting of the land, but also to the offspring that she gave birth to, the children who helped make the Indo-Guyanese the largest ethnic group in the nation. In these sections, the focus shifts from disjointed images of the body to the tears the female ancestor shed for the home country, which "Have watered/The blades/Thou didst sow/In my land" (Singh 1971, 61–64). Singh recognizes the sorrow the woman feels at leaving India, but indicates that for her descendants, this sorrow has given way to a sense of belonging, as the poet refers to Guyana as "my land."

The poem concludes by depicting the woman's offspring, who have spread across the land and think of her with gratitude. Here the poet makes explicit the connection between the woman's cultivation of the land and her fecundity, exclaiming that if she could see "The land's abundance/Of growing things/And thy offsprings" (Singh 1971, 47–49), she would not mourn for her lost home but instead celebrate what she was creating. The rhyme and matched rhythm of the phrases "growing things" and "offsprings," particularly in a poem that is otherwise written in free verse, tightly connect these two concepts. Here the brief lines emphasize the honor that Singh bestows upon the first migrant woman, giving each of the benefits that this ancestress has brought to Guyana its own line in the poem. The final lines shift to a religious tone, describing the first woman migrant in saint-like terms. Singh writes that the woman's descendants will place Hindu prayer beads on her head, which has become "hallowed" (Singh 1971, 82) because of the burdens that she has had to bear, and that they seek her "benediction" (Singh 1971, 88). Her martyrdom, Singh suggests, will be remembered and honored, which in turn indicates that an independent Guyana was worth some sacrifice.

Though this poem has dark moments, such as the reference to the sexual assault, its tone is overall joyful and hopeful, an homage to the first woman laborer and the abundance that she brought to Guyana. This optimistic quality can be seen as a reflection of the early, heady days of nationalism. Singh wrote this poem in 1970, four years after Guyana gained independence, and so the poem offers a celebration of the lives of the women who braved the *kala pani* to reach Guyana and settle the new land. Similar themes emerge in a lesser-known poem by Singh that deals with indenture.

"I See Bent Figures" (1971) also honors migrant laborers, in this case depicting them working in rice fields, as opposed to cane fields. This highlights the fact that migrants played a vital role in producing necessary food products, not just sugar, a luxury item. The tone of the poem, while still commemorative, is grimmer than that of "Per Ajie." Unlike "Per Ajie," where Singh focuses on her female ancestor and recognizes her as an individual, in "I See Bent Figures," the laborers are ungendered and depersonalized, viewed as the colonial master saw them. Rather than seeking to recover the lives of the women laborers, here Singh considers the laborers as a whole, and recognizes the physical impact of their long years of toil.

As in "Per Ajie," there is a significant emphasis on the body in conjunction with descriptions of the land, though this poem focuses more on the difficult labor that the migrants experienced and the role they played in feeding the nation. Each stanza is made up of a single sentence broken into five lines, the first of each stanza being "I see." This repetition frames the experiences of the laborers as they move through their time on the estates and into old age, bearing witness to their contributions and their suffering. Singh first describes the "fruitful grass" (Singh 1971, 5) the migrants plant, but here body parts are used as measurements rather than reminders of women's sexuality or reproductive qualities. The figures are "knee-deep in flooded fields" (Singh 1971, 2) and create holes that are "thumb-deep" for rice plants (Singh 1971, 3). Bodies are also sources of pain: the laborers "straighten and bend backwards" (Singh 1971, 7) in an effort to ease the pain of long hours bent over plants, and massage sore spots to release "Tensions of emaciated bodies" (Singh 1971, 10).

The poem then skips ahead to show the migrants decades later, "spindle-legged oldsters wheezing and coughing" (Singh 1971, 12), discarded by society. The concluding stanzas of the poem, like those of "Per Ajie," pay tribute to these workers, naming them "the feeders of nations" (Singh 1971, 23). Singh places the laborers as part of a long and unending tradition of people working the fields, completing brutal and thankless labor in order to feed the world's peoples: "the eternals of society" (Singh 1971, 23). Although this poem recognizes the painful experience of indentured laborers, it still contains a sense of gratitude to the migrants, a belief that their sacrifice was worthwhile. Singh's project is to recuperate the lives of her ancestors and bring attention to the vital role of the Indians in the Caribbean. Later poets seem less concerned with this project, instead focusing on their individual connections with their ancestors.

Nationalism in Tension with Empowerment of Women: Mahadai Das

Mahadai Das makes similar moves in her work, drawing attention to the suffering of the ancestors who indentured and calling on Indo-Guyanese women to feel pride in the role that they played in birthing their nation. Das is the author of "They Came in Ships," probably the most well-known piece of literature addressing Indo-Caribbean indenture. This seminal poem appears in most collections of Caribbean literature, and the 1998 anthology of Indo-Guyanese writing, *They Came in Ships* (Peepal Tree Press, 1998) takes its name from this poem.[5] Born in 1954 in Eccles, Guyana, Das led an active and varied life—she received her BA from the University of Guyana, she served as a volunteer member of the Guyana National Service in 1976, and she was a dancer, an actress, and a beauty queen. In some respects, her life was the opposite of Singh's, who was in a wheelchair from a young age, but Das, too, suffered from physical ailments. After attending Columbia University for her MA and beginning a PhD at the University of Chicago, she fell ill and had open-heart surgery. She died at the age of 48 of a heart attack.

Das was a member of the Messenger Group, the literary collective founded by Rajkumari Singh, and her work incorporates similar themes as Singh's, what Jeremy Poynting terms the "Indo-Guyanese, feminist, and radical nationalist perspectives" (Poynting 1990, 103). Denise deCaires Narain writes that Das' poetry is "characterized by a restless determination and energy as well as by unexpected and startling imagery" (deCaires Narain 2010, 11). Her early work is often criticized for its rough quality and naïve political ideology. Poynting regrets that in her first collection, *I Want to Be a Poetess of My People*, "few poems…survive the political sloganeering of the period" (Poynting 1990, 103) but he urges readers to recognize the difference between "the work of a young writer finding her voice, what was written in politically difficult times and betrayed by history, and what amongst the later poetry might have been revised to good

---

[5] Interestingly, *They Came in Ships* is also the name of a 1989 guidebook for Americans searching for their European ancestors, though this is undoubtedly a coincidence.

effect if her health had been better" (Poynting 2010, 8). There is certainly a shift from her work of the mid-1970s, which expresses idealistic support of Forbes Burnham and his government, to her work of the mid-1990s, where she demonstrates cynicism toward government and an awareness that the postcolonial government of Guyana was reproducing the same autocratic, repressive tendencies of the British colonial administration.[6]

Critics analyzing her early work tend to explore the tensions between her initial dedication to nationalism and her feminist ideology. Letizia Gramaglia and Joseph Jackson argue that Das' "effort to foreground the relationship between land and people through the use of gendered metaphors ultimately works against" the "ecological and feminist perspective" of her poetry (Gramaglia and Jackson 2013, 129–130). In response, Anita Baksh argues that Das was working within the constrictions of her time, and that "the contentious relationship between gender and power that underlies Das' work reflects the conflicted position women occupied in the public sphere at the time…Read in this context Das' claiming of poetic authority and highlighting of gender become courageous acts of feminist empowerment" (Baksh 2016, 85). Yet, Das' earliest poems can be further problematized by considering women's experience of indenture, as she often brushed aside the historical realities of women's experiences in order to trumpet nationalism.

I focus on poems from Das' earliest collection, *I Want to Be a Poetess for My People*, in which she deals most directly with the themes of indenture and nationalism. In the introduction, Poynting notes that "there are at least a couple of poems in *I Want to Be a Poetess for My People* that I know Mahadai Das felt embarrassed to have written" (Poynting 2010, 8). He does not identify those poems, but one suspects they are "He Leads the People" and "Does Anyone Hear the Song of the River Wending its Way Through the Jungle?" which honor the newly developed Guyanese government. DeCaires Narain writes that Das' "public endorsement of the PNC…would have alienated many Indian Guyanese, signaling both a rejection of traditional definitions of Indian womanhood and a willingness to embrace African Guyanese cultural identity" (deCaires Narain 2004,

---

[6] As noted earlier, Burnham's tenure was initially viewed with hope, but his time in power came to be characterized by sweeping autocratic moves such as the National Security Act, which gave police the power to search, seize, and arrest anyone for little cause, by voter intimidation and fraud, and by violence. The Commission of Inquiry into the assassination of historian Walter Rodney found Forbes Burnham responsible, as he reportedly felt threatened by Rodney and the opposition party that he was organizing.

171). In later collections, Das is much more cynical toward and critical of national projects, but in these early poems, we see the same sweeping metaphors connecting women's roles to the cultivation of the land and the birthing of the next generation of Indo-Guyanese as in Singh's poems.

Though Das is best known for "They Came in Ships," treated later in this section, I begin with her lesser-known (and more awkwardly titled) poem "Cast Aside Reminiscent Foreheads of Desolation." This piece deals specifically with women's experience of indenture and has many parallels with "Per Ajie." Like Singh, Das draws explicit connections between female laborer's fertility and their role in working the land, thus helping to found a new nation. She writes, "your curved back in the fields revitalized sugar./Brought forth, out of your womb a new industry"[7] (3–4). Both poems demonstrate optimism for the nation's future expressed in the celebration of women's bodies, women's fertility, and women's labor.

A central difference comes in the purpose of each poem—Singh seeks to increase awareness of the central role that women migrants played in building Guyana, while Das exhorts the current generation of Indo-Caribbean women to dedicate themselves to their new homeland. The formal differences between the poems highlight their distinct purposes. Where Singh's lines are short and simple, evoking gentle waves lapping on a shore, Das' are long and often dense, frequently punctuated with exclamation marks. Her ideas are framed by imperatives, as in the line "Cast aside your apologetic philosophy of uprooted destiny!" (Das 2010, 6) One imagines Das standing on a crate and holding a megaphone, rallying the crowd of women before her.

As noted earlier, literary critics Letizia Gramaglia and Joseph Jackson use an eco-critical, feminist lens to explore Das' poetry, and they express concern with her treatment of women migrants. In their discussion of "Cast Aside," they point to "Das' choice to characterize women through male-centered roles—as wives, mothers and daughters" (Gramaglia and Jackson 2013, 127), and problematize the connections she draws between women's ability to procreate and her role in giving birth to a new nation, which put her work "at risk of reinforcing patriarchal symbolisms"

[7] Like "Per Ajie," the language here is rather stilted, especially in comparison to the more straightforward language of Das' "They Came in Ships." These poets employed a more stylized language when speaking directly of women, which could be an attempt to sound more formal and authoritative in order to lend their subject an air of solemnity, or could be due to an unconscious tendency to follow the habit of male British poets, who used more florid language when writing of women.

(Gramaglia and Jackson 2013, 127). This is an important critique, but there is an additional, underexplored aspect of the poem that is equally troubling.

Das urges Indo-Guyanese women to dedicate themselves to their new country instead of looking back to India as the homeland, and she employs a metaphor of familial relations to make her argument. India, she suggests, is like the father one lets go of in order to embrace one's husband, the husband representing Guyana: "No bride regrets her entry/Into the arms of her husband./Yet, she never ceases to love her father" (Das 2010, 7–9). In fact, it is likely that many brides in the Indo-Caribbean community regretted their entry into the arms of their husbands, given the high and often fatal levels of domestic abuse that women faced.[8] It is also startling that Das suggests that a woman's role is to move from father to husband, as many traditional Indian practices, such as the marrying of a child bride, can be seen as an effort to impose patriarchal control over women.

As "Cast Aside" continues, Das extends the familial metaphor, stating that no woman regrets her "married state" (Das 2010, 26) because it is the only way for her to enjoy the "fruits of motherhood" (Das 2010, 28). This statement, too, is full of historical ironies, given that many partnerships (and children) under indenture occurred outside of officially sanctioned marriage, due to strict colonial laws that made marriage very difficult.[9] The awkwardness of the metaphor is borne out by the clashing of gender in the lines, "This land has bequeathed you new meaning./She is your husband" (Das 2010, 24–25). As Denise deCaires Narain points out, the "strains…in the marriage metaphor" suggest "an uneasy tension between the speaker's concern to address both women's and nationalist concerns" (deCaires Narain 2004, 171).

This brushing aside of historical factors is especially striking given that in this collection "Cast Aside" appears immediately after "They Came in Ships." In the latter poem, Das points to the violence and degradation that women experienced in the fields: "Was your blood spilled so that I might reject my history?/Forget tears in shadow—paddy leaves" (Das 2010, 57–58). This indicates that Das was aware of the vulnerability of

---

[8] As noted in previous chapters, the low numbers of women on plantations, combined with the oppressive conditions of indenture and the sense of women as representing Indian culture in a foreign land, led to high and often fatal levels of abuse when women sought to break out of traditional gender roles, as when they sought out a new partnership, were suspected of seeking out a new partnership, or sought out education or work.

[9] See Chap. 2.

indentured women, but overlooked that history in "Cast Aside" in favor of a nationalist sentiment. "They Came in Ships," which is a more historical accounting of indenture, offers a more comprehensive and complex portrait of women's experiences.

"They Came in Ships" is one of the most frequently cited texts of Indian indenture. In *The Routledge Reader in Caribbean Literature*, it is placed before Singh's "Per Ajie," even though it was published six years later, indicating the pivotal role this poem has played. Its renown is due in part to its far-reaching scope; critics note that it conveys the broad range of experience of Indian laborers. Véronique Bragard identifies the many historical allusions in the poem and suggests that Das "addresses a foreign audience in an attempt to raise historical awareness" (Bragard 2008, 74) of the denigration of Indian migrants. Anita Baksh adds that this poem "indicates Das' mission to insert Indians and women into Guyanese historical narratives (Baksh 2016, 83–84).

Scholars have also drawn attention to the ways that this poem complicates images of female migrants. Baksh notes that Das' "description of women as 'dancing girls' and 'stolen wives' disrupts myths of Indian female migrants as being sexually promiscuous" (Baksh 2016, 84). Gramaglia and Jackson argue that Das "challenges the stereotype of the submissive and compliant Indian woman by reaffirming a matrilineal genealogy of strong, proud and independent female workers who crossed the *kala pani* in search of a new life" (Gramaglia and Jackson 2013, 123). In contrast to "Cast Aside," they note, "In this poem the bond between women and nature is no longer defined within the prescribed parameters of patriarchal dichotomies, but becomes the expression of women's emancipation through the agency of migration and the economic empowerment of labor" (Gramaglia and Jackson 2013, 124). "They Came in Ships" seems to avoid many of the nationalist sentiments expressed in "Cast Aside" in favor of a more individualized exploration of indenture.

"They Came in Ships" covers parallel themes as Singh's poems, speaking of the suffering and dehumanization of the laborers. The tone is more somber than that of "Cast Aside," reflected by its shorter lines and simpler language. Das, like Singh, focuses on eyes, on voices, and on tears and blood as a reminder of the invisibility and voicelessness of the laborers, which Das seeks to remedy. Eyes play a particularly strong role in the poem, appearing at three points in the poem and creating connections across generations. As the laborers arrive, their dehumanization has rendered them little more than animals in the view of the colonizers: "Brown like cattle./Eyes limpid, like cattle" (Das 2010, 12–13). The sentence fragments and repetition emphasize Das' points and create a slow and heavy pace, like the footsteps of the laborers as they disembark. Das then imagines the "gaunt gaze" of her forefather after suffering through indenture and losing his innocence (34), and, finally, the poet describes her own, inner eye, searching the past and seeking to meet the gaze of her ancestors and her unborn children (35). The gaze that Das turns on her ancestors is an attempt to acknowledge the unseen role the laborers played in the history of the Caribbean and to return their humanity to them.

As in "Per Ajie," where Singh writes of tears that "Have watered/The blades/Thou didst sow/In my land" (61–64), Das, too, focuses on the spilling of bodily fluids. Unlike Singh, though, she does so to remember the suffering of the laborers, rather than to celebrate their role in cultivating the land. Das writes "Was your blood spilled so that I might reject my history?/Forget tears in shadow—paddy leaves" (Das 2010, 57–59)." The assonance of the e sound in "tears," "paddy," and "leaves" effectively links the woman's pain with her labor in the fields. The irony here is that if the female migrant is successful in her labor and earns enough money to escape poverty, future generations will not have to labor and will have the luxury of forgetting their history.

Later in the poem, Das shifts from increasing the visibility of the laborers to amplifying their voices. She writes of hearing "voices crying in the wind" (Das 2010, 61), but also of "Cuffy shouting" (Das 2010, 62). As Cuffy was the leader of a slave rebellion in Guyana, this reference connects in solidarity the enslaved Africans and the indentured Indians. Singh also describes William Des Voeux, the British official who protested the poor treatment of Indians: "Des Voeux cried/I wrote the Queen a letter/For the whimpering of the coolies/In their logies would not let me rest" (Das 2010, 68–71). While Des Voeux "cried" and Cuffy "shout[ed]," expressing full-throated anger and pain, the laborers could only "whimper," a sound associated with animals. This wording reminds the reader that a white man had to speak on behalf of the laborers, as they had few options to communicate their own suffering to those in power.

Both Das and Singh wrote poems that highlight the oppressive and destructive nature of indenture, but when focusing on women laborers, their bodies, and their relationship with the land, both poets write in a celebratory and optimistic tone. This suggests a hopefulness about the nation-building projects of the early postcolonial period. These poets recognize that women suffered under indenture but suggest that if given their proper due (albeit in the realm of nurturing), Guyana would prosper. Later Indo-Caribbean poets, however, demonstrate a disillusionment with national projects. When writing about women's relationship with the land, they search for a connection with the past, rather than projecting an excitement about the future.

THE IMPOSSIBILITY OF AUTHENTICITY, THE IMPOSSIBILITY OF BELONGING: DAVID DABYDEEN

David Dabydeen's period of writing, as well as the themes of his work, overlap with those of Mahadai Das.[10] His poetry collection *Coolie Odyssey* was published in 1988, a little over a decade after Das' *I Want to be a Poetess for my People*, but even that brief passage of time was enough to create a seismic shift in literary depictions of indenture. As noted earlier, the 1970s and early 1980s saw increasing unrest in Guyana, including the assassination of the leftist scholar and activist Walter Rodney. As a result, poetry by authors like Dabydeen becomes noticeably darker. Even when depicting female laborers, who had been held up in earlier texts as symbols of hope and national growth, these poets focus more on the problematic gender roles and hierarchical class structures that permeated indenture than on the contributions these women made.

Dabydeen's sweeping poem "Coolie Odyssey" is similar in subject matter to "They Came in Ships," centering on his experiences as a contemporary poet looking back at the lives of his forefathers and their emigration to Guyana. In mood, however, the poem is quite different, focusing on displacement rather than rootedness. Dabydeen's images of women's bodies and their connections to the land are bleak, indicating that his relationship to Guyana is an uneasy one. This tension is attributable partly to his departure from the country at a young age. At 13, Dabydeen traveled to England to join his father, and he settled there, attending first Cambridge, then the University College of London, and, finally, accepting a teaching position at the University of Warwick. Additionally, his view of the government of Guyana is highly critical: Dabydeen has referred to "the dereliction of Guyana under the autocratic rule of Forbes Burnham"

---

[10] David Dabydeen, though discussed in Chap. 4 as a novelist, is better known for his poetry. In 1984, his collection *Slave Song* won the Commonwealth Poetry Prize, an award given jointly by the Commonwealth Institute and the National Book League to a first book of poetry by an author from one of the Commonwealth countries.

(Dabydeen 2016). His connections to his ancestors and to Guyana are thus looser, more questing. Rather than holding up female ancestors as models of fertility and perseverance in order to inspire his readers, he seeks a connection to them and to his homeland, which he ultimately fails to find.

In the preface to *Coolie Odyssey*, Dabydeen notes that much of the book was written on trains around the United Kingdom and planes to the Caribbean, highlighting the transient and diasporic nature of his life and the frequency with which these themes arise in his poetry. Referring to the title of the collection, he writes, "The journey is from India to Guyana to England, and it is as much a journey of words as deeds" (Dabydeen 2006, 5). On the theme of diaspora, critic Jean Small adds, "The dream fantasy which motivates the journey and sustains the existence of a colonized people pervades the entire collection of poems" (Small 1995, 135). This can be seen in particularly stark terms in the poem that shares its title with the collection.

"Coolie Odyssey," which is dedicated to Dabydeen's mother,[11] is a juxtaposition between his current-day experience as a poet, his return to the Caribbean for a funeral, and the journey and arrival of his ancestors to Guyana. The poem, much like *The Counting House*, is told from a fragmented perspective that forces us to consider the nature of authenticity and accuracy. In addition to shifting back and forth between the perspective of the speaker, presumably David Dabydeen himself, and his ancestors, the poem shifts between the perspective of "Old Dabydeen," most likely Dabydeen's great-great-grandfather, and his wife.

It is worth noting that Dabydeen is the only one of the poets treated in this chapter who explores the experience of both male and female ancestors. The way in which he does so, however, serves to both highlight and challenge the stereotypes of women migrants. We begin with Old Dabydeen's perspective and take it as truth, but then we hear the perspective of Chandra, his wife, which complicates the narrative. The ordering of these stories is akin to the tradition of a woman walking several paces behind a man, but the revulsion and irreverence that Chandra expresses toward her husband demonstrate that she is far from a meek and docile wife.

---

[11] The collection as a whole is also dedicated to his mother, who died in 1985. This was one year after the publication of *Slave Song*, and one wonders whether she had the chance to read *Slave Song* or learn of her son's acclaim.

Old Dabydeen's perspective is a disgruntled one, and he offers stereotypical judgments of other ethnicities and of his wife. He "called upon Lord Krishna to preserve/The virginity of his daughters/From the Negroes" (Dabydeen 2006, 53–55), reflecting the view of Africans as hypersexual and the need to maintain racial purity, a theme taken up in *The Counting House*. Additionally, in his view, Chandra was "a fearful bride barely come-of-age" (Dabydeen 2006, 35) when he married her, demonstrating the standard depiction of the submissive Indian wife. He considers her infertile, "cursed…Like the blasted land/Unconquerable jungle or weed" (Dabydeen 2006, 29–31) because she gave birth to several girls and only one son. In this poem, when women's bodies are compared to the land, it is to denigrate both, to offer a sense of doom rather than one of hope.

The few references to women's bodies relate directly to birth, and in particular, to Old Dabydeen's disappointment in raising primarily girls. He describes Chandra "swelling with female child" (Dabydeen 2006, 36) and the "Guilt [that] clenched her mouth" (Dabydeen 2006, 37) for bearing so many girls. The word "swelling" connotes some sort of malady, like a tumor or an infection. Meanwhile, the clenching of her mouth acts in opposition to this image: her mouth shrinks while her belly grows. The baby is described as a "burden" (Dabydeen 2006, 40), "wrapped hurriedly in a bundle of midwife's cloth" (Dabydeen 2006, 39) and taken to the home of Chandra's mother to keep her safe, presumably to protect her from Old Dabydeen's rage once he learns that he has another daughter. In this depiction, mothers and grandmothers must conspire to keep girl babies safe.

Old Dabydeen views his own life in terms of misery and sacrifice. He suffers the physical punishment and premature aging of the labor he performs to provide for himself and his many girls: "He stamped and cursed and beat until he turned old/With the labour of chopping trees, minding cow, building fence" (Dabydeen 2006, 42–43) and providing "his daughters' dowries"[12] (Dabydeen 2006, 44). The list-like, repetitive structure of his tasks mimics the repetitive nature of the tasks themselves, while the alliteration of "daughters' dowries" binds the women to the monetary burden they have created. In a line that directly follows this

---

[12] Patricia Mohammad has noted that the low numbers of women meant that dowries were often reversed, so this may be an imaginary melding of Indian traditions and Indo-Guyanese lived experience.

mention of his daughters, Old Dabydeen dies dreaming of India, which suggests that he sees his life in Guyana as cursed. Perhaps if he had not crossed the *kala pani*, he seems to think, he would not have suffered this life of wretchedness.

The reader may think, here we have a familiar figure and a man worth pitying, an Indian laborer who worked until he died, who had a meek and quiet wife, and who suffered due to his bad luck of bearing mostly girl children. This image conforms to stereotypical depictions of laborers that appeared in texts written during the height of indenture, such as *Those That Be in Bondage*. However, the poet then shifts to the perspective of Chandra, who has outlived her husband, and she has quite a different view on their lived experience. As she sprinkles rice to feed the chickens, the speaker describes her as "Ever so old and bountiful" (Dabydeen 2006, 56). Far from being infertile, she is "bountiful," a term that could refer both to the many children she bore and to her capacity to grow rice, which in turn will feed the chickens, which in turn will feed her and her family. This view of fertility, contrasting with that of the earlier poets, seems less tied to the land, and more defined by her many children and her ability to provide for them.

Additionally, Chandra's view of her husband clashes sharply with the view that he had of himself. As she passes her husband's grave, rather than remembering him working endlessly to cultivate the land and provide for his family, she describes him as "idle as usual in the sun" (Dabydeen 2006, 58). Rather than honoring him in her thoughts, she compares him to a "low-caste sow" (Dabydeen 2006, 60), and describes him with the delightfully onomatopoeic and alliterative phrase "squelching and swallowing" (Dabydeen 2006, 60). The next stanza moves on to a different scene, the arrival of the first laborers to Guyana, and so Chandra has the last word, cursing her husband and relieved that he is dead. By offering conflicting accounts of a shared life, Dabydeen not only challenges traditional views of indentured men and women, he also challenges the idea that we can ever accurately represent the past, a theme that appears throughout the poem.

Dabydeen, like Das, filters the narrative of his ancestors through his own life, describing his process of trying to recapture their experience. He imagines their fateful moment of landing: "Coolies come to rest/In El Dorado" (Dabydeen 2006, 63–64). This phrase is full of paradoxes: as field laborers, the migrants will hardly be resting. Additionally, by using the name of the mythical city of gold that Spanish conquistadors searched for, Dabydeen alludes to the tales that migrants were told about the wealth of the colonies and the riches they would earn. In stark contrast, the next line captures the unglamorous reality: "Their faces and best saris black with soot" (Dabydeen 2006, 65). This section of the poem ends with another reference to gold, as the laborers get their first view of the fields: "Canefields ripening in the sun/Wait to be gathered in armfuls of gold" (Dabydeen 2006, 74–75). Dabydeen acknowledges the beauty and bounty of the land, which laborers may initially have admired. However, that beauty belies the labor that is required to harvest the cane, and the fact that the wealth the cane brings will go to the plantation owners, not the laborers.

Immediately after this description of his ancestors' arrival, Dabydeen describes his own journey back to Guyana from England. The jarring switch to first-person perspective emphasizes the full force of the displacement that he feels. In a twist on his ancestors' journey, he is traveling across the Atlantic Ocean, but from England, the colonial hub, rather than from India. He writes, "I have come back late and missed the funeral" (Dabydeen 2006, 76). "Come back late" refers to a literal tardiness, but also to a broader sense of belatedness, a feeling that he has been gone too long and this is no longer his home. His journey is quite different than that of his ancestors, which he refers to in an ironic description: "You will understand the connections were difficult./Three airplanes boarded and many changes" (Dabydeen 2006, 77–78). By modern standards, this may seem a taxing journey, but when contrasted with the three- to six-month boat voyage taken by the laborers, it hardly seems worth a complaint, an irony of which Dabydeen is surely conscious.

This section contains a similar thread to that of "They Came in Ships," that if the laborers are successful at providing a better life for their children and their children's children, their progeny will have the luxury of forgetting them. Dabydeen writes, "The ancestors curl and dry to scrolls of parchment./They lie like texts/Waiting to be written by the children/For whom they hacked and ploughed and saved" (Dabydeen 2006, 83–86). He refers to himself here, the boy who escaped and returns to seek out the stories of his ancestors. He compares this quest to that of the Spaniards seeking El Dorado, noting that he and poets like him seek "To make bountiful our mind in an England/Starved of gold" (Dabydeen 2006, 96–97). By returning to the theme of gold and El Dorado, Dabydeen ties this passage to the description of his ancestors' arrival. Just as they mistook Guyana's cane for gold, seeing the wealth that would only be reaped by the colonizers, he seeks the warmth of family connections, searching for a sanctuary from cold England.[13] The repetition of the word "bountiful," which Dabydeen used to describe his ancestress, further highlights his longing for kin.

Ultimately, however, Dabydeen fails in his pursuit. He hears the voice of his ancestors telling him, "*Me dead./Dog-bone and dry well/Got no story to tell*" (Dabydeen 2006, 89–91). No matter how much he tries to embody these men and women in his poetry, they remain nothing more than scraps of paper and dried-out bones. Abigail Ward argues, "Dabydeen's work suggests that, rather than the absence of a story to tell, it is perhaps more accurate to posit the inadequate means of either accessing or expressing the stories of these Indian indentured ancestors" (Ward 2011, 86). Like the section in which the poet describes Old Dabydeen and his wife, this stanza acknowledges the impossibility of truly representing the lives of the dead.

Further, Dabydeen indicates that the attempt to do so is exploitative, laying bare the migrants' suffering for the amusement of the (primarily British) reading public. In the final stanza of the poem, Dabydeen writes, "We mark your memory in songs/.../Poems that scrape bowl and bone" (Dabydeen 2006, 112–114). His efforts to commemorate his ancestors are a cannibalistic act, scraping at the bottom of the bowl or the surface of a bone for a little more flesh to feed his audience, whose "applause flutter[s] from their white hands/Like so many messy table napkins" (Dabydeen 2006, 120–121). This image is the last of the poem and completes the view of Britain consuming India, in previous centuries by devouring the labor of Indian migrants on its Caribbean plantations, and today with a proprietary interest in Indo-Guyanese culture. Dabydeen, like Singh and Das, seeks to bring his ancestors to life, but he suggests that he (and other poets of his ilk) does so for selfish reasons, to feed them to the British, who are hungry for stories of peasants and poverty. This cynical image rejects the tendency of Indo-Caribbean authors to memorialize their ancestors as heroes and reflects the poet's lack of a sense of belonging in either Guyana or England.

Dabydeen's dismissiveness regarding the opportunities afforded to migrants can be seen in two other poems in this collection, "Coolie Mother" and "Coolie Son," which appear side by side. Unlike "Coolie

---

[13] This line works on another level, as well—as England has lost most of its colonies by the time Dabydeen writes this poem, it is starved of the gold that it earned from its colonies, and seeks instead a kind of cultural gold, mining for the authentic in the stories of peasants.

Odyssey," these poems are written entirely in Creole, capturing the rhythms and language of the Guyanese working people and acknowledging their influence on his own writing.[14] "Coolie Mother" describes a destitute woman named Jasmattie who works day and night in order to give her son a chance at a better life. The toll of the labor Jasmattie performs is illustrated in descriptions of her broken body: "She foot-bottom crack and she hand cut up" (Dabydeen 2006, 8), and she coughs up blood and spits it onto the ground. This is her connection to the land—rather than taking joy in cultivating it, she seems to battle against it, scraping out a living and mashing her blood into the earth. The hard sounds of "crack" and "cut" lend an aural quality to her physical pain, conveying her suffering to the reader through as many senses as possible.

Jasmattie works so hard so that she can send her son to school in Georgetown, and so that he won't be viewed as a coolie: "*Must* wear clean starch pants, or they go laugh at he,/Strap leather on he foot and he *must* read book" (Dabydeen 2006, 14–15, emphasis original). She wants him to do well in school and escape poverty by attending a university in England, all so that he does not turn into his "rum-sucker chamar dadee" (Dabydeen 2006, 18), his alcoholic, low-caste father. While the description of Jasmattie focuses intently on her body—her hands, her feet, and the blood she coughs up, the image of the boy only comes through in his trappings, which prove he is not a low-class laborer—the pants and shoes he wears, and the books he reads. Once you rise above the position of laborer, Dabydeen suggests, you are seen as more than a body, but until then, you are nothing but hands to draw water and feet to carry it.

The positioning of this poem right before "Coolie Son" offers a grim view of the upward mobility of the children of laborers. "Coolie Son," whose subtitle is "The toilet attendant writes home," is framed as a letter to a sibling, or perhaps a friend. It details the end result of Jasmattie's hard work: her son (or a boy much like her son) has successfully migrated to England, but can only find work cleaning toilets. He writes optimistically, "Soon I go turn lawya or dacta" (Dabydeen 2006, 15), but he admits that he has little money, and so he took the only job that he could find. His title sounds fancy, "Deputy Sanitary Inspecta" (Dabydeen 2006, 18), and he

---

[14] Benita Parry argues, "The many linguistic registers of his poetry enunciate a self dispersed between affiliation to Indian parentage, solidarity with Guyana's history of conquest, colonization and slavery, and a consciousness irreversibly marked and fissured by English education and residence, the disparate facets held together within a black identity" (Parry 1988, 2).

writes proudly of the "Tie round me neck" (Dabydeen 2006, 19), which sounds ominously like a noose, as well as the "Brand-new uniform" and the "big bunch of keys" (Dabydeen 2006, 20). As in "Coolie Mother," the focus is not on his body but on his trappings: his uniform and his keys. But here, those trappings work ironically. Even without the subtitle, the reader recognizes that he is in a janitorial position, and so the irony of the last line, "If Ma can see me now how she go please" (Dabydeen 2006, 21) is intensified by the juxtaposition with the previous poem and the sense that all of the mother's hard work has amounted to nothing. She had cursed his low-caste father, and done everything she could to make sure her son did not become his father, but her son has ended up in a job that, in India, is given to people of the lowest caste.[15] The poem "Coolie Son" echoes the displacement that Dabydeen expresses in "Coolie Odyssey." Neither he nor the toilet attendant can truly belong in England.

As noted in Chap. 4, Dabydeen has expressed dismay at the current state of politics in Guyana, describing his homeland as "a dangerous pit, fitter for the habitation of the unscrupulous, immoral, and criminal" (Dabydeen 1993, 28). This view is reflected in the harsh depictions of women's connections to the land. Rather than celebrating the bounty and potential of Guyana through imagery of women's fertility, Dabydeen draws attention to the ongoing bleakness of the lives of the peasant class. It is worth noting that the cynicism that Dabydeen expresses toward national projects matches the more cynical views of Das' later poetry, such as "For Maria De Borges." Published in 1988, the same year as *Coolie Odyssey*, this poem describes a factory owner in a metropolis plundering a women's body for treasure, an allegorical dismemberment that represents the exploitation of women migrants: "At gunpoint he steals rubies in my cheeks,/my full curve of hip" (Das 2010, 59–60).[16] Thus, the shift in tone among the poems of indenture may be a difference of era rather than of

---

[15] Dabydeen plays with this theme in another poem in the collection, "The Untouchable." In a twist on the term "untouchable," Dabydeen describes the lust that an Indian laborer feels for a young white woman he saw briefly through the plantation house window. As in the other poems described in this chapter, we get a vivid description of the woman's body, her creamy skin, "her ankle small and pretty" (Dabydeen 2006, 13). But here the description only serves to highlight how off-limits this woman is, how he will be beaten if the master finds him day dreaming about the young white woman. This makes her "the untouchable."

[16] Brinda Mehta suggests that Indo-Caribbean women writers experience a form of exile that is often demonstrated by images of physical dismemberment in their work. Of "For Maria De Borges," she notes, "Feelings of alienation have led to a psychic splitting, in which women are partitioned and deprived of multiple parts of themselves" (Mehta 2004, 163).

poet. It is certainly possible that if Singh had lived longer, she too would have turned to a more cynical view of nationalism and a more brutal description of women's bodies.

NIHILISM AND REINCARNATION: LELAWATTEE MANOO-RAHMING

Lelawattee Manoo-Rahming, like David Dabydeen, dedicates her collection of poetry, *Curry Flavor*, to her mother. Though her poetry shares similar themes to those of Das and Singh, focusing on the body of a female ancestor as a way of celebrating her fertility and her intrepidness, Manoo-Rahming's work ultimately demonstrates the same sense of displacement and pessimism as that of Dabydeen. As in Dabydeen's case, this can perhaps be attributed to the changes in the political climate of the Caribbean in the decades after decolonization. Born in Trinidad in 1960, Manoo-Rahming grew up in a period of political upheaval in that nation. As noted earlier, Trinidad and Tobago did not experience the same level of autocracy as Guyana after achieving independence, but the 1960s and 1970s saw a series of strikes as part of the Black Power Revolution, whose proponents viewed then prime minister Eric Williams as "the enabler of the imperial economic presence that he had denounced so persistently and vehemently" (Palmer 2006, 302). In 1970, Williams responded by declaring a state of emergency, and soon after, there was a short-lived mutiny within the army. Economist Scott B. MacDonald writes, "The growing apprehension over the increased authoritarianism of Trinidad and Tobago's government was heightened in 1971 when most of the political parties...boycott[ed] the general elections. The PNM won every seat in Parliament, which ushered in a period of de facto one-party rule and put Trinidad's democratic system on the brink of complete breakdown" (MacDonald 1986, 162). The government regained some economic and political stability in the late 1970s, but Manoo-Rahming would certainly have been influenced by this period of political turmoil and the ongoing tensions in the region.

The quality of disillusionment found in Manoo-Rahming's poetry could, as in Dabydeen's case, also be attributed to her peripatetic life. Though born in Trinidad, she attended school at the University of Miami, and she now lives in Nassau, Bahamas. In an interview with Giselle Rampaul, she admits that she might not have become a writer if she had not moved to the Bahamas, where, for the first time, she was in the minority as a person of Indian descent and felt the need to research her cultural identity and the history of indentured labor (Manoo-Rahming 2013). This outsider feeling echoes that of Dabydeen in England. On the other hand, Manoo-Rahming lives in another Caribbean nation, rather than the heart of the colonial empire, which may explain why her work is not quite as grim as that of Dabydeen.

"Ode to My Unknown Great-Great Grandmother," like all of the indentured poems discussed thus far, imagines the moment of arrival of the first Indian laborers to the Caribbean. In an interesting shift on this theme, Manoo-Rahming describes the experiences of an ancestor who was not herself an indentured laborer, but was born on a ship to two indentured migrants heading to Trinidad. Manoo-Rahming writes, "The first to belong nowhere/Born on the wide Kala Pani/between Calcutta and Port-of-Spain" (Manoo-Rahming 2000, 1–4). Her great-great-grandmother is the ultimate example of a migrant caught between two cultures, as she came into the world belonging to neither the country that her parents had left behind nor yet to her soon-to-be home.

Echoing this sense of dislocation, the tone of the poem is somewhat fragmented. On the one hand, Manoo-Rahming honors her female ancestor, just as Singh and Das do, and the images of this woman's body connect her to her new land. Her great-great-grandmother's "eyes were the first to embrace" the twin peaks of Trinidad's highest mountains (Manoo-Rahming 2000, 16), and her "bare feet" were the first to walk from one tip of the island to the other (Manoo-Rahming 2000, 23), claiming it for herself. The synesthetic image of embracing the land with her eyes conveys the immediacy and the physicality of her ties to it. Of this imagery, Joy Mahabir writes, "'to belong nowhere' makes it possible to belong everywhere in the Caribbean space, since the ocean inevitably touches every Caribbean island, creating points of convergence and departure" (Mahabir 2013, 147). Manoo-Rahming thus celebrates both the rootlessness and rootedness of her great-great-grandmother. Rather than describing her ancestor's connection to the land as a metaphor for her fertility, Manoo-Rahming imagines her as a pioneer. Véronique Bragard suggests that the poem "Posit[s] the communal mother as one of the first explorers of the New World landscape" and "generates an image of creative adaptability in which women actively participated" (Bragard 2008, 105). The references to the female ancestor's body and to the land announce that she found a place in this new home.

Like Dabydeen's "Coolie Odyssey," though, this poem has a touch of pessimism, even nihilism, which has been underexplored by critics. Manoo-Rahming writes, "My eyes are the last to gaze/upon the Scarlet

Ibis/roosting in the Caroni Swamp" (Manoo-Rahming 2000, 28–30) suggesting that her intrepid ancestor will have no more descendants roaming the hills of Trinidad. The poem is full of specific references to the iconic animals and landmarks of Trinidad, which increase the sense of the poem as a eulogy for or goodbye to the island. The speaker desires to pass on her ancestor's spirit to a child, to "reincarnate/you in my womb" (Manoo-Rahming 2000, 25–26), but she has "failed" (Manoo-Rahming 2000, 27). The poet does not indicate the form of this failure, whether she has been unable to give birth to any children or unable to pass on her ancestor's spirit to her children. It is also possible that the poet, having left Trinidad to settle in another Caribbean nation, mourns the cutting of ties to her homeland, and thus her ancestors. In the final line of the poem, she concludes, "My ashes are the last to belong somewhere" (Manoo-Rahming 2000, 36), imagining her death as the end of any sense of rootedness or lineage. This is the only line that is composed of a complete sentence, emphasizing the sense of finality. Manoo-Rahming, far from celebrating women's fertility in birthing a new nation, expresses sorrow at her inability to recreate her great-great-grandmother's ties to the land. Like Dabydeen, she seeks connection to an individual ancestor, and ultimately, fails.

This poem contrasts sharply with "Incarnation on the Caroni," the piece that appears immediately before it in the collection. "Incarnation" suggests the opposite of "Ode," announcing the rebirth of the speaker's great-grandmother, whose soul "stays with me here/on the banks of the Caroni River" (Manoo-Rahming 2000, 30–31). Her life force rises like "wood-smoke" (Manoo-Rahming 2000, 32) and then comes down in a "rainy drizzle" (Manoo-Rahming 2000, 33) and saturates the speaker, entering her womb. The rhythm of these lines is lilting and the words gentle, imitating the language of a mother speaking to her child. There is a sense of continual rebirth in this poem: the speaker's unborn baby will be the fourth incarnation of her ancestor, offering a sense of hope and continuity. Further, the ancestor finds release in this rebirth: "After three incarnations,/your soul is freed" (Manoo-Rahming 2000, 17–18). Joy Mahabir writes of this poem, "Indo-Caribbean people have changed the mythical and religious constructions of space brought from India, so that the soul of the grandmother, now free after three incarnations, chooses not to be taken by the Hindu deity Vishnu. Instead, the soul desires incarnation in the Caribbean, choosing to re-enter life on the banks of the river" (Mahabir 2013, 145). The cycles of birth and rebirth strengthen the speaker's ties to her homeland, as "grandmothers become granddaughters" (Manoo-Rahming 2000, 16). Importantly, this poem venerates the matrilineal. By contrast with Old Dabydeen and his wife Chandra, who feel ashamed to have daughters, the speaker and her ancestor revel in the continuance of the female line.

As with "Ode," though, there is an underlying darkness to this poem. The speaker lists the painful experiences that her indentured ancestors faced, such as the fraught journey to the Caribbean. She notes that she has not suffered any of these miseries: "My eyes have never crossed the black water; *kala pani* of fear and change" (Manoo-Rahming 2000, 1–2), and "my nose has never devoured rotting bodies…/thrown overboard without Krishna's blessing" (Manoo-Rahming 2000, 4–5). Manoo-Rahming uses sensory imagery, not to form connections with her ancestors, as Das does, but to emphasize the distance between the speaker's life and theirs.

However, the celebratory quality of the poem triumphs over the grim remembrance of past suffering. In spite of the lack of shared experiences across generations, Indian culture has been preserved, as the speaker has vicariously felt some of the joys of her ancestors by participating in the ritual to commemorate Indian Arrival Day. "I echoed your emancipation cries," the speaker proclaims (Manoo-Rahming 2000, 13), memorializing the freedom that her ancestors experienced at the end of indenture, which in turn led to the growth of Indo-Caribbean communities in Trinidad. Frank Birbalsingh writes, "This link between the poet and her homeland seems indivisible" (Birbalsingh 2012). But this is only true of *this* poem; in "Ode," the link is fractured at best. This startling shift in tone indicates that there is no single way to approach the past or to explore one's heritage.

There is certainly more joyfulness and hope in these poems than in those of Dabydeen. Manoo-Rahming rejoices in the landscape of her homeland, in the waters of the ocean, in the blood of the womb and the exultation of rebirth. Yet in her poems, there is also a sense of fragmentation and distance, themes that do not appear in the work of poets writing immediately after decolonization. With the fading of the hopes for a halcyon postcolonial Caribbean, Dabydeen and Manoo-Rahming turn inward, seeking a sense of rootedness within the bloodlines of their own families. These themes are especially prevalent in Manoo-Rahming's "Ode," in which the speaker celebrates the arrival of her ancestor to the Caribbean but suggests that she will be the last of her line to walk the paths of the Trinidad hills. Rather than viewing women's fertility in terms of the birthing of a land and a people, she, like Dabydeen, focuses on the more intimate connections between generations of a single family, hoping for, and sometimes failing in, the more modest goal of passing on the spirit of her ancestors.

CYCLES OF TOIL AND SHAME: EASTON LEE

There are few examples of poetry reflecting on the experience of Chinese indenture, as has been discussed in previous chapters; Easton Lee is one of the few authors to address the Chinese-Caribbean experience. Born in Jamaica in 1931 to a Chinese father and a Jamaican mother, Lee grew up surrounded by cane fields, and the formative nature of these years can be seen in poems like "Cane Piece Blues," discussed below. He did not start publishing poetry and short stories until the 1990s: *From Behind the Counter*, his first collection of poems and the collection within which "Cane Piece Blues" appears, was published in 1998. Thus, though he is of the same generation as Rajkumari Singh, this poem is written well after the national movements that rocked the Caribbean in the 1960s and 1970s. The descriptions within "Cane Piece Blues" of women's labor, both on the land and giving birth, contain a similar pessimism as the work of Dabydeen and Manoo-Rahming.

There has been little critical attention to Lee's work, but Lee-Loy writes broadly, "The image of Chinese alienation is renegotiated by Chinese West Indian authors such that…alienation is not used as a means of marking the outside borders of the nation" (Lee-Loy 2010, 106). In a review of *From Behind the Counter*, literary critic Rex Nettleford adds, "People like Easton Lee have spent a lifetime demonstrating that the heterogeneous experience is life-giving rather than life-threatening" (Nettleford 2004, 93). Both scholars point to the tendency of Chinese-Caribbean authors to reach across boundaries and to recognize the value in difference. Lee himself expresses this view, noting that his poems position the traditional Chinese shop counter not as a barrier between the shopkeeper and the customer, but as "a meeting place" (Lee 2014), a central location where community members could share food and conversation. Though this is less apparent in "Cane Piece Blues" than in some of Lee's other poems, the text does not identify the ethnicity of the speaker, a young woman who works in the cane fields, and so a wide range of readers are able to identify with her.

"Cane Piece Blues" does not deal with indentured labor per se, but, as noted, does address the experiences of cane laborers. The poem begins with images of "green fields stretching arrowing for miles" (Lee 1998, 3).

The unpunctuated phrase "stretching arrowing for miles" conveys the endlessness of the cane, the feeling that it continues without break or pause.[17] The whole piece, which covers several years, seems to take place in these fields, indicating the dominance that sugarcane held over the lives of the laborers who harvested it. This is emphasized by the black-and-white photo that accompanies the poem, a claustrophobic image of sugarcane shot from lowdown and close-up so that the stalks fill the frame and press down upon the viewer. The poem contains no descriptions of the workers' homes, and many of the laborers mentioned in the text are seasonal workers, which creates a sense of rootlessness. Lee, like so many Caribbean authors, eventually settled outside of his homeland and now lives in Florida, which helps explain the lack of a sense of belonging within the poem.

Like the poems discussed previously, "Cane Piece Blues" draws connections between women's fertility and their toil in the fields. The poem's speaker describes how her "innocent mother" (Lee 1998, 7) was seduced over and over by seasonal workers who promised to return but never did, leaving her to care for the children that she bore them. In this poem, the *busha*, or field boss, most likely a white man, is not evil so much as he is indifferent, like Gladstone in *The Counting House*. He pays attention only to how well the cane is growing and does not notice or care that seasonal workers are taking advantage of one of his laborers. While the boss may not be directly responsible for this mistreatment, he is complicit in a system that developed out of colonialism, slavery, and indenture, a system that degrades women, dehumanizes laborers, and condemns female sexuality, and thus has created the conditions that led to this mistreatment.

One of the results of these conditions is that bearing children is depicted as a burden. It is an obligation, similar to the hard labor in the fields, both of which turn the speaker's mother "old before her time" (Lee 1998, 19). The promises of the seasonal workers, like the beauty of the cane fields, tempt and mislead, and Lee's description of the "sweet sugar cane turned sour vinegar" (Lee 1998, 17) represents the mother's hopes and dreams, which have soured over time. This imagery places Lee squarely in the camp of authors disillusioned with the nationalistic view of women as birthers of a nation.

---

[17] The poem is written primarily in enjambed lines and without punctuation, giving the piece a stream-of-consciousness quality.

The poem also suggests a cyclical nature of trauma, similar to the trauma described in *Monkey Hunting* and *Jahajin* in Chap. 6. The speaker writes that she, like her mother, was swayed by the seductive promises of a seasonal laborer who swore to return. Her sexual awakening is inextricably linked to the sweet promise of the cane fields, which is "intoxicating pungent/fresh-cut under hot sun" (Lee 1998, 21–22). This awakening is tied to agriculture in an additional way, as she describes her ensuing pregnancy as "a pumpkin belly growing/growing with the seed he planted" (Lee 1998, 32–33). Like her mother, she feels no pleasure in her pregnancy, but sits in the cane fields, wondering whether the father of her child will return and hiding her "swelling shame" (Lee 1998, 37). Just as the sugarcane repeats its cycle of growth, seed formation, and harvest, she has repeated her mother's experience of seduction, pregnancy, and abandonment. The shame that she feels suggests that she will face scorn from her mother and perhaps other members of their community when they learn of her pregnancy.

"Cane Piece Blues" concludes on a bitter note, in which the speaker's tears do not "soften/the hard unforgiving earth" (Lee 1998, 45–46). This is no nationalistic celebration of the bounty of the land and the honor of childbirth. Women laborers, Lee observes, led hard lives, suffering from exploitation and societal condemnation as much as from the challenging work they performed. The similarity in tone between this poem and those of Dabydeen, and, to a lesser extent, Manoo-Rahming, suggests that Lee is making a similar move away from the nationalist projects of the 1960s and 1970s, seeking instead to understand the individual experiences and suffering of female ancestors who toiled in the fields.

Further, the parallel tropes in the work of these authors suggest a commonality of experience across Indian and Chinese migration. As discussed in previous chapters, there were extensive divergences between the state-sponsored, large-scale migration of Indian indentured laborers and the privately organized Chinese system of indenture. Yet, Indian and Chinese migrants alike were exploited by colonial systems and suffered under the hierarchical structures of empire that treated Asians as less advanced than Europeans and women laborers as pawns in power struggles between men. Lee, like the other authors described here, recognizes the exploitation of the female laborer that developed out of these systems and draws attention to the ways that societal norms continue to reflect colonial paradigms long after independence.

"A Single Linear Story": Conclusion

The connections that the poets in this chapter draw between the body of the female laborer and the land that she works are not unique to representations of indentured laborers; women's ability to give birth is often connected to the fertility of the land. However, the conditions of indenture and imperialism, in which fewer women migrated than men and women became representatives of their national culture (both the nation of origin and the adopted homeland), intensified this symbolic link. Yet the link serves different purposes at different moments in history. Those authors writing in the immediate wake of decolonization reclaim the labor of the woman's body under the flag of anti-colonial nationalism, while those writing even a decade or two later emphasize the exploitation of migrant women through a postcolonial exploration of familial genealogy.

Historian Bridget Brereton notes that "post-colonial states typically struggle to create a 'universalist' historical narrative, a single linear story which captures the 'whole' past of the new nation" (Brereton 2010, 219), and Singh and Das search for that "'universalist' historical narrative" to draw together the people of Guyana. By contrast with many anti-colonial authors, particularly male authors, these poets position women at the center of this linear narrative, the heroes of the new nation. Energized by the nationalist movements of the 1960s, they reclaim the bodies of women migrants, honoring the sacrifices these women made and urging their female descendants to devote themselves to birthing a new nation. Unfortunately, the sweeping parallels drawn between the woman's body and the land tend to repeat colonial tropes, attaching a significance to the female laborer as representative of her nation.

As nationalist movements fractured and postcolonial governments replicated the autocratic tendencies of colonial governments, many Caribbean citizens became disillusioned. Combined with the fragmenting of national identity that accompanied the increasing globalization of the late twentieth century, this disillusionment led authors like Dabydeen, Manoo-Rahming, and Lee to turn to the lives of their female ancestors as a source of regeneration, a way of connecting the past to the present and finding a sense of belonging. In the final chapter of this book, I turn to contemporary novels by female authors that similarly wrestle with issues of nationalism and migrant identity, and draw on the notion of kinship as a strategy for addressing these thorny topics.

BIBLIOGRAPHY

Baksh, Anita. 2016. Indentureship, Land, and Indo-Caribbean Feminist Thought. In *Indo-Caribbean Feminist Thought: Genealogies, Theories, Enactments*, ed. Gabrielle Jamela Hosein and Lisa Outar, 73–92. New York: Palgrave Macmillan Press.

Birbalsingh, Frank. 2012. Lelawattee Manoo-Rahming's *Curry Flavour*. *Stabroek News*, January 9. www.stabroeknews.com/2012/features/in-the-diaspora/01/09/lelawattee-manoo-rahming%E2%80%99s-curry-flavour/.

Bragard, Véronique. 2008. *Transoceanic Dialogues: Coolitude in Caribbean and Indian Ocean Literatures*. New York: P.I.E. Peter Lang.

Brereton, Bridget. 2010. 'All Ah We Is Not One': Historical and Ethnic Narratives in Pluralist Trinidad. *The Global South* 4 (2, Fall): 218–238.

Dabydeen, David. 1993. Indo-Guyanese Resistance. In *Indo-Caribbean Resistance*, ed. Frank Birbalsingh, 27–32. Toronto: TSAR.

———. 2006. *Coolie Odyssey*. London: Hansib.

David Dabydeen. 2016. An Interview with David Dabydeen on Literature and Politics. Interview with Ruzbeh Babaee. *International Journal of Comparative Literature & Translation Studies* 4 (3). http://www.journals.aiac.org.au/index.php/IJCLTS/article/view/2598.

Das, Mahadai. 2010. *A Leaf in His Ear: Selected Poems*. Leeds: Peepal Tree Press.

deCaires Narain, Denise. 2004. *Contemporary Caribbean Women's Poetry: Making Style*. New York: Routledge.

———. 2010. "Introduction." In *A Leaf in His Ear: Selected Poems*, 11–21. Leeds: Peepal Tree Press.

Donnell, Alison, and Sarah Lawson Welsh. 1996. 1966-1979: Introduction. In *The Routledge Reader in Caribbean Literature*, ed. Alison Donnell and Sarah Lawson Welch, 282–297. New York: Routledge.

Gramaglia, Letizia, and Joseph Jackson. 2013. The Broad Breast of the Land: Indo-Caribbean Ecofeminism and Mahadai Das. In *Critical Perspectives on Indo-Caribbean Women's Literature*, ed. Joy Mahabir and Mariam Pirbhai, 121–137. New York: Routledge.

Lazarus, Neil. 1990. *Resistance in Postcolonial African Fiction*. New Haven: Yale University Press.

Lee, Easton. 1998. *From Behind the Counter: Poems from a Rural Jamaican Experience*. Kingston: Ian Randle Publishers.

———. 2014. Let Me Tell You How I Began: A Conversation with Easton Lee. Interview with Tzarina T. Prater. *SX Salon* 15 (February). http://smallaxe.net/sxsalon/discussions/let-me-tell-you-how-i-began.

Lee-Loy, Ann-Marie. 2010. *Searching for Mr. Chin: Constructions of Nation and the Chinese in West Indian Literature*. Philadelphia: Temple University Press.

Macdonald, Scott B. 1986. *Trinidad and Tobago: Democracy and Development in the Caribbean*. New York: Praeger Publishers.

Mahabir, Joy. 2013. The *Kala Pani* Imaginary: A Survey of Indo-Caribbean Women's Poetry. In *Critical Perspectives on Indo-Caribbean Women's Literature*, ed. Joy Mahabir and Mariam Pirbhai, 141–161. New York: Routledge.
Manoo-Rahming, Lelawattee. 2000. *Curry Flavour*. Leeds: Peepal Tree Press.
———. 2013. Interview with Lelawattee Manoo-Rahming. Interview with Giselle Rampaul. June 6. http://www2.sta.uwi.edu/podcasts/index.php?option=com_content&view=article&id=84:podcast-37-interview-with-lelawatee-manoo-rahming&catid=36:the-spaces-between-words-conversations-with-write.
Mawby, Spencer. 2012. *Ordering Independence: The End of Empire in the Anglophone Caribbean, 1947–1969*. New York: Palgrave Macmillan.
McClintock, Anne. 1995. *Imperial Leather: Race, Gender, and Sexuality in the Colonial Contest*. New York: Routledge.
Mehta, Brinda. 2004. *Diasporic (dis)locations*. Kingston: University of the West Indies Press.
Nettleford, Rex. 2004. The Book Launch of Easton Lee's *Encounters*. *Caribbean Quarterly* 50 (2): 91–93.
Palmer, Colin A. 2006. *Eric Williams and the Making of the Modern Caribbean*. Chapel Hill: The University of North Carolina Press.
Parry, Benita. 1988. Between Creole and Cambridge English: The Poetry of David Dabydeen. *Kunapipi* 10 (3): 1–17.
Poynting, Jeremy. 1986. East Indian Women in the Caribbean: Experience, Image, and Voice. *Journal of South Asian Literatures* 21 (1): 133–180.
———. 1990. 'You Want to Be a Coolie Woman?': Gender and Ethnic Identity in Indo-Caribbean Women's Writing. In *Caribbean Women Writers: Essays from the First International Conference*, ed. Selwyn Cudjoe, 98–108. Wellesley: Calaloux Publications.
———. 2010. Publisher's Note. In *A Leaf in His Ear: Selected Poems*, 8–9. Leeds: Peepal Tree Press.
Singh, Rajkumari. 1971. *Days of the Sahib*. Georgetown, Guyana: Rajkumari Singh.
———. 1996. I am a Coolie. In *The Routledge Reader in Caribbean Literature*, ed. Alison Donnell and Sarah Lawson Welch, 351–353. New York: Routledge.
Small, Jean. 1995. Review of *Coolie Odyssey* by David Dabydeen. *Caribbean Quarterly* 41 (3): 135–138.
Ward, Abigail. 2011. *Caryl Phillips, David Dabydeen and Fred D'Aguiar: Representations of Slavery*. New York: Manchester University Press.

CHAPTER 6

At the End of Their Tether: Women Writing about Indenture

INTRODUCTION: FINDING CLARITY IN THE PRESENT

Jan Lowe Shinebourne's novel, *The Last Ship* (2015), begins with the story of Clarice Chung, who, as a child, migrated aboard the last ship to bring Chinese laborers to British Guiana in 1879. Clarice describes to her children the terrible conditions of the voyage and the brutal treatment her relatives received on the plantation: "They had to work in the open in the canefields exposed to the blazing sun and driving rain, and in the sugar factory where there were many accidents that left people permanently injured, even limbless" (Shinebourne 2015, 25). Her son, horrified by this tale, denies its validity and latches on instead to Clarice's stories about her noble ancestry. He repeats these stories to his own daughter, Joan, explaining that they are descended from Emperor Chengzong and showing her an old scroll of the emperor's image. Decades later, Joan travels to Hong Kong to trace her ancestry, only to find that her family was not descended from the emperor at all, and that the scroll, far from being a present from the emperor, is "tourist rubbish…that could be bought cheap in any market in Hong Kong" (Shinebourne 2015, 150–151). The story that Clarice's descendants chose to believe was a false, idealized version of the past, whereas they ignored the real suffering that their ancestors experienced. This blindness has repercussions: aside from Joan, all of the family members revere Clarice because of her noble ancestry and forgive her cruelty, even replicating it toward future generations. It is only when Joan learns of this deceit that the cycle is broken.

© The Author(s) 2018
A. Klein, *Anglophone Literature of Caribbean Indenture*,
New Caribbean Studies,
https://doi.org/10.1007/978-3-319-99055-2_6

The themes that arise in this novel, including the impact of forced labor on future generations and the importance of resisting the impulse to erase the degradation of one's ancestors, are concerns that appear in many writings by women authors depicting indenture. These include several novels: Patricia Powell's *The Pagoda* (1998), Ryhaan Shah's *A Silent Life* (2005), and Ramabai Espinet's *The Swinging Bridge* (2013), as well as Gaiutra Bahadur's nonfiction text, *Coolie Woman* (2013), a historical account of women's experience of indenture framed through Bahadur's research into the life of her great-grandmother. These texts are all fairly recent: until the tail end of the twentieth century, there was no fiction about Caribbean indenture by women and little nonfiction or poetry, but in the twenty-first century there has been a wave of female authors writing literature that either directly or indirectly deals with Caribbean indenture.

The previous chapters explored the ways that the gendered, racialized hierarchies of empire are replicated in the politics and literature of the contemporary Caribbean. While these hierarchies are insidious, this chapter turns to texts that offer a ray of hope, a means of moving beyond such repressive ideologies. In it, I consider the themes of generational trauma and the political act of remembering in two novels by women authors, *Jahajin* (2007), by Peggy Mohan, and *Monkey Hunting* (2003), by Cristina García. Both novels directly describe the indenture experience, but their geographic locations, plot, and protagonists differ dramatically. *Jahajin*, set in the present, focuses on an unnamed female protagonist from Trinidad of Indian and Canadian descent. While earning a PhD in linguistics in the United States, she returns to Trinidad to record older Indians speaking in Bhojpuri, a dying language originally from North India. In the process, she uncovers the largely untold story of female indentured laborers, including her own great-great-grandmother, Sunnariya. *Monkey Hunting* begins in the 1860s with a destitute Chinese farmer named Chen Pan, who is indentured in Cuba. The novel switches back and forth between Chen Pan and two of his descendants: Chen Fang, his granddaughter, who is raised as a boy in China, and Domingo Chen, his great-grandson, who moves from Cuba to New York in search of a better life.

In spite of their differences, the two stories are strikingly similar in their structure and theme. Both novels move across locations, set in areas termed the "global south," including India, Trinidad, Vietnam, and Cuba, as well as Western nations such as the United States and Canada. In addition, both blend narratives from different eras in order to emphasize the ties between successive generations. This structure, in which the past melds with the future, shows the ways that the systematic violence and gender oppression of indenture ripple forward in time, impacting generations to come. Many contemporary female authors have employed such a technique in their fictional depictions of indenture. *A Silent Life* and *The Swinging Bridge*, as well as *Jahajin* and *Monkey Hunting*, meld the past and the present to draw attention to the recurring nature of oppression.[1] While David Dabydeen also employs a fractured timeline in *The Counting House*, the events all take place within the lifetime of the main characters. His novel gives voice to the laborers who have been written out of history, showing the ways that imperialism affected Indians in the past. The female authors, on the other hand, follow generations of a single family to show the echoes of indenture in the present and to express a collective frustration with ongoing, repetitive patterns of violence against those who are othered, particularly women.

In order to understand these cycles of domination and find models of resistance, Mohan and García suggest that we actively engage with our history. In particular, they focus on the importance of building family connections across generations to develop a deeper understanding of the past and combat the tendency toward blinding nostalgia. In *Jahajin*, for example, the narrator comes to understand the trauma and constraints that her female ancestors experienced and is able to recognize and avoid similar constraints in her own life. In *Monkey Hunting*, García suggests that cultivating a pragmatic sense of altruism is the best way to cope with and move past the cruelty of systematic forms of oppression and to build equitable and sustaining family relationships. Both authors employ a poetics of kinship, indicating that healthy familial bonds offer benefits beyond the expected warmth and support one receives from loved ones.

As many scholars have noted, nostalgia[2] often plays a crucial role in the aftermath of colonialism, though there is debate over how beneficial that role is. Sociologist Janelle Wilson acknowledges nostalgia's potential dan-

---

[1] Contemporary indenture narratives by male authors, such as Amitav Ghosh's Ibis trilogy and Sharlow's *The Promise*, tend to employ straightforward chronology.

[2] The word "nostalgia" was first coined in seventeenth-century Switzerland by the physician Johannes Hofer. He used the term to identify the extreme homesickness felt by Swiss mercenaries, and classified it as a (treatable) medical condition. By the nineteenth century, nostalgia had ceased to be viewed as a disease, and was seen instead as an emotion, a longing for a particular time, rather than a particular place. Today, theorists focus on the cultural, as well as the individual experience of nostalgia. For instance, psychologist Janelle Wilson writes, "While [nostalgia] began—conceptually and experientially—as solely a private phenomenon centered on one's longing for home, it has become...a more public experience" (Wilson 2005, 30).

gers but argues that it "can serve the purpose of forging a national identity, expressing patriotism" (Wilson 2005, 31).[3] Colonized nations seeking self-government or newly independent nations have often looked to a precolonial past as an idyllic time in order to build a sense of national pride. In some cases, this has been a powerful tool to combat colonial stereotypes of the inferiority of the colonized peoples. For example, the Negritude movement of Francophone African and Caribbean writers like Léopold Sédar Senghor and Aimé Césaire celebrated the mystery, rhythms, and sensuality of Africa, traits that had been reviled by the colonizers.

Other critics, however, note that this kind of nostalgia has been used to consolidate the power of a small, elite group. Of early twentieth-century Indian and African independence movements, Elleke Boehmer writes:

> As well as being male, nationalist leadership at this time was…middle class, highly educated—also urbanized, liberal-minded, cosmopolitan, and often more proficient in European than indigenous forms of expression… Nostalgia and reconstruction, therefore, helped legitimate…the more 'advanced' of an elite's progressive or modernist attitudes. (Boehmer 1995, 122)

Boehmer indicates that nostalgia helped native leaders create a sense of identity and togetherness even when they were starkly divided from the majority of the people by wealth, education, and status.

Mohan and García engage with these ideas, suggesting a move away from nostalgia, which creates a crystallized version of the past. Nostalgia, they indicate, often requires selective memory, erasing the pain and suffering of oppressed groups, including women, ethnic minorities, and political dissidents, in order to create a peaceful, comforting memory of the past. Mohan focuses on individual nostalgia, showing that ignoring the trauma in the lives of one's ancestors leads to repeating the mistakes of prior generations, thus threatening one's future. García, on the other hand, draws attention to nostalgia on a cultural level. *Monkey Hunting* depicts multiple postcolonial contexts to demonstrate that nostalgia is often used to legitimate those in power or as an attempt to regain power. The best way to escape this trap, García suggests, is to acknowledge the traumas of the past, but to combat the prejudices and injustices of the

---

[3] Similarly, historian Svetlana Boym argues that "for many displaced people from all over the world, creative rethinking of nostalgia was…a strategy of survival, a way of making sense of the impossibility of homecoming" (Boym 2001, xvii).

present by developing a pragmatic altruism, in which one balances a generousness toward those in need with an awareness of one's limitations.

In a sense, García and Mohan deploy a similar strategy as that of David Dabydeen and Lelawattee Manoo-Rahming, the contemporary poets described in Chap. 5. All four authors emphasize the importance of connecting with one's ancestors, but the novelists described here are less interested in locating a sense of belonging than in disrupting cycles of oppression. Additionally, while Dabydeen and Manoo-Rahming suggest that the desire to know one's ancestors will ultimately be frustrated, as it is impossible to truly understand their experiences, García and Mohan are more optimistic about this project. *Monkey Hunting* and *Jahajin* both feature protagonists who reach across generations to form meaningful connections that enrich and enlighten their own lives. The differences between the poems and the novels could be a result of the more autobiographic nature of poetry, particularly true of the poems described in the previous chapter. The fictional nature of the novel form allows for an aspirational approach to history, in which an author explores potential remedies for postcolonial trauma, whereas Dabydeen and Manoo-Rahming draw on their own thwarted attempts to reach back in time.

García and Mohan are not naïve: they acknowledge the persistence of gendered and racialized repression, as well as the role that nostalgia plays in perpetuating this repression. Like the hierarchies of empire, nostalgia is seductive: historian David Lowenthal argues that it offers "an ordered clarity contrasting with the chaos or imprecision of our own times" (Lowenthal 1989, 30). Yet, García and Mohan offer a means to resist this seduction, urging readers to acknowledge the chaos and imprecision of the past in order to find a clarity in the present.

Jahajin: Actively Engaging with the Past

Jahajin is a highly autobiographical novel, shaped around Mohan's own experiences as a PhD candidate in linguistics and her interviews with older Indo-Trinidadians. In a review of the book, Rukmini Bhaya Nair draws attention to the overlap between the author's life and that of the main character: "In trendy postcolonialese, it is what's known as 'autoethnography,' a hybrid genre where the author's fictionalised biography intimately mirrors the story of her community" (2008). Mohan adds, "I have lived so long with *Jahajin* that I am not sure any more what actually happened and what is purely my invention" (Mohan 2010).

The hybrid quality of Mohan's novel, blending fiction, autobiography, and oral accounts, makes use of the forms that Indo-Caribbean women's narratives have often taken. As discussed in Chap. 2, bonded laborers, particularly women, had little access to education or public forms of expression, and so there are no known novels or autobiographies written by indentured women. The few published texts produced by laborers, such as Munshi Rahman Khan's *Autobiography of an Indian Indentured Laborer*, were written by men. Men testified in court more frequently than women, and thus their experiences are more comprehensively documented in colonial records. Yet women did pass on cultural knowledge and stories through other genres, such as Alice Singh's diary and the matikor ceremony, a female-centered ritual performed before weddings to instruct the bride-to-be in sexual matters through song, dance, and acting out scenes.

The cross-genre nature of *Jahajin* celebrates these forms of expression and highlights the importance of oral narratives, including the interviews that inspired this novel, in recuperating women's stories and combating the dangers of nostalgia. The emphasis on alternative, women-centered narratives is reflected in the intimate style of the novel and the nested quality of the stories. The transcriptions, which make up a large portion of the novel, include chitchat and interruptions, as when a dog steals a roti from the kitchen. Dialogue also plays a heavy role in the plot, particularly in establishing the narrator's evolving views on gender roles. For example, during a visit to the home of a friend, the narrator, her cousin Dylan, and her friend Sheila extensively debate the significance of an Indian folk tale, comparing it to the narrator's own relationships with men.

The narrator, like Mohan, was born and raised in Trinidad to a father of Indian descent and a Canadian mother, and is earning her PhD at the University of Michigan in linguistics. She has returned to Trinidad to record Indian immigrants speaking in Bhojpuri, a language from North India, from where many of the laborers came. In Trinidad in the 1970s, Bhojpuri was a dying language, replaced by Hindi and Creole English. In her quest to preserve and study the language by recording the last of the native speakers, the narrator inadvertently also preserves the story of these laborers, the last living men and women to experience indenture. Staying at her parents' house while she performs her work, she feels caught between the pressure from her family to leave Trinidad and pursue her scholarly career, and her desire to find a place for herself and to shape her own life.

The novel weaves together three different stories: the narrator's experiences as she records the voices of older Indo-Trinidadians and develops a love affair with Fyzie, her local guide; the indenture narrative recounted by Deeda, a 109-year-old woman who indentured with Sunnariya, the narrator's great-great-grandmother; and a folk tale that Deeda tells about a monkey boy and girl who become human and encounter great obstacles in their quest to be together. The three stories overlap in clear ways—in each, a female protagonist goes on a great voyage; in each she struggles against cultural norms around gender and class in an effort to carve out a measure of independence; and in each she searches for a way to hold on to that independence as she becomes entangled in a romantic relationship. These parallels emphasize that many Indo-Caribbean women have faced similar tensions, caught between the desire to strike out on one's own and the pressure to shape one's identity around a male partner.

The critical attention on this book focuses on the relationships formed between the female characters—the solidarity of the women who indentured, but also the bonds of women across generations. Mariam Pirbhai writes, "In accessing these women's stories in their own voice, so-to-speak, the narrator discovers not only the history of one *jahaji-bhain* but also an animated record of the new sisterhood formed among early women migrants, and alongside what was, for some, an emerging spirit of female emancipation" (Pirbhai 2012, 32). Abigail Ward argues that Peggy Mohan "examines how women, in particular, have been edited from official versions of both Trinidadian and Indian migratory histories" (Ward 2013, 271). As these scholars indicate, *Jahajin* is notable for the degree of attention given to the stories of the women who indentured. Though other novels such as *The Counting House* feature female characters, their stories are framed as one half of the story of a man and a woman who indenture, as opposed to being worthy of a tale of their own. As noted in the introduction, most indenture narratives depict women traveling with a partner or men traveling alone, when in fact the majority of women who indentured did so alone. *Jahajin* is one of the few novels to represent this fact.

The emphasis on recovering women's stories contributes to the novel's argument that certain forms of remembering can perpetuate systems of oppression. Through the narrator's growing awareness of the experiences of the female laborers and how that experience has been filtered by later generations, *Jahajin* highlights the ways that nostalgia can erase the suffering of oppressed groups, including minorities and women. Mohan advocates a move away from sentimental views of previous eras and toward an active engagement with the past, modeled in the relationships formed between the narrator and the other women in the novel. These relationships develop through her interviews with Bhojpuri speakers, which draw a web of connections between her, her grandmother, her great-great-grandmother, and Deeda, her interviewee. As the narrator is drawn closer to the women of earlier generations, she begins to resist her family's gender-inflected expectations that she be self-sacrificing, studious, and chaste, and she notices the sexism that she faces in academic and social settings. The novel ends on an ambiguous note, as it is unclear whether the narrator will be able to escape the fate of her ancestors, who suffered sexual assault, the constraints of gender norms, and unhappy marriages. However, there are hints that the awareness she has gained will help her dodge these traps.

The folktale and the oral narrative of indenture act as a bridge between the past and the present, highlighting the connections between the generations of Indo-Caribbean women. *Jahajin* opens with the narrator recording the folk story of the monkey couple, as told by Deeda.[4] When Deeda pauses in telling her story, the scene dissolves; the narrator is now at home translating the story with the help of her grandmother, Ajie. This is the first of several shifts between the narrator's present-day story, the folktale, and Deeda's story of her indenture, shifts that draw together the female characters in the novel. Deeda, the storyteller, indentured with the narrator's great-great-grandmother, Sunnariya, and so her description of their experience of bonded labor ties together generations of women from two different families. In addition, Ajie helps her granddaughter to translate the stories, so on a literal level the narratives have brought together these two women.

The ties between women of different generations are strengthened by the many overlaps between the three storylines. The girl monkey-turned-human leaves behind her mate on a journey to explore the world. In her travels, she is wooed by a prince, but demands some degree of independence from him. We later learn that this parallels Deeda's story, as she left

---

[4] Monkeys play a key role in both *Jahajin* and *Monkey Hunting*, which is not unusual in Indian indenture narratives. Hanuman, the monkey god in the Hindu pantheon, is a key part of the Ramayana, a Hindu epic that tells the story of Rama, a prince who is exiled from his homeland, and Sita, his devoted and chaste wife. It was often used as a source of inspiration and comfort by the laborers, particularly males, because of the many parallels with their own story. Novels by contemporary Indo-Caribbean women often subvert the Ramayana, as in Ryhaan Shah's *A Silent Life*.

behind her husband when she migrated to Trinidad, then declined to return to India with a high-caste man named Mukoon Singh. The monkey girl also asks the prince for 12 years alone, which almost exactly matches the period of Sunnariya's indenture: "their indentureship was not, in the end, for the five years they had expected or the ten years they had ultimately signed for. Esperanza Estate managed to extend their indentureship period until it finally lasted eleven years and five months" (Mohan 2007, 182). This was a common experience for laborers, as employers often extended the time of the contract through dubious practices such as adding days missed for illness.

These connections between the narratives give the narrator a richer, deeper understanding of her family's history and the history of indenture, which in turn helps her recognize her own tendency to romanticize the past. At one point, the narrator asks Deeda whether food didn't taste better when it was all made fresh at home, by hand. Deeda dismisses this idea, focusing instead on the unseen labor of women that was intrinsic to traditional cooking: "She gave me a skeptical look and told me that she didn't care at all. All that good food I was talking about, for her it was just a lot of hard work, and she was tired of that. Any amount of curry powder was better than always being poor, and tired" (Mohan 2007, 50). Deeda's pragmatic response shakes the narrator out of her misty view of the past: "All my middle class angst and nostalgia suddenly seemed like an affectation, and insensitive to boot" (Mohan 2007, 50).

In addition to the burdensome nature of these traditional ways of doing things, Deeda also hints at the economic damage that can be caused by traditional gender roles: the effort it took to feed a family by cooking from scratch was energy that could have been spent on earning extra income through farming, gardening, craftwork, or selling merchandise. Historians such as Marina Carter have noted that women frequently supplemented the family income through such tasks, and that this in turn led to the purchase of land (Carter 1994, 124). This suggests that families were more likely to rise above subsistence-level agriculture when the women in the family were able to take part in trade work.

The details that Deeda shares about her days of indenture help the narrator combat this middle-class nostalgia. For example, she describes the violent treatment the laborers received on the voyage to Trinidad: "all the goras, the white sailors, were watching us carefully, waiting to flog people if they caused any disturbance on the boat" (Mohan 2007, 61). Upon arrival, Beharry, a seasoned laborer, encourages the migrants to rub oil into their hands and place them over a fire in order to toughen their skin before they begin cutting cane. Deeda captures the repetitive, grueling nature of the work in short, choppy sentences, as if, years later, just talking about it is exhausting: "Strip cane. Make bundles. Move on...Hands were hurting...Sit down and think. Head spinning now! Drink some water. This is too much, too much. Try again. Get up and keep working" (Mohan 2007, 122–124). Although we hear extensive accounts of the laborers' suffering, the British are largely absent from the novel, mentioned only in passing and never named. This focus contrasts sharply with earlier depictions of indenture in which the relationships between the British and the Indians are the central concern, and reshapes the story of indenture as the story of the laborers.[5]

We see the narrator's emerging views on the hazards of nostalgia when she presents her research to a group of linguists. The scholars in the audience challenge her seeming indifference to the death of Bhojpuri. Remembering her conversation with Deeda about meals made from scratch, she draws a connection to the shrinking numbers of Bhojpuri speakers. She realizes that all of the people who spoke this language were poor and lacked education. Languages like Hindi and English were often learned in school, and so those who spoke them were the ones who had escaped from fieldwork and other forms of subsistence labor. Its death might mean the rising of an Indian middle class. The narrator responds, "'It isn't up to us, you know. It is the poor people who still speak the language who will decide if they want to pass it on or not...They will decide, and you and I will only talk about it'" (Mohan 2007, 51). The scholars who decry the death of Bhojpuri have the luxury of choosing to study it, as opposed to the native speakers who had no access to other languages.

Deeda's stories about her past help the narrator come to a new understanding of women's roles during indenture. In one interview, Deeda lists off the women who indentured with her, "who all had come as widows, who had come with parents, who had run away from hard times, and who had simply walked out of the house. And a kind of woman who never got married at all" (Mohan 2007, 204). The narrator is struck by this new view of women migrants:

---

[5] Mohan indicates that the women she interviewed hardly ever spoke about the British: "They really didn't see anybody who wasn't relevant to them. And as far as they were concerned, the entire life on the estate was Indians...they talked of [the British] the way you would talk of maybe seeing Haley's Comet or something. Something that passed by" (Mohan 2014).

The migration came across to me as a story of women making their way alone, with men in the backgrounds, strangers, extras. In the history books it had always been the other way around: it was the men who were the main actors. But there was also the unwritten history of the birth of a new community in Trinidad. And it was women at the centre of the story. (Mohan 2007, 204)

The narrator thus realizes that Indian women performed a crucial community-building role in Trinidad.[6]

Here, Mohan draws attention to the ways that nostalgia, whether for cooking or for a language, often depends on selective memory, erasing suffering and inequality to create a warm, comforting image of home. Both the linguists' attachment to Bhojpuri and the narrator's longing for food made by traditional methods depend on a middle-class existence, a life removed from manual labor. Yet, there is a difference in their responses. The narrator's yearning is tied to family and childhood: she has a desire for an intimate meal prepared at home, rather than the impersonal, bland food made from products purchased at a supermarket. On the other hand, the scholars who mourn the disappearance of Bhojpuri seem to be longing for a connection to their ancestral homeland and resisting the cultural adaptations that those of Indian descent have made in Trinidad, even if those adaptations indicate a rise in social status. This hints at a generational difference in one's focus on the past, as the older linguists, who are fewer steps removed from the migration, seem to have a stronger desire to maintain connections to their homeland.

There is also a gendered element to this nostalgia, as the tasks of keeping the home, cooking food, and even teaching language to children are often seen as the domain of women, and thus it is the exploitation of women that gets forgotten in these romanticized views. This erasure is emphasized through Deeda's stories, which offer a vivid view of the denigration that the laborers, and particularly the women, experienced. Deeda alludes to the harassment that women faced on the journey when she describes their quarters on the boat: "The women had to sleep the whole night with lamps on, so that none of the sailors could come in the dark and try to interfere with us. That was a rule" (Mohan 2007, 54). Historians Verene Shepherd and Gaiutra Bahadur note that these partitions did little to protect women from sexual assault on the voyage. In

---

[6] Peggy Mohan makes this argument in more depth in her article "Indians Under a Caribbean Sky" (2001).

Maharani's Misery, Shepherd relates the harrowing story of a young woman named Maharani who was forcefully assaulted on board a ship and later died from her injuries, while Bahadur gives several cases of British sailors, officers, and even the ship's surgeon harassing and assaulting Indian women and girls. In almost all cases, the perpetrators escaped with mild or no consequences (Shepherd 2002, Bahadur 2013).

In addition, Mohan draws attention to the prevalence of sexual assault on the estates, as well as its devastating impact. An overseer, drunk one afternoon, comes across Sunnariya in the cane fields and attempts to rape her. She is traumatized when she returns to Deeda: "The look in her eyes was something I will never forget. As if she didn't care anymore. As if there was nothing worse that could happen to her now" (Mohan 2007, 151). Her distress is further indicated by the way she changes her story each time she tells it: in one version saying she had tricked him and escaped, and in another saying that he had been too drunk to do anything to her. She seeks to gain control over the situation and to shape it into a narrative that she can live with. In each version of the story, she manages to escape the overseer's attempts, and Deeda reports, "It did not look as though the overseer had managed to rape her," but the depth of Sunnariya's shock suggests that may not be the case.

Mohan said of the actual events that inspired this section of the story, "People keep editing their memories…that we aren't the kind of people to whom such things could happen. So Sunnariya is just too classy a lady to have been abused or assaulted, and we don't know to this day what it was" (Mohan 2014). This suggests that the erasure of Sunnariya's assault may have been a community choice, an unwillingness to believe that such a thing could have happened to one of their own and a desire to keep Sunnariya's honor intact. Woven in to this silence are the issues of gender and class, as denying Sunnariya's rape sustains the myth that only low-class, promiscuous women are sexually assaulted. By remembering Sunnariya's assault, the novel helps to break such silences and erase the blame that is often placed upon victims of sexual violence.

The after-effects of the attack on Sunnariya also demonstrate that indenture was not a complete domination of a passive people. Mukoon Singh, Sunnariya's father, kills the overseer, and the Indian community is complicit in this act of revenge: "The guards on the estate knew, everyone who was Indian knew that he would come like this in the middle of the night…so they had quietly slipped away, disappeared" (Mohan 2007, 154). The plantation officials, fearing retribution from Sunnariya's family, do not dare send her to the fields again, and instead assign her the role of the *khelauni*, the woman who watches over the children of the laborers. Their response shows that their power over the laborers is far from complete.

This moment in the novel offers an interesting commentary on the restrictive nature of masculine gender roles. The government officials, aware that they bear some responsibility for the situation, offer Mukoon Singh a compromise: if he surrenders, he will not be punished, but he must return to India. Certainly, it is the terrible actions of the overseer and the lack of justice for laborers that puts Mukoon Singh in this difficult situation, but before he killed the overseer, Mukoon Singh lay his pagri[7] next to the sleeping Sunnariya and said to her "I will take this back from you... when I bring back your honour" (Mohan 2007, 154). His emphasis on his daughter's honor raises the question of whether Sunnariya and Deeda wouldn't have been happier to have him within their family even if it meant the overseer went unpunished. Because he has killed the overseer, he will be an ocean away and unable to care for Sunnariya. In addition, he and Deeda had been moving toward a partnership, a dream that they must now give up. This suggests that gender roles for men, such as the need to protect women's honor, can be equally confining as gender roles for women.

Deeda's vivid stories about the racialized and gendered oppression of the laborers help the narrator recognize the lingering effects of these dynamics in contemporary Trinidad. Shortly after listening to the tale of Sunnariya's assault, the narrator visits the Sevilla Club, which had once been one of the leisure locations for estate management. There she experiences a milder version of the entitlement that the overseer seemed to feel over Sunnariya. A Scottish overseer, seeing the narrator walking through the club in her bathing suit, looks her up and down and asks, "'Are you a member here?'" (Mohan 2007, 164). She is distressed and quickly leaves the club to go home, trying "to dispel the image of the overseer focusing his eyes on me through an alcoholic haze, sizing me up. Deciding if I belonged or not. Like, was I some Indian girl poaching on his property?" (Mohan 2007, 165). Abigail Ward notes that Mohan walks a fine line in this moment of the novel to demonstrate the dangers of overidentification with victims: "Whilst the narrator's meeting with the Scottish man appears to be reminiscent of Sunnariya's encounter with the overseer, it is short-

[7] Turban.

lived, and a clear distinction is made between the trauma experienced by Sunnariya and the narrator's empathy for her indentured ancestor" (Ward 2013, 279).

Yet, there are places when the narrator's identification with the laborers is problematic. For example, Ward points to a moment in which the narrator equates translating the stories with cutting cane. "The narrator's involvement in translating Deeda's stories seems to have drawn her into experiencing a postmemory of indenture, where she is left exhausted after her physical toil of translating-as-working-the-cane" (Ward 2013, 280). This identification is somewhat troubling, as choosing to translate a text as a scholarly project, while mentally and physically draining, cannot be equivalent to a full day of field labor, especially given that the punishment for shirking this labor would be a beating or jail. In fact, this moment is an example of the very nostalgia that the novel critiques. The narrator, who is translating the interview with her historian friend Rosa, is perhaps seeking the same close bond of friendship that Deeda and Sunnariya formed through their shared suffering, without acknowledging the differences between her experiences and theirs.

At the same time, the novel levels a harsh indictment of the ways that nostalgia contributes to patterns of restrictive gender roles. As a result of the silence around her assault, Sunnariya blames herself, marries immediately after, and withdraws from public view, falling into the conventional view that a woman is safer in the home. The novel, however, does not condone this view: Sunnariya has an unhappy marriage, as her husband turns out to be an alcoholic, and she dies young while giving birth to her fifth child. This death begins a chain reaction, as Sunnariya's oldest son becomes responsible for raising his brothers and sisters, as well as his own children. Overwhelmed by his caretaking obligations, he marries off his daughter at age 14. Her marriage, like Sunnariya's, is an unhappy one: she "had been chosen by her in-laws in the hope that a fair pretty girl would be able to wean their son away from an unsuitable relationship with a woman on one of their estates" (Mohan 2007, 197). After divorcing her husband, Ajie takes a job in a store, where she sits in a cage with the store's cash. This less-than-subtle metaphor represents the confined life she lives and the view of women as a commodity, like money. The frustrating similarities in the lives of the narrator's female ancestors point to the self-perpetuating quality of traditional gender roles.

Through her interviews with Indian migrants, the narrator starts to realize that when she was a child, her life was constricted in similar ways. Instead of exploring her neighborhood or the island, as her male cousins have done, she was pushed into the role of the diligent student. She is living her life for others, as the women in her family have done before her, and she resents it. Remembering that her father was happier about her graduation from college than she was, she thinks, "I had known then that I was making up for all the things that hadn't happened in his life" (Mohan 2007, 80). This is certainly about more than her gender, as parents generally want their children's lives to be better than their own, but the self-sacrifice and constraint that is expected of her has the tinge of Sunnariya's self-sacrifice and constraint, and that of Ajie before she determined to divorce her husband and start a new life on her own. It is only when the narrator begins an active engagement with her family's past that she begins to push back against these expectations.

This conflict comes to a head in a decision that the narrator must make about her future. In Michigan, she was involved with an Indian man named Nishant, but she was unsure of her feelings for him. In Trinidad, she begins a relationship with Fyzie, the man her father engaged to take her around the island to visit older Indian men and women. Her family, particularly her grandmother, objects to this relationship. It later becomes evident that Ajie is upset because she doesn't want her granddaughter trapped in an unhappy relationship, the way she had been. Her anger at her granddaughter can be seen as the fear that she will repeat this same pattern, settling down with a man who is known to have casual relationship with other women and living an unhappy life as a result.

The narrator faces a danger in becoming involved with Nishant, as well. The narrator's cousin Dylan compares Nishant to the prince in the Saranga the story, ready to sweep up the narrator and take her away to a privileged but confined life. This seems an apt comparison, as Nishant is determined to return to India, which would limit the narrator's career options: "There were no foreign wives who had managed to find their feet in a career in India. Someone like me might have a hard time finding work: the job scene in Indian academia was xenophobic" (Mohan 2007, 162). If she travels to India with him, she will have to give up her career, and she will be pushed into the traditional gender role of the passive wife. This parallels the decision that Deeda has to make when Mukoon Singh asks her to return to India with him. She is tempted, but is aware that her lower caste, a difference that was erased in Trinidad, would cause tension should she return to India with him. She wants to hold on to the freedom she has gained in Trinidad, and so she politely declines his offer.

As the narrator considers this possibility, she imagines the division between Trinidad and India as a handwoven cloth: "India was on the other side of a porous handloom curtain. Once I crossed that curtain to settle in India, coming back would not be easy...A purdah,[8] I thought. Like Ajie's orhnis.[9] Woven in the mind. But stronger than a curtain you could touch" (Mohan 2007, 163). Once there, it would be difficult to regain the independence that she developed in Trinidad. She would be swallowed up and lose her sense of self, just as Deeda would have been had she returned with Mukoon Singh.

Mohan's comparison to handwoven cloth here is noteworthy. She references curtains and orhnis, cloths that are meant to protect women from the eyes of men, but are also identified with the traditional Indian craft of homemade textiles. As part of his nationalist campaign, Gandhi advocated a return to older Indian crafts, such as the handloom and the chakra. This was intended to develop the economy in rural areas and make India self-sufficient, rather than relying on the mass-produced British textiles and other goods that had flooded the markets. While Gandhi advocated women's rights and wanted everyone in India—male, female, wealthy, poor—to learn to weave as an equalizer, he also exhibited some nostalgia for traditional gender roles. He was reportedly charmed to see "lovely maidens of Assam weave poems on their looms" (Mahmud 2004, 46). Mohan pushes against such comforting, idyllic image of women weaving, demonstrating that it idealizes a moment when women faced oppressive cultural practices, such as the systematic seclusion of women.

The narrator feels caught between these two choices: Will she stay in Trinidad with Fyzie, the unreliable ladies' man, in a relationship similar to Ajie's marriage, or will she marry Nishant and move to India, following the path that Mukoon Singh offered Deeda? Deeda's decision to remain in Trinidad offers the narrator another model, which is to make her way through life without a partner. The narrator gains a bit of a reprieve when she wins a scholarship to travel to India to continue her research, which she accepts almost without thinking about it. She recognizes that her choice to go may be a reaction to her family's pressure to succeed, "to turn my face away from happiness into the winds of a cold future" (Mohan 2007, 199). However, she is determined to end the cycle: "I was not

---

[8] A practice among Muslims and some Hindus of secluding women.
[9] A long scarf or veil that Indian women wore to cover their hair and the upper part of their body.

going to make the next generation sail the high seas for me. The curse had to end" (Mohan 2007, 200). Her engagement with the stories of her ancestors has helped her recognize this "curse" and hopefully break it.

For the narrator, returning to India is not a homecoming. Though she forms connections with the people she meets, she is also struck by the pervasive gender and class hierarchies she witnesses. Sociologist Gayatri Gopinath notes that images of diaspora and homecoming are often gendered. For instance, the lyrics and video of a bhangra song by Malkit Singh, a Punjabi folk singer, depict a diasporic male figure returning to his homeland of India, which is represented by a mother figure. She further suggests that "'India' be written into the diaspora as yet another diasporic location, rather than remaining a signifier of an original, essentialized identity around which a diasporic network is constructed and to which it always refers" (Gopinath 1995, 313). Mohan similarly troubles the idea of an idealized homeland, indicating that laborers and other migrants who romanticize the notion of homecoming may have brushed over the gender and class oppressions that existed and continue to exist in their native land.

At the same time, the narrator's trip to India demonstrates that her interviews with older Indo-Trinidadians have helped her to recognize those lingering caste, class, and gender prejudices. She is struck that railway porters in India are called coolies, a word that was banned in Trinidad after Independence because of its derogatory nature. In Deeda's home village, where the narrator has gone to record older Indians speaking Bhojpuri, she sees indications of ongoing degradation of the lower class. The pradhan, the village headman, summons an old man who deferentially squats and waits for his instructions. When the pradhan leans forward to get the old man's attention, "the old man grimaced and flinched back from the expected blow" (Mohan 2007, 263). Attempting to sidestep this power dynamic, the narrator asks to speak to the old man alone, but the pradhan resists, trying to maintain control of the situation. It is only when another man, Nishant's father, steps in, that the pradhan agrees to leave the two alone.

The novel concludes with the narrator playing the ending of Deeda's folktale for the old man. In the story, the two lovers escape the king on a flying cot and return to his home, where they live happily ever after, suggesting a subversion of both social hierarchies, in which the king is all-powerful, and of gender roles, as the woman's bold life choices have led to happiness for both her and her mate. The story also links together different eras and distant geographic locations. The old man's recognition of the story connects his village to Trinidad, albeit briefly. When the narrator hits stop on her tape player, "the bridge across two great oceans to Deeda's little house in Orange Valley disappeared" (Mohan 2007, 267). The scene closes with the narrator, Nishant's father, Nishant's sister, and the driver getting into a car together, echoing Saranga's magic carpet cot ride.

The ending is not as conclusive for the narrator as it is for Saranga. She is staying with Nishant's family, who assume an impending marriage, yet her fate is not set. Thanks to her work with the indenture narratives, she has several models of Indo-Caribbean women's lives to learn from. Sunnariya retreated into seclusion and suffered a short, unhappy life, married to an alcoholic. Ajie, too, endured an unhappy marriage, but managed to leave her husband. While the folktale is somewhat subversive, it still ends with Saranga's marriage as a happy ending. More subversive yet is Deeda's story—she left her husband behind to seek a better life, rejected a life with another suitor, and raised her son by herself, living a long and seemingly happy life. The narrator recognizes the dangers in living her life for others, and so it seems possible that she might find a way to avoid this fate.

Prior to her interactions with Deeda, the narrator, along with others of her generation, feels pride in her ancestors, yet feels wary of being associated too closely with them. When Fyzie and the narrator steal cane from an estate, echoing Sunnariya's theft generations ago, the narrator's cousin Dylan remarks wryly "'You can take the coolie out of the cane field but you can't take the cane field out of the coolie'" (Mohan 2007, 95). The narrator reflects:

> We lionized our ancestors who had worked in the cane fields, yet on the other hand we kept our own evolved selves light years away from the sugar estates. Our hearts bled for the poor aging cane cutters, the last repository of "our" culture. But to go near the life of the estates was to place your feet too close to the quicksand. (Mohan 2007, 95)

She had previously viewed her ancestral connections to field labor as "quicksand," a deadly and suffocating trap. Through her work, she has come to see her ancestors as real people with real experiences, as opposed to symbols of a terrible fate or repositories of culture. This in turn helps her to recognize that she is not as far from the life of the estates as she might think, and that the barriers the female laborers faced have not been entirely dismantled.

We see this warning repeated in other novels that touch on Indo-Caribbean indenture. These include *The Swinging Bridge* (2003), by Ramabai Espinet, and *A Silent Life*, by Ryhaan Shah (2005), both of which focus on a present-day Indo-Caribbean woman uncovering the stories of her female ancestors. In *The Swinging Bridge*, Mona, a Trinidadian currently living in Canada, returns home to fulfill her brother's deathbed request that she buy back the family land.

In the process of doing so, she uncovers the story of Gainder, her great-grandmother who indentured in Trinidad, as well as disturbing stories of the abuse that she and the other women in the family faced.[10] Both Gainder's story and the instances of violence have been left out of the family history in order to present an image of middle-class success. This image is contrived, though; as in *Jahajin*, the patterns of domination and abuse repeat in later generations. Mona's father is an alcoholic who viciously beat his family members, and Mona witnesses her uncle attempting to kiss her mother, then later is the victim of his sexual assaults. It is in the recovery of Gainder's story and in the home of Bess, an illegitimate cousin, that Mona finally finds a sense of safety and belonging.

A Silent Life, by Ryhaan Shah, similarly highlights patterns of abuse and the importance of uncovering the stories of generations of women. The narrator, a Guyanese woman named Aleyah, learns to recognize restrictive gender norms in her own life after piecing together the lives that her grandmothers led. Aleyah's paternal grandmother, Gaitree, was badly beaten by her mother-in-law in India and ran away from her family to indenture in Guyana. Her maternal grandmother, Nani, had a past as a community organizer of field laborers. She fell silent when her husband, ashamed of his inability to fill traditional gender roles, hanged himself. Similarly, when Aleyah becomes more and more successful in her career, her husband, who has been unsuccessful in his own field, grows angry and demands that she refuse a dream job. Aleyah sinks into a deep depression in which she finds herself unwilling to speak. The gender roles in Indo-Caribbean families, Shah suggests, have not changed dramatically in two generations, and women are still expected to be the silent, passive partners

---

[10] Rodolphe Solbiac notes that when Joshua, Mona's great-grandfather, destroys pages that contain the *rands*' songs, "the act is a patriarchal erasure of the memory of Indian independent female migration. This act is perpetrated in order to preserve the male mythical discourse that presents Indian migration to Trinidad as a family process exclusively" (Solbiac 2012, 238).

in a marriage. While the female characters do not experience the same level of physical or sexual abuse as the characters in *The Swinging Bridge* or *Jahajin*, there is a systematic, cultural silencing of their voices that is shown to be destructive not only to the women, but also to those around them.

Nostalgia requires a separation of the past and present, a sense that the previous era was not only preferable, it has ended, and is disconnected from the present. *Jahajin*, *The Swinging Bridge*, and *A Silent Life* all weave together stories of the present and stories of the past in order to demonstrate patterns of patriarchal oppression and the continuing impact of indenture on gender relations in the present.[11] Through their engagement with the stories of their ancestors, the narrators in these novels come to recognize that the allure of nostalgia, the image of a simpler, more authentic time, hides the fact that the past is deeply implicated in the present. Faulkner famously wrote, "The past is never dead. It's not even past" (Faulkner 2011, 73). Perhaps with the new understanding that these narrators hold, they will be able to break the cycles of the past that is not past.

Monkey Hunting: Cultivating Pragmatic Altruism

Monkey Hunting, by Cristina García, also focuses on cycles of trauma, but unlike Mohan's work, treats large-scale, systematic forms of oppression such as the slavery-like Spanish indenture system, the repression that occurred during the Cuban Revolution and the Chinese Cultural Revolution, and the aggression of American neo-imperialism. A rare fictional representation of the experience of Chinese laborers, it is a sprawling book that begins in nineteenth-century China with Chen Pan, a young farmer who indentures in Cuba. The novel follows his descendants through the nineteenth and twentieth centuries with scenes that take place in Cuba, the United States, China, and Vietnam. The scenes are held together by their emphasis on rebellions and revolutions; the story skips across history, pausing at moments of upheaval such as the Spanish-American War, the Boxer Rebellion and the Cultural Revolution in China, and the Vietnam War.

Like Mohan, García's work is influenced by her multinational background. Born in Cuba, she settled in the United States, where she currently writes fiction full time. Though written in English, her novels primarily focus on Cuba, and she notes, "I always thought of myself as Cuban" ("…

---

[11] Even Gaiutra Bahadur's nonfiction book, *Coolie Woman* (2013), could be included in this category. This book moves back and forth between Bahadur's own experiences of migration, racism, and sexism, and the information she has uncovered about her great-grandmother.

And There Is Only" 607), in part because she grew up speaking Spanish and hearing stories about Cuba. García has reported tension with other Cubans, including those who live in Cuba and the United States, who question her decision to write in English or her lack of engagement with anti-Castro movements. In response, she has said that in her novels, she tries to emphasize that, "there is no one Cuban exile" ("At Home" 75).

García has received much critical acclaim and is probably best known for her novel *Dreaming in Cuban*, which was nominated for the National Book Award in 1992. *Dreaming in Cuban* is critical of both Cuban socialism and American capitalism, pointing to the repression of dissent in the first and the money-driven interventionist policies of the second. Her second novel, *The Agüero Sisters*, focuses more on family than national politics. Published in 1997, it tells the story of two Cuban sisters unearthing the violence of their family's past. García said in an interview, "Traditional history, the way it has been written, interpreted and recorded, obviates women and the evolution of home, family and society, and basically becomes a recording of battles and wars and dubious accomplishments of men" ("...And There is Only" 610). All three novels thus explore underrepresented and repressed populations in Cuban history, and García has described them as a loose trilogy meant to capture the wide variety of the Cuban experience ("An Interview" 178).

Monkey Hunting's depiction of Caribbean indenture diverges in key ways from that of *Jahajin*. Most notably, *Monkey Hunting* is set in Cuba when it was still a Spanish colony, and focuses on Chinese indenture, rather than Indian. While Indians made up the vast majority of the approximately 500,000 indentured laborers who migrated to the Caribbean, the 18,000 indentured Chinese constituted a significant number (Look Lai 1993, 19). In 1877, the height of Chinese habitation in Cuba, there were more than 40,000 Chinese living on the island.

There were several important differences between the two systems. Unlike the Indian migrants, who went primarily to British colonies, the Chinese generally traveled to Spanish colonies such as Peru and Cuba, although some went to British colonies including Jamaica, Guyana, Trinidad and Tobago, and Suriname.[12] Another distinction was the number

[12] The Chinese migration to the Caribbean in the nineteenth century was part of a broader Chinese migration throughout the globe. The mid-nineteenth century was a period of turmoil for China, as the Qing Dynasty was losing power in the face of Western imperialism and widespread social unrest. Roughly two-and-a-half million Chinese workers left China in the nineteenth century for overseas destinations, including Australia and California, during the gold rush.

of females who migrated. While both British colonizers and Indian migrants were dismayed by the low numbers of Indian women who migrated, women still made up a sizable portion of those who indentured, between 30% and 40% (Look Lai 1993, 46). However, migration of Chinese females was incredibly rare, to the point that the British Consul at Canton wrote, "Chinese women never emigrate" (quoted in Look Lai 1993, 47). This was in part because of the societal pressure in China, even greater than in India, for women to remain within the domestic sphere. Additionally, there was a stronger expectation among the Chinese laborers of returning to their homeland after completing their period of indenture. British colonizers encouraged Indians to settle in the colonies, sometimes offering them land in lieu of the return passage, while the Chinese migration process, controlled by Chinese middlemen, was much more of a back-and-forth system. Even though Chinese migrants did often stay in the colonies, the expectation of return was a persistent one that prevented men from bringing their wives, or women from traveling alone.[13]

Some historians suggest that the Chinese system of indenture was harsher than the Indian system, and "almost indistinguishable from slavery itself" (Look Lai 2010, 52). Unlike the colonial system of British indenture, China's overseas migration was primarily run by Chinese businessman. Only about 11% of the Chinese migrants were contract or indentured laborers (Look Lai 1993, 38), which meant that they had few protections and no authority to appeal to. Walton Look Lai argues that the privately run nature of Chinese migration led to an unmatched level of abuse: "There was nothing in the British Empire labor tradition to compare with what was standard practice in Cuba or Peru" (Look Lai 2010, 52). Further blurring the boundary between Chinese indenture and slavery, Chinese laborers often worked alongside enslaved persons on plantations rather than replacing them. The first Cantonese laborers arrived in Cuba in 1847 to work the sugar plantations, but slavery was legal in Cuba until 1886, so there was a significant period of overlap. *Monkey Hunting* begins in 1857, during this period of overlap, and it emphasizes the similarities between the treatment of the enslaved laborers of African descent and the Chinese workers.

[13] *Monkey Hunting*'s focus on a male laborer and his descendants separates it from the female-centered *Jahajin*. Because so few Chinese women indentured, we only see female Chinese characters in the scenes that take place in China. For Chen Pan, Chinese women exist primarily in wisps of memory—his mother, the dancing girl in Amoy who takes all of his money, and the women of the old imperial court whom he dreams about, women best admired from afar.

Reviews of *Monkey Hunting* emphasize the evocative language and the engaging exploration of history, but generally fault the lack of character development. Jennifer Schuessler writes, "The poetry is there, but not the spark of life that allows the Chen family to survive and transcend its forced march through endless war and revolution" (Schuessler 2003). Michiko Kakutani adds, "Like so many of the characters in this author's earlier fiction, these people find that the large convulsions of history reverberate noisily through their lives…This novel lacks the fierce magic and unexpected humor of Ms. García's remarkable 1992 debut novel, *Dreaming in Cuban*" (Kakutani 2003). In his article, "Search for Utopia, Desire for the Sublime: Cristina García's *Monkey Hunting*," Sean Moiles challenges this view of *Monkey Hunting*, arguing that the novel's minimalism "rejects grand historical narratives and teleology—and the sublime advances a political worldview at odds with both 1960s nationalist radicalism and assimilationist, pro-market, multicultural platforms" (Moiles 2009, 182). I find both views of the novel accurate—the minimalism may serve a purpose in taking to task nationalist epics, but our insight into the lives of the characters feels somewhat glancing, which minimizes the emotional connection we feel for them.

Like *Jahajin*, *Monkey Hunting* shifts back and forth between the present and the past, following several generations of one family. The novel begins with Chen Pan's story of indenture, and focuses on two of his descendants: Chen Fang, his granddaughter, who lives through the Cultural Revolution in China, and Domingo Chen, his great-great-grandson, who migrates from Cuba to New York and then fights in the Vietnam War. With this structure, García draws attention to the cycles of domination that persist across the globe and throughout different eras. While Mohan focuses on the dangers of dwelling on an idealized version of the past, García warns that it is equally dangerous to erase the past. She draws parallels between the cultural revolutions that erupt across the world, revolutions that break the links between the present and the past and shatter the relationships between the various members of Chen Pan's family.

Following this different focus, the fractured timeline serves a different purpose in *Monkey Hunting* than *Jahajin*. Mohan treats indenture as a starting point, a break in the history of a people. She shows the rippling effects of the indenture system and imperialism, including systemic abuse of women. By contrast, García depicts indenture as one of many forms of oppression that developed out of imperial violence. Marta Lysik writes that *Monkey Hunting* "brings to the foreground various forms of slavery:

chattel system in Cuba, forced marriages, foot-binding and cross-dressing in pre-Cultural Revolution China, and prostitution during the Vietnam War" (Lysik n.d., 1). García indicates that one must continue to challenge these forms of domination through revolutionary acts on a national level and revolutionary acts of kindness on a personal level.

This difference can be attributed, at least in part, to their different nations of origin. Peggy Mohan has stated in an interview that in Trinidad, her home country, indentureship and colonialism are viewed as things of the past. "We see in a sense that it's been fortunate that we are here...that we are in the Caribbean or Mauritius rather than in villages in India...that the problem is essentially over. A little bit of history" (Mohan 2014). García, on the other hand, sees her home nation of Cuba continuing to struggle under multiple forms of dominance. She has criticized both the Cuban government for the increased "repression of dissidence" (García 2007, 185) and the US government for its disregard of human rights and Cuban sovereignty in Guantánamo Bay (García 2007, 184).[14]

As in *Jahajin*, nostalgia is a key theme in García's novels, as many critics have noted. Dalia Kandiyoti examines the role of commodified nostalgia in García's novel *The Agüero Sisters*. Cuban businesses manufacture products that appeal to consumers' desire for an idyllic view of their nation's past. Kandiyoti adds that García and the other authors she examines "take care to validate loss, mourning and suffering evoked in the original definition of nostalgia. What they oppose are the stale, stultifying forms of nostalgia that serve consumerism and dominant exile politics" (Kandiyoti 2006, 82). Sean Moiles builds on this argument, exploring the way that García writes against nostalgia in *Monkey Hunting*. He argues that "Chen Pan learns to embrace new possibilities following the rejection of codified nostalgia" (Moiles 2009, 177), when he gives up hope of returning to China and finds a new home in Havana. Missing from these interpretations is García's view of *how* we move forward, how we proceed once we have rejected nostalgia.

There are hints at the answer in García's earlier work. In *The Agüero Sisters*, García emphasizes the hazards of erasing one's past. Dulce, a young Cuban woman, mourns the lack of information she has about her own

---

[14] García sees this as part of a pattern of America's imperial incursions into Cuba. In 2007, she stated that the Spanish-American War had been a period "of enormous upheaval, and the changes came on the very edge of a big empire—the United States—that was increasingly placing its weight around the world" (García 2007, 177).

family: "There should be rituals like in primitive societies, where the elders confer their knowledge in their descendants bit by bit. Then we could dismiss all the false histories pressed upon us, accumulate our true history like a river in rainy season" (García 1997, 144). Nostalgia, García suggests in *Monkey Hunting*, creates these false histories. It involves a kind of willful blindness, caused either by a selfishness that ignores the suffering of others, or an idealism that ignores the reality of the situation.

The key to moving forward from nostalgia, then, seems to be in finding a balance between blind selfishness and blind idealism, a kind of open-eyed, pragmatic altruism. This can be seen most clearly in the role of Chen Pan, the main character of the story. As a child, his father was considered a hero because he tried to save a young girl from being raped by bandits and was killed in the process. His mother objects to this act, complaining that he abandoned his family. She tells her children, "'Avert your eyes to the sorrows of others and keep your own plates full'" (García 2003, 19). Chen Pan finds a middle ground between these two approaches, hopeless heroism and cold-hearted self-interest, by helping others but also maintaining a sense of self-preservation. It is evident that he passes this worldview on to his descendants. Pipo Chen, Chen Pan's grandson, offers his own son a more empathetic version of the advice that Chen Pan received from his mother, saying: "*Don't watch with interest the suffering of others*" (García 2003, 151, emphasis original). The theme of vision is one that repeats throughout the novel, emphasizing the importance of seeing with clarity both the suffering of others and the obstacles in one's path. The characters in the novel who find the most happiness are those who, like Chen Pan, are generous and kind in the face of brutality, nurturing relationships with lovers, parents, and children, yet not martyring themselves for others or for ideological causes.

The erasures of the past inherent in cycles of colonialism and revolution play out in the microcosms of family relationships in *Monkey Hunting*. There is a great deal of misery in the novel, which grows primarily out of the systematic forms of oppression it depicts, including slavery, indenture, and totalitarianism. In addition to the physical brutality of such subjugations, these systems of repression act like acid upon interpersonal connections, leading to blindly selfish behaviors such as parents abandoning their children. This in turn separates generations, thus obscuring the past on both a national and an individual level. These concerns can be seen in testimonials given by real Chinese laborers in Cuba. Lisa Yun notes that "broken family and social disintegration were major preoccupations in the testimonies," and that "the Chinese expressed grave concern over obligations to parents [and] children left behind" (Yun 2008, 99).

Many postcolonial critics have explored the links between family relationships and societal tensions. Frantz Fanon notes, "There are close connections between the structure of the family and the structure of the nation" (Fanon 1967, 141). He writes that a white child finds the same laws and principles of his society within his family. By contrast, for a black child, the values of his family are seen by the white world as abnormal, and so once he has contact with the white world, he must choose to reject either his family or his society. In *Carnal Knowledge*, Ann Laura Stoler seeks to understand "why connections between parenting and colonial power, between nursing mothers and cultural boundaries, between servants and sentiments, and between illicit sex, orphans, and race emerge as central concerns of state and at the heart of colonial politics" (Stoler 2002, 8). These critics draw attention to the ways that colonialism corroded or sought to control family relationships, a central concern of *Monkey Hunting*.

This theme of the erosion of family ties appears in the opening scenes of the novel. The story begins with a brief description of Chen Pan in China at the moment that he decides to indenture. A farmer with a wife, his crops have failed, and he is convinced by a recruiter to leave his family and indenture in Cuba. This man, dressed in a "Western-style suit and a ring on his little finger flecked with diamond chips" represents the influence of European imperialism and capitalism (García 2003, 5).[15] In China, the British attempted to avoid using paid professional recruiters in favor of voluntary recruiters, such as missionaries, in order to prevent fraudulent recruitment practices, though they were not always successful. By contrast, the private companies that recruited labor for Cuba or Peru were paid based on how many laborers they recruited, which often led to highly deceptive practices and even kidnapping. The man in the Western suit tempts Chen Pan with stories of mineral-rich drinking water that will make him twice as strong, beautiful Cuban women, warm temperatures, and easy wealth. Chen Pan agrees to indenture, imagining himself returning a few years later with wealth and status, bringing honor to his family. In fact, he is leaving forever his wife and his parents.

---

[15] Chen Pan's voyage further emphasizes the links between imperialism and capitalism. Though he is traveling to Cuba, a Spanish colony, he does so on a British boat. As Mark Tumbridge notes, British boats were allowed to carry laborers for rival empires in the interest of making a profit (Tumbridge 2012, 244).

The brutal conditions of Chen Pan's voyage indicate that the indenture of the Chinese in Cuba was only nominally different from slavery. The laborers suffer from hunger, cold, and thirst, and many die from illness and beatings, or commit suicide. The ship is "outfitted like a prison, with irons and grates," and, on board, the crew threatens the laborers "with muskets and cutlasses and rattan rods, shackled those whom the ropes didn't tame" (García 2003, 8). Lisa Yun notes that mortality rates on board these ships were actually higher than that of the African slave trade, between 12% and 30%, sometimes reaching as high as 50%, and that approximately 16,400 Chinese died on European and American coolie ships to Cuba (Yun 2008, 18). She describes the retrofitting that some ships underwent in order to transport laborers, making them very similar to slave ships: "The infamous iron hatch was utilized to imprison coolies below the deck and to insure the protection of the armed crew above. The hatches were symbolic of Chinese coolie traffic as pirated slave traffic" (Yun 2008, 27).

In these moments on the boat, as the nature of his indenture dawns on Chen Pan, we see his emerging sense of practical morality. This develops out of his reflections on the different worldviews of each of his parents. Even before his attempt at heroism, his father had been idealistic in the face of defeat. A poet and an educated man, he took the Imperial exams for 20 years, but failed to earn a post and was forced to be a farmer instead. Chen Pan's mother, though callous in response to her husband's death, raises a practical point in her dismissal of his heroism: "'What father leave his children nothing but his good reputation to eat?'" In his response to the harsh conditions on the boat, Chen Pan seems to combine the approaches of his parents, rather than dwelling on what he has lost. Like his mother, he has a sense of self-preservation: he determines that "he would survive unless someone managed to kill him" (García 2003, 15) and that if "any of the other city cocks so much as jostled his elbow, he would knock them unconscious with a blow" (García 2003, 12). Yet, he is also kind, like his father—when the ship's doctor cures him of a fever, he tries to pay the man with "one of his precious Mexican coins" (García 2003, 14).

On the plantation, there is even less distinction between indenture and slavery than on the boat. As noted earlier, bound Chinese laborers and enslaved Africans often worked side by side on the plantations. Chen Pan soon realizes that "he was in Cuba not as a hired worker but as a slave, no different from the Africans" (García 2003, 9). The labor is endless, the quarters where the laborers are locked in at night are filthy, laborers are whipped for defiance or even speaking their own language, and, as on the voyage, men, both African and Chinese, frequently commit suicide to escape their pain and humiliation. Sean Moiles notes that "the novel's portrayal of Chinese and African enslavement on a sugar plantation rejects the myth of pre-Castro Cuba as a prelapsarian paradise" (Moiles 2009, 181), drawing attention to García's fierce resistance to a nostalgic view of Cuban history.

In Chen Pan's early days on the plantation, we see him benefiting from his openness and generosity, particularly in the camaraderie he forms with the Africans. The other Chinese ridicule Chen Pan for this association, mocking the Africans with racialized insults. In spite of this, Chen Pan and the Africans become friends, and they share elements of their cultures with each other. The Africans offer Chen Pan the yams they roast, show him how to swing a machete, and give him healing leaves for his wounds when he is whipped. In exchange, Chen Pan teaches his friend Cabeza Chinese exercises to do in the morning in order to gather strength. Through this creolization and mutual friendship, a theme that continues throughout the novel, García emphasizes the benefits of solidarity between races.

While Chen Pan is generous with the other laborers, he is not subservient to the management. In a scene that gives the novel its title, he wins the admiration and gratitude of the Africans when he kills the cruel Creole overseer by hurling a rock at his head. Chen Pan's action echoes a similar moment back in China, when he threw a stone at a mischievous monkey who was gorging himself on the fruit from the family's kumquat tree and trying to mount the local dogs. The implication is that the overseer is no better than this monkey, stealing the labor of the workers and attacking the women. Chen Pan's act of violent resistance echoes real incidences of laborers overpowering and even killing managers. Lisa Yun notes that the laborers' "predicament of unending bondage combined with a high mortality rate led to the preponderance of explosive resistance and chaos" (Yun 2008, 174).

Chen Pan manages to escape into the woods, where he lives for nine months. This length of time hints at a rebirth, a theme that is strengthened by an owl that scolds him in the voice of his mother. Chen Pan attempts to appease the owl with offerings of food and shelter, demonstrating the guilt he feels for leaving his family and his inability to let go of his life in China. Finally, a near-death experience releases him from his nostalgic attachments to his past. He chops off his queue, the rope of hair that acts as "a definite signifier of Chineseness," thereby cutting ties to his former life in literal and figurative ways (Moiles 2009, 177). He leaves the jungle and becomes a success story, owning his own secondhand shop in Havana.[16]

Chen Pan's accomplishments come as a direct result of his ability to be simultaneously idealistic and realistic. He wins the protection of Count de Santovenia, a Spanish nobleman, by saving him from a bandit, which in turn allows Chen Pan to open his store. Chen Pan's decision to help the count, however, is a curious one. As a laborer, he killed a Creole overseer for his cruelty. Shortly before he rescues the count, he sees an overseer herding a chain gang of enslaved people through the streets of Havana. As he watches, he touches the knife in his jacket and thinks that the overseer's time will come. Yet, he rescues a count who leads a lavish lifestyle in a palace where he "once hosted a three-day feast that ended with a sunset ride in a gas-filled balloon" (García 2003, 64).[17] While de Santovenia may not have been directly involved in Chen Pan's suffering, as a planter, he was in a sense more responsible for the indenture system than the overseer who Chen Pan killed or the overseer in charge of the chain gang. If anything, one might expect Chen Pan to side with the bandit.

Sean Moiles argues that Chen Pan is influenced by his father's chivalry, which "provide memories that inspire Chen Pan's own heroic acts" (Moiles 2009, 173). Attempting to rescue a ten-year-old girl from rape, though, does not seem equivalent to saving a count who flaunts the wealth that he earned through the exploitation of his laborers. Chen Pan's motivations are not described, and so it is indeed possible that he aided the count out of a sense of honor and a desire to follow in his father's heroic footsteps. It also seems possible that Chen Pan made a calculated decision to help a man who could help him. This, then, could be seen as another combination of his father's model of idealism and his mother's sense of self-preservation.[18]

---

[16] Mark Tumbridge points out that Chen Pan's escape, success, and long life, like the success of Phularjee and Munshi Rahman Khan, are not the norm: "His eventual success is a departure from the everyday fight for survival of the majority of Chinese indentured labourers in Cuba" (Tumbridge 2012, 245). Lisa Yun notes that in the 1899 Census, only 13% of Chinese Cubans were listed as merchants, "while 73% remained day laborers and servants" (Yun 2008, 218).

[17] The Count de Santovenia was a real nobleman in Cuba, a planter named Nicolás Martínz de Campos, who bought the title of count in 1824 for somewhere between $25,000 and $30,000 (Thomas 1998, 142).

[18] When the story is passed on, these events change shape: Chen Pan's granddaughter, Chen Fang, is told that Chen Pan "became rich after saving a Spanish lady's honor, although he never succeeded in marrying her" (García 2003, 91), pointing to the quixotic nature of memory and the ways that history is shaped by what we want to remember.

With his wealth, Chen Pan is equipped to help others, as he does when he buys Lucrecia, an enslaved woman, and her son Victor from a man named Don Joaquín. We later learn that Lucrecia is actually Don Joaquín's daughter, that he had brutally assaulted her mother, and that he then assaulted Lucrecia after her mother's death. Slavery has perverted the ties of family to the point that Don Joaquín will not even acknowledge that Lucrecia is his daughter, strangling her and threatening to kill her when she calls him "Papa." When selling her to Chen Pan, Don Joaquín equates her with an animal: "'You can cancel the milkman with this heifer in the house…breed [her] with a few young bucks and populate your own plantation!'" (García 2003, 67). In contradistinction to this callous prediction, Chen Pan, Lucrecia, and Victor form a new kind of family, based on an equality of relations that none has yet experienced. Lucrecia demands that she purchase her freedom rather than letting Chen Pan free her outright, so he helps her find ways to support herself and is rewarded for his kindness. The two eventually become lovers, then husband and wife, and have three children together: Lorenzo, Desiderio, and Caridad.

Lucrecia's generosity and balanced worldview enable her to move beyond the traumatic experiences of her childhood, and she is perhaps the happiest character in the novel. She is deeply syncretic in her beliefs, borrowing from Christian, Santeria, and Buddhist traditions: "In her opinion, it was better to mix a little of this and that, like when she prepared an *ajiaco* stew…she lit a candle here, made an offering there, said prayers to the gods of heaven and the ones here on earth" (García 2003, 129). She refuses to pledge herself to just one, politely declining when Protestant missionaries attempt to convert her: "If she believed anything, it was this: Whenever you helped someone else, you saved yourself" (García 2003, 129). This philosophy directly contradicts that of Chen Pan's mother to "'avert your eyes to the sorrows of others and keep your own plates full'" (García 2003, 19).

Lucrecia finds a sense of belonging in her ties to her family and adopting Chen Pan's homeland as her own: "Sometimes Lucrecia questioned the origin of her birth, but she didn't question who she'd become…She was thirty-six years old and the wife of Chen Pan, the mother of his children. She was Chinese in her liver, Chinese in her heart" (García 2003, 138). Her attitude toward the fatal illness that she develops at age 48 reflects the peace of mind that she has achieved. While Chen Pan mourns, Lucrecia views it as a part of a cycle, requesting that she be buried in the garden to help the vegetables grow and urging Chen Pan to find another wife after she dies. She tells Chen Pan, "More than half my life has been happy...How many people can say that?" (García 2003, 180). The openness and kindness that she and Chen Pan demonstrate toward each other lead to a rewarding and long-lasting relationship, one of the few in the novel.

Although Chen Pan faces significant racism and hostility in his adopted homeland, he resists the lure of a nostalgic idealization of China. He longs to see his birth country, but he also recognizes the futility of trying to return to his home. One of his friends, Arturo Fu Fon, spends a great deal of time and money on a trip to China, but finds upon arrival that his whole family has died, and he immediately returns to Cuba. This, like the narrator's visit to India in *Jahajin*, underscores Stuart Hall's argument in "Cultural Identity and Diaspora" that members of a diaspora can never truly find the home that they left, because these places are constantly changing, rather than frozen at the moment of their departure (1990).

With Chen Pan's story, García draws clear connections between the family and the nation. The tragedies and joys of his family parallel his own involvement in Cuban struggles for independence and nationhood. Shortly after Chen Pan purchases Lucrecia and Victor, Victor succumbs to yellow fever, and Chen Pan is devastated. Victor's death coincides with the beginning of the Ten Years War (1868–1878), in which Cubans fought for independence from Spain. Chen Pan seeks solace in the revolution, buying 50 machetes and delivering them to Commander Sian, one of the 400 real Chinese who fought in the Ten Years War. Sean Moiles notes, "through the actions and reflections of Chen Pan, García inserts into historical narrative the Chinese contributions to anticolonial struggles in Cuba" (Moiles 2009, 174). After returning from this unsuccessful rebellion, he begins to build a new family with Lucrecia. Thirty years later, once he has formed a family, he longs to join the Cuban War of Independence, in which Cuba finally pushed out the Spanish, but settles for sending money to the rebels.[19] With such echoes between the events in Chen Pan's home life and the events in Cuba, García reminds us that the cruelty of repressive regimes filters into the most intimate of connections.

[19] Chen Pan makes his wealth by buying the furniture and goods of the Spaniards who have fallen upon hard times or who are fleeing Cuba, then selling those goods to other foreign clients. He thus supports the Cuban independence movement with money earned from the very people the rebels fight against. This, then, is another example of his pragmatic idealism—Chen Pan burns to aid the nationalist revolution but has the business acumen to take advantage of his opponents' weakness.

The second storyline of the novel follows Chen Fang, Chen Pan's granddaughter, and it takes place entirely in China. Chen Fang's performance of gender simultaneously demonstrates the fluidity of masculinity and femininity and the rigidity of gender roles in nineteenth-century China. Furthermore, her abandonment of her own child and the negative consequences that follow parallel the erasure of the past that occurs under the Chinese Cultural Revolution. Both events emphasize the devastating impact of blinding oneself to the past.

Chen Fang's narrative is the only one in first-person perspective, which gives her tale a sense of immediacy and intimacy. She tells her story from prison, a victim of Mao's attack on intellectuals. The first half of this section, in which she describes her childhood, is in past tense, whereas the second half is in present tense, capturing her miserable days in the jail cell and her reflections on what has come to pass. Her suffering thus has an endless quality, as though she always has and always will be imprisoned. We sense that Chen Fang is near death as she tells her story, giving it the feel of a testimonial, that she is bearing witness to the societal strictures that led her to this wretched position.

Chen Fang is Lorenzo's daughter, and part of the family Lorenzo started while visiting China to learn medicine. Lorenzo left his family to return to Cuba before Chen Fang's birth, an abandonment that has far-reaching repercussions. Chen Fang's mother, distraught at birthing a third daughter, chooses to raise her as a boy, supporting the view of gender as a social construct.[20] Chen Fang's childhood is one of relative freedom. Unlike her sisters, her feet are not bound, she is able to play in the fields instead of helping with domestic tasks like cooking and sewing, and Lorenzo believes that she is a boy and sends money for her education. She knows little of Cuba, having heard that it is a magical place with "fish that rained down from the sky during thunderstorms," and gold so plentiful it was used for "buttons and broom handles" (García 2003, 92). Included in this list of fantastic tales is that "in Havana, the women choose whom they want to marry and when," indicating that she finds it equally unbelievable that women would have this level of choice as that fish would fall from the skies (García 2003, 92). Chen Fang's set of fantasies about Cuba thus emphasizes the binding nature of women's roles in early twentieth-century China.

---

[20] Chen Fang's story shares many similarities with that of Lowe in Patricia Powell's *The Pagoda*, discussed in Chap. 4. The similarities between Powell and García's novels demonstrate a growing interest in challenging the view of gender as biological and drawing attention to the low status of women in nineteenth-century China.

Chen Fang's early happiness and freedom make it all the more painful when she is forced into the constricting role of wife and mother. When she is 16, World War I interrupts her father's remittances, and her mother must find a husband for her. Chen Fang says, "It was not easy to become a woman" (García 2003, 96), echoing Simone de Beauvoir's quote, "One is not born, but rather, becomes a woman" (Beauvoir 2011, 283). Chen Fang cannot cook or sew, and her mother-in-law criticizes her unbound feet, calling them "'clumsy hooves'" (García 2003, 96). She equates Chen Fang with a cow, as Don Joaquin did with Lucrecia; both Don Joaquin and Chen Fang's mother-in-law use insults that reduce women to their breeding capabilities. Chen Fang comes to feel that "There is no harder work than being a woman. I know this because I pretended to be a boy for so long" (García 2003, 96). Men, she says, hide their weakness, whereas "For women, there are no such blusterings, only work" (García 2003, 96). Years later, she attributes her life's uncertainty to her existence outside the structures of gender norms: "In China women do not stand alone. They obey fathers, husbands, and their eldest sons. I lived outside the dictates of men, and so my life proved as unsteady as an egg on an ox" (García 2003, 226).

Just as Lorenzo left his family to return to Cuba, Chen Fang ultimately abandons her own child to take a job as a teacher at a foreigners' school in Shanghai. She quickly regrets the decision to leave her son with her mother-in-law: "I thought I would be pleased to leave him, to seek my freedom. Instead I swallowed my bitter heart again and again" (García 2003, 100). This decision haunts her later, when she learns that her son has become a leader of the Cultural Revolution that persecutes her. Like Chen Pan and Lucrecia, Chan Fang finds temporary comfort in a relationship that rejects societal notions of who should love whom. Dauphine, a French woman who is temporarily living in China, connects her, not only to love and joy, but to her family in Cuba, as well. Dauphine has spent time in Havana and has photographs of the city, "including one of an old Chinese man in a doorway smoking an opium pipe," whom Chen Fang imagines knows her father or grandfather (García 2003, 141). These small moments seem to shorten the distance between China and Cuba and to offer the possibility of reforming ties with this side of her family.

Chen Fang's happiness is short-lived, though, pointing to the cyclical nature of trauma. Dauphine returns to France, and Chen Fang suffers under Mao's Cultural Revolution, which sought to root out bourgeoisie, traditional, and capitalist influences. Through Chen Fang's story, García depicts the inculcation of youth and the targeting of educational institutionsthat was a vital part of the Cultural Revolution. An army official comes into the school once a week and shouts at the students, "'You must plant gardens with bayonets!'" (García 2003, 227). Chen Fang is accused of being a foreign spy and a capitalist, and her students are encouraged to beat her and make accusations against her. She bemoans the mob mentality of the revolution, that the other teachers and her neighbors are quick to add allegations. She likens this to the old days, when millers blinded "the mules they used to turn their grindstones. Is this what we have become? A country of blind mules?" (García 2003, 228). The theme of blindness is further emphasized when she is placed in jail and the guards immediately break her glasses. These references echo the trope of vision that ties together all three storylines. Mao's persecution of the educated, an attempt to blind the Chinese people to all but his ideology, is similar to Chen Pan's mother's selfish admonition to "'avert your eyes to the suffering of others and keep your own plates full'" (García 2003, 19).

The party's attack on tradition also parallels the patterns of abandonment in Chen Fang's family. In the final scenes of her story, she is 72 years old and has been in prison for three years. Of the dehumanizing treatment she receives, she thinks, "These days, everything old is to be destroyed: old customs, old habits, old culture, old thinking" (García 2003, 228). This cutting of ties to the past resonates with her own cutting of ties to her son, which is made explicit when Chen Fang learns that her son has become an important party member. She has heard that he "made his reputation running an important southern province. A reputation, no doubt, built on corpses" (García 2003, 230). Had she raised her own son, the novel suggests, he would not have turned into such a monster. She considers using his name to escape the physical discomfort of her cell and her brutal interrogations, but fears that the repercussions might be severe. "What would become of him if it were known that his mother was a traitor? Would he have to shoot me to prove his allegiance to the Revolution?" (García 2003, 231). Her son's cruelty and the party's repression are both intrinsically tied to an erasure of the past.

Chen Fang's story ends with a flicker of hope that points to the importance of uncovering the buried past. She imagines that if she ever gets out of prison, she will travel to Havana and seek out her father. She will find a balcony and watch the rain "splattering the city, replenishing the sea," and then she will write a letter to her son in Shanghai (García 2003, 233). Her vision of her own replenishing, then, comes from reforming the severed connections with her father and son, connections that were both cut because she was born a woman, not a man.

The story of Domingo Chen, Chen Pan's great-grandson, is a final demonstration of the stubbornly pervasive nature of imperialism and racism. Pipo, Domingo's father, is part of the second family that Lorenzo started after returning to Cuba, and Pipo migrates with Domingo to the United States during the early days of the Cuban Revolution. Domingo's section of the novel opens with Domingo in his apartment, listening to the radio: "the bad news was blaring—subway decapitations and hijackings to Cuba and all the tragic state of Vietnam" (García 2003, 44). The news thus connects into a web of violence his current city, his homeland, and the nation that he will soon visit as a member of an invading army. The destructive experiences that Domingo has in each of these places tie them together into a critique of American neo-imperialism, as well as the repression of dissent that occurred during and after the Cuban Revolution.

As Domingo pours sugar into a pot of tea in his apartment in New York City, he contemplates the labor that went into it: "To work the sugarcane fields, his father had told him, was to go wooing mournful ghosts. The chain gangs of runaway souls, ankles ulcerated and iron-eaten and wrapped in rags. Or the luckier suicide ghosts who'd killed themselves dressed in their Sunday best" (García 2003, 49). The stories that have been passed down to Domingo capture with poetic accuracy Chen Pan's brutal experience of indenture, as depicted in the opening scenes of the novel. While Chen Pan's descendants do not face the same level of physical abuse as the indentured laborers, nor have they escaped racism or oppression.

As Domingo was growing up in Cuba, his mother supported the Cuban Revolution, while his father was loyal to the Americans. The enmity that developed between his parents acts as a condemnation of both nations. Domingo's mother blamed the Americans for the deformed babies she delivered, believing that the US Naval Base in Guantánamo Bay had polluted the Río Guaso, which irrigated the nearby fields. This in turn led to congenitally joined triplets, a baby with an eye in its umbilical cord, and a boy "whose heart had steamed furiously outside his chest. A moment later, his tiny heart had exploded in her face like a grenade" (García 2003, 206). The comparison of the baby's heart to a weapon of warfare emphasizes the constant threat of the American military presence. Pipo had no such hatred for the Americans and worked as a short-order cook in Guantánamo, a position that brought him negative attention from revolutionary leaders after the Cuban Revolution. When Pipo was arrested on charges of anti-revolutionary activity, his wife testified against him, a return to the theme of the corrosive effect of repressive political policies upon family ties. Pipo was placed in an insane asylum, where he was beaten and given electroshock therapy. The United States' aggressive incursion into Cuban affairs and the Cuban government's cruel treatment of American sympathizers are thus equally to blame for the destruction of Domingo's family.

Pipo's connections to the Americans eventually helped Pipo leave Cuba with Domingo, but the United States is no paradise for them. Domingo works long hours washing dishes in a restaurant, and his father struggles to find his place and overcome the trauma he has experienced. Pipo finally commits suicide one evening by jumping onto the subway tracks, challenging the view of America as a democratic refuge for those fleeing Latin American dictatorships. Domingo joins the American army shortly after his father's suicide, but he faces racial prejudice from the officers as well as the nurses who treat him when he is wounded in Vietnam.

Just as Domingo's childhood in Cuba acts as a critique of American involvement in Cuba, the cruelty and senseless violence that he witnesses in the Vietnam War is a condemnation of that neo-imperial offensive. The irrational, barbaric nature of the war is indicated at several points: a soldier named Lester Gentry machine guns an old woman and two small children, while a lieutenant interrogates a prisoner by "plung[ing] a knife into [his] thigh and slash[ing] him down to his knee" but gets no answers (García 2003, 111). Most of all, the insanity of the war is reflected when Domingo Chen's platoon is attacked by a gang of monkeys who bite and scratch him, then steal his flak jacket and his gun. The monkeys can be seen as a symbol of the Viet Cong fighters who, though fewer in number and less heavily armed than the Americans, used guerilla warfare tactics and persevered against the Americans in a war of attrition. The American military's blindness to this reality is represented by the major who refuses to believe Domingo's story.

Chen Pan's glasses, a symbol of clear vision, play a key role in this section of the novel. Domingo Chen keeps them in his flak jacket while he is in Vietnam and attributes to them his luck in surviving various close calls. Sean Moiles notes that throughout the novel, physical objects that have been passed down through generations have a positive impact on those who carry them: "García implies that these historical traces invite the imagination to search for possibilities outside the rigidity of top-down political, economic, social, and cultural systems" (Moiles 2009, 173).

However, Domingo's luck does not last forever, and he is injured by a land mine. In the recovery ward, he finds himself thinking of the advice of his father, Pipo, advice that had been passed down to him from Chen Pan: *"Don't watch with interest the suffering of others"* (García 2003, 151, emphasis original). Domingo finds himself struggling with this advice in the hospital ward: "Everywhere he looked, crisply gauzed catastrophes looked back" (García 2003, 151).

Domingo finds consolation with a prostitute named Tham Thanh Lan, but unlike the relationship between Chen Pan and Lucrecia, theirs is not an equal partnership. Tham Thanh Lan, like Lucrecia, is caught in a form of abusive, sexualized slavery. Her body has been colonized by a jealous general in the South Vietnamese army, who tattooed his identity numbers on her thigh, and she is scarred from where he penetrated her with his dagger. Domingo cannot fully liberate Tham Thanh Lan from this slavery, though. In part, this is because she depends on Domingo for financial stability, and in part because the American domination of Vietnam seeps into their interactions. Domingo takes over her life, moving into her apartment, sending away her other clients, and buying her "things she didn't need: hair curlers and a waffle iron, lemon-cake mix and a brand-new sewing machine" (García 2003, 204). Upon learning that Tham Thanh Lan is pregnant, he feels tied to her by a mixture of obligation and pleasure. He tells her he will marry her, but feels that he "needed to go away, to leave her like another country" (García 2003, 217). For him, she is tied to the trauma of the war, trauma that still haunts him.

In considering his options, Domingo thinks of the stories he has heard of American soldiers taking home Vietnamese fiancées or wives. He imagines these women attempting to assimilate by "bleaching their hair, wearing blue jeans and cowboy hats, renaming themselves Delilah," or, like Bibi in *Those That Be in Bondage*, "dressed up like China dolls at their husbands' insistence, paraded around small towns in Texas and Mississippi" (García 2003, 208) or even committing suicide. As he contemplates leaving Tham Thanh Lan, he equates a life with her to a life of bonded labor. He considers that when Chen Pan arrived in Cuba, the cost to buy eight years of bound labor was 150 pesos, and that in twice that time his son will be grown. He hides $1012, all his money, in her apartment and leaves, seemingly justifying his exit by buying his freedom. It is tempting to see similarities between this departure and the United States' withdrawal from Vietnam, which many South Vietnamese who had fought with the United States described as abandonment.

In one of the final sections of the novel, Lorenzo and Chen Pan take a train trip to Havana for the birth of Lorenzo's child, Pipo (who later becomes Domingo's father). The 17-hour voyage has a liminal quality, a sense of a time and space apart. The train scenes act as a web, pulling together the present and the past, and the three different storylines of the novel. Five generations of Chen Pan's family are present in these scenes in one form or another. On the train with him are his son Lorenzo and his grandson Meng, but other family members are in his thoughts. At one point, Chen Pan hears "a muted hooting, as if an owl were trapped among the luggage racks" (García 2003, 191), which harks back to the time he spent in the forest, followed by an owl that he believed to be the ghost of his mother. Later, he thinks hopefully of Chen Fang (who he believes to be male), "Perhaps one day the boy would come to Cuba and teach them all Chinese" (García 2003, 187), which connects to Chen Fang's own desire to travel to Cuba, meet her father, and learn Spanish. Even the unborn Domingo is present in a sense: Chen Pan falls asleep and dreams of the future, of the train turning into a plane, which can be seen as a premonition of the plane trip that Domingo and his father Pipo take to the United States.

These train scenes also draw together the racial groups of Cuba into a shared history. On the train itself, Chen Pen, Lorenzo, and Meng share a cabin with a Belgian couple and a Spanish bureaucrat, and Chen Pan sees Creole women in other cars. Notably, we do not see any characters of African descent on the train, pointing to the ongoing wealth inequality between the races, a legacy of colonialism and slavery. The Afro-Cubans certainly have a presence in the train scenes, though, as the trip occurs during the 1912 uprising, alternately called the Race War or the Armed Uprising of the Independents of Color. Protesting a law that effectively banned their political party, supporters of The Independent Party of Color, one of the first black political parties in the Caribbean, rebelled, attacking primarily foreign sugar mills and plantations.[21] The train ride takes place in the midst of this uprising, and García uses this moment to reflect on both the racialized stereotypes that maintain tensions between races, and the possibility for solidarity between members of oppressed groups.

---

[21] After two months, the Cuban army, bolstered by American marines sent to protect North American property, violently put down the rebellion, killing between 2000 and 6000 Afro-Cubans. Official Cuban sources put the number at 2000, but other sources estimate somewhere between 5000 and 6000. See Aline Helg's *Our Rightful Share: The Afro-Cuban Struggle for Equality, 1886–1912*, p. 225 (1995).

On the train, the Europeans and Creoles spread exaggerated rumors that the Afro-Cubans are preparing to slaughter every Creole in the country and "that a posse of *negros* had raped a schoolteacher in Ramón de las Yaguas and had partially cannibalized her flesh" (García 2003, 186). García is careful to contrast these reports with Chen Pan's more tempered view of the events. He dismisses the racist rumors, wondering, "How was it that fear so clotted rational thinking?" (García 2003, 187). In response to the violence that they witness outside the train, Chen Pan wants to explain to Meng "that *los negros* were protesting for their rights to form a political party, that they would pay for their protesting with their lives and the lives of many innocent others. What choice did they have? Revolutions never took place sitting quietly under a mango tree" (García 2003, 193–194). There is also an implied solidarity between the protestors and the Chinese former indentured laborers like Chen Pan. As the train passes fields of sugarcane, Chen Pan fantasizes about buying the plantation where he had been a laborer, a parallel to the Afro-Cubans' desire to take over or destroy the plantations.

The liminal space of the train also encourages Chen Pan to reflect on the diasporic citizen's quest for belonging. He wonders where his son Lorenzo is truly at home and concludes, "Lorenzo's skin, Chen Pan supposed, was a home of sorts, with its accommodations to three continents" (García 2003, 192). Just as Lucrecia experiences a sense of Chinese-ness bodily, in her heart and her liver, Lorenzo carries his sense of identity with him, equally Chinese, African and Cuban. Chen Pan, Lucrecia, and Lorenzo are able to find a sense of balance, between the cultures that are a part of them, and between idealism and practicality.

In spite of these hopeful moments, there is an element of bleakness in *Monkey Hunting*. Throughout the novel we see patterns of parents erasing connections with their offspring, or children cutting ties with their parents. Don Joaquin denies that Lucrecia is his daughter, Lorenzo leaves behind his Chinese family, Chen Fang abandons her son, and Domingo walks out on Tham Thanh Lan, who carries his child. These moves echo the erasures of the past and blindness to the present that occur on a national scale throughout the novel. China purges tradition and history in the Cultural Revolution, and Cuba creates an idealized version of the past in order to build nationalism during the Cuban Revolution. García also warns against the self-interested blindness of neocolonialism in America's aggressive protection of U.S. financial interests in Cuba and its involvement in and then abandonment of the conflict in Vietnam.

The cycles of trauma and domination that grow out of imperialism repeat throughout the novel, and it is certainly understandable that some of the characters, who are, as one critic put it, "beaten up by history" (Schuessler 2003) turn to nostalgia to escape their pain. Yet the characters who find the most happiness in the novel, Chen Pan, Lucrecia, and Lorenzo, are able to resist that nostalgia. They move forward with an open-eyed realism combined with a generous idealism. These characters acknowledge the traumas of the past and the present but hold on to a vision for the future.

Conclusion: Casting Off the Burden of Nostalgia

In *Futurity*, literary critic Amir Eshel examines fiction that, like *Jahajin* and *Monkey Hunting*, engages with the traumatic world events of the modern era and wrestles with "the sense of a world deprived of the future" (Eshel 2013, 3). Eshel argues that these novels open up a range of possible futures by beginning a conversation about what caused such catastrophic events and how to prevent them from recurring. While these texts "express uncertainty and skepticism about our ability to shape our future, they also examine the human action necessary to overcome this doubt" (Eshel 2013, 4). *Jahajin* and *Monkey Hunting* similarly express a sense of unease about the future, but open a conversation about the best way to achieve a future free of despotism. They recognize the persistence of culturally sanctioned violence against women, minority ethnic groups, and additional "othered" groups and note that these hostilities are fueled by selective blindness about individual and national history. Yet, as these texts indicate, individuals can combat such blindness, and rebellions, while often flawed, can succeed: the state-sponsored systems of indenture and slavery ended in the Caribbean, and Trinidad, British Guiana, and Cuba achieved independence. The key is to remain clear-sighted in the face of both triumphs and tragedy and to avoid the lure of nostalgia.

In *The Last Ship*, discussed in the opening of this chapter, Joan discovers that her paternal ancestors were not in fact aristocrats from North China, but Hakka from southern China, an ethnic group that Joan's paternal grandmother had frequently belittled. Far from being dismayed by this news, Joan finds it "a relief not to have to carry the burden of a fantastic myth, which, all along, had been a delusional lie" (Shinebourne 2015, 151). Joan finds symbolic release from this false past by throwing into the ocean the Chinese coins and seeds that had been passed down to her, and burning the mass-produced scroll of Emperor Chengzong's image in a monastery furnace. It is important to note that it is only the nostalgic view of history that Joan rejects; she still finds comfort in her connections to her maternal grandmother, Susan Leo. Though Susan had been scorned by the rest of Joan's family because of her poverty and her affinity for Indian men, she treated Joan with kindness and taught her that happiness could be found in even the simplest of lifestyles. This points to the necessity of recognizing patterns of blindness and repression, of exploring the past to better understand the present and consider ways to break such cycles in the future.

BIBLIOGRAPHY

Bahadur, Gaiutra. 2013. *Coolie Woman: The Odyssey of Indenture*. Chicago: The University of Chicago Press.
Boehmer, Elleke. 1995. *Colonial and Postcolonial Literature: Migrant Metaphors*. Oxford: Oxford University Press.
Boym, Svetlana. 2001. *The Future of Nostalgia*. New York: Basic.
Carter, Marina. 1994. *Lakshmi's Legacy: The Testimonies of Indian Women in 19th Century Mauritius*. Stanley-Rose Hill, Mauritius: Editions De L'Océan Indien.
De Beauvoir, Simone. 2011. *The Second Sex*. Translated by Constance Borde and Sheila Malovany-Chevallier. New York: Vintage.
Eshel, Amir. 2013. *Futurity: Contemporary Literature and the Quest for the Past*. Chicago: University of Chicago Press.
Fanon, Frantz. 1967. *Black Skin, White Masks*. Translated by Charles Lam Markmann. New York: Grove Press.
Faulkner, William. 2011. *Requiem for a Nun*. New York: Vintage Books.
García, Cristina. 1992. *Dreaming in Cuban*. New York: Knopf.
———. 1997. *The Agüero Sisters*. New York: Knopf.
———. 2003. *Monkey Hunting*. New York: Knopf.
———. 2007. An Interview with Cristina García. By Ylce Irizarry. *Contemporary Literature* 48 (2): 175–194.
Gopinath, Gayatri. 1995. 'Bombay, U.K., Yuba City': Bhangra Music and the Engendering of Diaspora. *Diaspora: A Journal of Transnational Studies* 4 (3): 303–323.
Hall, Stuart. 1990. "Cultural Identity and Diaspora." In *Identity, Community, Culture, Difference*, Jonathan Rutherford, 222–237. London: Lawrence & Wishart.

Helg, Aline. 1995. *Our Rightful Share: The Afro-Cuban Struggle for Equality, 1886–1912*. Chapel Hill: University of North Carolina Press.
Kakutani, Michiko. 2003. Historic Convulsions Seen in Personal Terms. *The New York Times*, June 24. https://www.nytimes.com/2003/06/24/books/books-of-the-times-historic-convulsions-seen-in-personal-terms.html.
Kandiyoti, Dalia. 2006. Consuming Nostalgia: Nostalgia and the Marketplace in Cristina García and Ana *Menéndez. MELUS* 31 (1): 81–97.
Look Lai, Walton. 1993. *Indentured Labor, Caribbean Sugar*. Baltimore: The Johns Hopkins University Press.
———. 2010. Asian Diasporas and Tropical Migration in the Age of Empire: A Comparative Overview. In *The Chinese in Latin America and the Caribbean*, ed. Walton Look Lai and Tan Chee-Beng, 35–64. Leiden: Brill.
Lowenthal, David. 1989. Nostalgia Tells It Like It Wasn't. In *The Imagined Past: History and Nostalgia*, ed. Christopher Shaw and Malcolm Chase, 18–32. Manchester: Manchester University Press.
Lysik, Marta. n.d. Multiple Trajectories of Slavery: Cristina García's *Monkey Hunting* as a Transnational Neo-Slave Narrative. https://www.academia.edu/511061/_Multiple_Trajectories_of_Slavery_Cristina_Garc%C3%ADa_s_Monkey_Hunting_as_a_Transnational_Neo-Slave_Narrative._.
Mahmud, Jafar. 2004. *Mahatma Gandhi: A Multifaceted Person*. New Delhi: APH Publishing Corporation.
Mohan, Peggy. 2001. Indians Under a Caribbean Sky. *India International Centre Quarterly* 28 (3): 3–13.
———. 2007. *Jahajin*. New Delhi: HarperCollins and The India Today Group.
———. 2010. Writing. *Jahajin*, July 12. http://peggymohan.blogspot.com/2010/07/writing-jahajin.html.
———. 2014. Interview with Alison Klein. August 17.
Moiles, Sean. 2009. Search for Utopia, Desire for the Sublime: Cristina García's *Monkey Hunting. MELUS* 34 (4): 167–186.
Nair, Rukmini Bhaya. 2008. Ladies Coop. *Outlook India*, March 31. https://www.outlookindia.com/magazine/story/ladies-coop/237061.
Pirbhai, Mariam. 2012. "Recasting Jahaji-Bhain: Plantation History and the Indo-Caribbean Women's Novel in Trinidad, Guyana, and Martinique." *Critical Perspectives on Indo-Caribbean Women's Literature*, Joy A. I. Mahabir and Mariam Pirbhai, 25–47. New York: Routledge.
Schuessler, Jennifer. 2003. Fantasy Island. *The New York Times*, May 18. https://www.nytimes.com/2003/05/18/books/fantasy-island.html.
Shepherd, Verene. 2002. *Maharani's Misery: Narratives of a Passage from India to the Caribbean*. Kingston: University of the West Indies Press.
Shinebourne, Jan Lowe. 2015. *The Last Ship*. Leeds: Peepal Tree Press.
Solbiac, Rodolphe. 2012. Revising Female India Memory: Ramabai Espinet's Reconstruction of an Indo-Trinidadian Diaspora in *The Swinging Bridge*. In

Critical Perspectives on Indo-Caribbean Women's Literature, ed. Joy A.I. Mahabir and Mariam Pirbhai, 229–252. New York: Routledge.

Stoler, Ann Laura. 2002. *Carnal Knowledge and Imperial Power: Race and the Intimate in Colonial Rule*. Berkeley: University of California.

Thomas, Hugh. 1998. *Cuba Or The Pursuit of Freedom*. Boston: Da Capo Press.

Tumbridge, Mark. 2012. *Indenture Wreathed in Opium: Asian Presence in the Caribbean – Literary Representations of Indo-Caribbean and Sino-Caribbean Subjects from the 19th Century to the Present*. PhD diss., University of Warwick, Coventry.

Ward, Abigail. 2013. Assuming the Burden of Memory: The Translation of Indian Indenture in Peggy Mohan's *Jahajin*. *The Journal of Commonwealth Literature* 48 (2): 269–286.

Wilson, Janelle L. 2005. *Nostalgia: Sanctuary of Meaning*. Lewisburg: Bucknell University Press.

Yun, Lisa. 2008. *The Coolie Speaks: Chinese Indentured Laborers and African Slaves in Cuba*. Philadelphia: Temple University Press.

CHAPTER 7

Conclusion: Loose Threads

May 30, 2015, marked the 170th anniversary of the arrival of the Fatel Razack, the first boat to bring Indian indentured laborers to Trinidad. Each year, Trinidad celebrates this date as Indian Arrival Day, marked by religious ceremonies, speeches from prominent Indo-Trinidadians, and street parades that include floats modeled after the Fatel Razack. Similar holidays exist throughout the Caribbean: in Guyana, May 8 marks the beginning of Indian immigration in 1838, while in Suriname June 5 commemorates the 1873 arrival of Indians.

Chaman Lal, a Hindi professor at Jawaharlal Nehru University in India, suggests that these colonies should be placing more emphasis on Deliverance Day: January 1, 1920. This was the day that indentured labor came to a complete stop, and Lal equates it with Emancipation Day for enslaved Africans. He writes: "Indians in these countries never focused upon Deliverance Day, which is [a] much more historic day of their life... than so called Indian Arrival Day, which is the day to mark the beginning of untold sufferings, deceit" (Lal 2011).

Lal does not speculate on possible reasons for this focus on Indian Arrival Day as opposed to Deliverance Day, but I would argue that celebrating Arrival Day serves a few important functions. If we focus, as Lal does, on May 30 as the beginning of 75 years of exploitation and suffering, then all the more reason to remember this moment in order to prevent similar forms of abuse. At the same time, celebrating the arrival of

© The Author(s) 2018
A. Klein, *Anglophone Literature of Caribbean Indenture*,
New Caribbean Studies,
https://doi.org/10.1007/978-3-319-99055-2_7

Indians, as well as laborers from other nations, emphasizes their own agency in the story of indenture and highlights their contributions to Trinidad, Guyana, Suriname, and other former colonies, contributions that are often overlooked in the history of the Caribbean. Deliverance Day, by memorializing the end of British Imperial indentured labor, emphasizes the system that denigrated the laborers, rather than the laborers themselves—the choice they made to undertake a life-changing journey, the suffering they experienced, and the role they played in shaping the societies that they joined.

The narratives discussed in this book, like the observance of Arrival Day, act as a reminder of the abuses of empire and a testament to the suffering of the laborers, but also a celebration of their lives and stories. While Cristina García's *Monkey Hunting* offers a stark tale of the brutality of indenture, it also depicts a laborer resisting and escaping that brutality. In an interview, the former laborer Maharani tells of the field labor that was too much for her and of the pressure to marry, but also of how she defied that pressure. We see examples in these narratives of laborers fighting against racialized, gendered forms of oppression in highly public ways such as strikes and lawsuits against employers, and in more individualized acts, such as women leaving abusive husbands.

The issues raised in these narratives are strikingly relevant today, as contemporary forms of migrant labor abuse continue to rely on racialized and gendered views. Women, especially those in poverty, are particularly vulnerable to systems of human trafficking and sexual exploitation, as they were under the institution of British indenture. Author and activist Siddharth Kara interviewed Maya, a Nepalese woman whose parents, desperate for money, sold her to an agent on the promise that she would get a good job. The agent then sold her to a trafficker, who in turn sold her to a brothel in India. Maya says, "The *malik*[1] told me I owed him thirty-five thousand rupees [\$780], and I must have sex with any man who chooses me until this debt is repaid" (Kara 2009, 19). She eventually escaped and, at a shelter, learned that she had contracted HIV. When the shelter contacted her father, he told her not to come home: "He said I can never be married and because I have HIV, I can only bring shame" (Kara 2009, 20). The combination of Maya's gender and economic destitution made her a prime target for the sex trade, while her father's emphasis on honor and the implied blame that he places upon her indicate that women

[1] Brothel boss.

continue to be held responsible for the ills that befall them, particularly those related to sexual assault.

It may be comforting to believe that these kinds of things happen elsewhere, but these exploitations occur close to home, as well. Journalist John Bowe describes the experiences of a Thai man named Intajak (name changed), who paid a recruitment fee of $11,700 in exchange for a three-year contract job in the United States. After Intajak arrived in the United States, a representative of Global Horizons, the company that recruited him, took him to an apple orchard, where his passport was confiscated. Over a few months of working in this orchard, Intajak came to realize that, while he was paid minimum wage, there was no guarantee of steady hours, and he could be sent back to Thailand if his employers were unhappy with him. Bowe writes, "If the work ran out, or if he did anything to displease his bosses, he'd have no way to pay off the $11,700 he'd borrowed. Ever" (Bowe 2010).

Intajak was then sent to a pineapple plantation in Hawaii, where the pay was better, but the conditions more brutal. A Global Horizons agent carried a gun, a knife, or a baseball bat; beat one of Intajak's coworkers; and threatened to deport the workers if they didn't meet their quota. The workers slept in the dirt next to the parking lot in order to meet the van that would take them to work at 4:30 A.M., and their food rations were often insufficient or of poor quality. Intajak eventually ran away through the cane fields in a dramatic escape akin to Chen Pan's flight from the plantation in *Monkey Hunting*. Intajak says: "'I was sweating like crazy, and it was muddy and slippery...I really had no idea what was going to happen, or if I'd make it, or what would happen if I got caught'" (Bowe 2010). He managed to escape to Los Angeles, where he lives under an assumed name for fear of reprisal.

On March 19, 2014, a federal judge found Global Horizons liable for the abuse of its workers. In her decision, Judge Kobayashi said, "Global Horizons exploited the enormous debts the Thai workers incurred to pay the recruitment fees...Global Horizons specifically chose Thai workers based on a stereotype that Thai workers would be more compliant and less likely to escape or cause other problems" (EEOC v Global Horizons, Inc. 2014, 13–14). The mistreatment and racialized views of these workers are remarkably similar to the mistreatment and racialized views faced by Chinese and Indian laborers under the British imperial system of indenture, suggesting that we have not escaped these abusive labor practices and stereotypes.

Intajak and Maya's stories echo in troubling ways the narratives of indenture described in this book. The systems of migrant labor that exist today continue to exploit workers in many of the same ways as imperial indenture: utilizing debt bondage, taking advantage of those in economic need, incorporating racialized and gendered notions of labor, and even relying on technically legal but highly deceptive contracts and recruitment practices, as Global Horizons did. As in many forms of abuse, understanding and awareness have been crucial to the abolition of this exploitation. It was through the reports of men like Intajak that Global Horizons was held accountable for its crimes, just as the testimonials of laborers in the nineteenth and twentieth centuries helped bring to an end the imperial systems of indenture.

These narratives act as a window into the political views of the time and reveal the insidiousness of the hierarchies of gender, ethnicity, and class in rhetoric by both the dominant and oppressed groups. I focus on these hierarchies in the hopes that drawing attention to them will help to challenge remnants of imperial and indenture ideology in the Caribbean. These include the societal acceptance of domestic abuse, the assumption of a link between class and character, and tensions between Caribbean citizens of African, Indian, and Chinese descent. As I note in my fourth chapter, racial tensions still infiltrate political discourse in the Caribbean, and violence against women is disturbingly common.

We also see lingering attitudes of empire in contemporary rhetoric about indentured labor. In 1987, historian Basdeo Mangru published an essay titled "The Problem of Indian Wife Murders," in which he investigates the high rates of Indian women killed by their partners on the estates. His findings support the view that women, either by their presence or by their absence, were the source of the problem. For example, he blames the frequent relationships that developed between the British managers and the female laborers on the (lack of) Indian women's clothing: "One could hardly fail to visualize the problems inherent in a situation where Indian women, by their mode of dress, seemed to reveal to estate subordinates 'more physical charm' than what they had been accustomed to in Britain" (Mangru 2005, 36). He also argues that if colonial officials had recognized migrant marriages, potentially disloyal women would have been forced to stay with their husbands: "The refusal to recognize the validity of Indian marriages solemnized in accordance with custom and religion tended to weaken the marriage ties and facilitate the desertion of unfaithful wives to form new matrimonial connections" (Mangru 2005, 35).

These statements ignore the colonizers' brutalizing treatment of both male and female laborers, which modeled relationships of dominance and violence, as well as the very valid reasons women may have had for leaving their husbands, such as physical abuse. That a scholar working 70 years after the end of indenture would make such arguments suggests that imperial rhetoric, such as the scapegoating of women in discussions of contract labor, may be harder to escape than we imagine.

The novels, autobiographies, poems, and interviews that record the experiences of indentured laborers in the Caribbean help shed light on how such systems develop and the rhetoric that perpetuates them. Earlier authors such as Edward Jenkins and A.R.F. Webber, even when criticizing aspects of indenture, lay the blame on certain characteristics of the system rather than the practice of bonded labor. By contrast, contemporary authors Dabydeen and Sharlow openly criticize imperialism and indenture as exploitive systems, drawing attention to the vulnerability of the laborers and the wealth that colonizers gained from the immigrants' toil in the name of civilizing barbaric races. While Dabydeen and Sharlow are concerned with sexualized form of exploitation that women laborers experienced, they do little to challenge the patriarchal assumptions that lead to such exploitation, such as the view of women as representatives of nationhood. Female authors García and Mohan further expand fictional representations of indenture, depicting aspects of the system that have previously received little attention. These include women traveling alone, Chinese laborers, and the impact of indenture on generations of Caribbean men and women. The poetry of indenture reflects a shift from nationalist views of women migrants as birthing the land in both literal and figurative ways to a more intimate desire to connect with female ancestors in order to strengthen a sense of belonging. The autobiographies of Munshi Rahman Khan and Alice Singh, and the interviews with Maharani, Doolarie, and Achamma highlight the extent to which a laborer's class and gender shaped his or her experiences and perceptions of indenture.

It is unsurprising that there should be drastic differences between authors writing from such varying times and subject positions, but what is startling is the similarities of the authors' concerns. All of the texts emphasize the suffering that the laborers experienced, including those works by writers who supported empire, such as Jenkins and Rahman Khan. The narratives detail crushing hours and work tasks, substandard living conditions, deceptive labor practices, managers abusing their power, corporal punishment, and the generally precarious existence of the laborers, particularly women. The recognition of these circumstances, even in texts that supported empire, underscores the severity of conditions that many of the laborers experienced.

Gender also emerges as a central issue in each of the indenture narratives, as authors explore the ways that the gender disparity both improved and inhibited women's lives. Jenkins and Dabydeen portray the domestic abuse that was distressingly prevalent among the laborers, while Mohan shows that women migrants may have gained some agency, traveling alone, earning wages, and supporting themselves and their family. The interviews and autobiographies demonstrate the ways that women's metaphoric role shapes their material existence, as in extensive legislation around immigrants' marriages.

Equally vital to these narratives are issues of race and class. Interestingly, all of the fictional texts feature interracial, interclass relationships, indicating a flexible notion of kinship. Chaps. 2 and 3 of my book examine a relationship forming between a British manager and an Indian woman, but similar interactions appear in the other novels, as well. *Jahajin* depicts a Canadian woman from a wealthy family becoming involved with a working-class Indian man, while *Monkey Hunting* describes a Chinese man marrying a formerly enslaved African woman. Even the nonfiction texts include examples of such relationships. The persistence of this trope suggests that these relationships were and continue to be a source of tension for citizens of the Caribbean. At the same time, images of such relationships may offer a ray of hope, the promise of solidarity between people of different ethnic and class backgrounds.

It is my hope that the topics discussed in this book will open up areas for further investigation. There are many questions yet to be answered in the study of gender and race in indenture. For example, what does the changing role of the women who migrated teach us about how gender relations were influenced by colonialism, and how rapidly gender roles are shaped by societal factors? What do family and intimate metaphors mean for those who were in the periphery of empire versus those who were in power? How do the performance of masculinity and femininity manifest at different points in indenture narratives, and how do these performances intersect with race and class? What is the role of literature in understanding the abuses of the past and trying to prevent such abuses in the present?

I focus on texts dealing directly with Caribbean indentured labor, but broader exploration of indenture narratives may help us answer these questions. For instance, there have been no comprehensive studies of the literature of indenture in other British colonies. These include Totaram Sanadhya's indenture autobiography, *My Twenty-One Years in Fiji* (1991), and novels about contract labor in Mauritius, such as Deepchand Beeharry's *That Others Might Live* (1976) and the more recent *Sea of Poppies* by Amitav Ghosh (2008). An examination of these texts and the characteristics of the locations that produced them would lead to a deeper understanding of the function of gender and race within empire, and the impact of indenture across the British colonies. Fiji did not have the same history of imported slave labor as the Caribbean, as British rule in Fiji began in 1874, 40 years after Britain abolished slavery in its colonies. Native Fijians refused to work on cotton and sugarcane estates, and so indentured laborers were brought in, first from nearby islands such as the New Hebrides, and then from India. With these historical differences in mind, it would be interesting to consider how representations of interactions between native Fijians and indentured laborers differed from representations of former slaves and indentured laborers in Caribbean colonies.

Another worthwhile area of study would be the comparison of the literature of British Imperial indenture to texts about other indenture systems. William Moraley's autobiography, *The Infourtunate*, published in 1743, chronicles the experience of an Englishman indenturing in Pennsylvania and challenges the view of bound labor as an exclusively nineteenth-century system of Indian and Chinese migration (2005). Laure Moutoussamy's 2007 novel *Le "Kooli" de morne Cabri*, which tells the story of Indian indenture in Martinique, a French colony, could offer insights into how European imperial systems of indenture overlapped and differed.

It is critical that we pay attention to the lessons of these narratives. While contemporary institutions of human trafficking are not state sponsored in the same way as British imperial indenture, many governments facilitate such practices. All of the members of the Gulf Cooperation Council, including the United Arab Emirates (UAE) and Qatar, utilize the *kafala* system of migrant labor, in which private individuals sponsor migrant workers, mostly from India, Bangladesh, and Pakistan. The punitive laws limiting the rights of these migrants, combined with the privatized nature of the system, leave the laborers vulnerable to all kinds of abuse. In 2014, *The New York Times* reported on the exploitation of the migrant laborers who built the Abu Dhabi campus of New York University (NYU). Workers went on strike in 2013 to protest unfair employment practices, including 12-hour days, low pay, confiscation of their passports, and paying recruitment fees that were never reimbursed. The UAE government discourages such dissent—strikes are illegal and there is little legal recourse to laborers for contract violations. In response to the strike, the police arrested, beat, and then deported the strikers. While NYU had set forth a "statement of fair labor values" in order to protect the workers who built the Abu Dhabi campus, they did not monitor the pay or the conditions of the laborers (Kaminer and O'Driscoll 2014), and so both the UAE and the United States are complicit in the mistreatment of these workers.

The conditions under which migrant laborers are building the stadium for the 2022 World Cup in Qatar are infamous. Speaking about the intense pace of construction required to build the stadiums before 2022, and seeming to disregard concerns that have been raised about violations of the workers' human rights, architect Albert Speer Jr. said, "'Major events like the Olympics or the World Cup make the unthinkable thinkable. There are no taboos'" (Smoltczyk 2012). The Human Rights Watch estimates that hundreds of construction workers have died while building the stadium, most likely from heat exposure (Human Rights Watch 2017). Both the numbers and the causes of death are uncertain, though, due to the lack of transparency of the Qatari government. Laws were enacted in the UAE in 2015 and Qatar in 2016 in an attempt to curtail the mistreatment of laborers, but significant abuses remain. For example, the 2018 Human Rights Watch Report notes that "current heat protection regulations for most workers in Qatar only prohibit outdoor work from 11:30 a.m. to 3 p.m. from June 15 to August 31. But climate data shows that weather conditions in Qatar outside those hours and dates frequently reach levels that can result in potentially fatal heat-related illnesses without rest" (Human Rights Watch 2018).

Journalist Cynthia Gorney notes that "migration for better opportunity is as old as human history, but today it's likely that more people are living outside their countries of birth than ever before" (Gorney 2014). Within this massive labor migration, indentured servitude persists in various forms around the globe. Fictional and nonfiction narratives of indenture, such as the ones explored in this book, help us to understand how these abusive systems of labor develop and are perpetuated, and help make such practices "taboo." It is my hope that focusing on the rhetoric around Caribbean indenture will help us recognize the ongoing effects of indenture in that region but also the exploitative nature of various modern-day forms of labor around the globe.

Bibliography

Beeharry, Deepchand. 1976. *That Others Might Live*. New Delhi: Orient Paperbacks.
Bowe, John. 2010. Bound for America. *Mother Jones*, May/June. https://www.motherjones.com/politics/2010/04/immigration-law-indentured-servitude/.
EEOC v Global Horizons, Inc., 11-00257 LEK. (The United States District Court for the District of Hawaii 2014).
Ghosh, Amitav. 2008. *Sea of Poppies*. New York: Picador.
Gorney, Cynthia. 2014. Far From Home. *National Geographic*. January. https://www.nationalgeographic.com/magazine/2014/01/.
Human Rights Watch. 2017. Qatar: Take Urgent Action to Protect Construction Workers, September 27. https://www.hrw.org/news/2017/09/27/qatar-take-urgent-action-protect-construction-workers.
———. 2018. Qatar: Events of 2017. https://www.hrw.org/world-report/2018/country-chapters/Qatar.
Kaminer, Ariel and Sean O'Driscoll. 2014. Workers at N.Y.U.'s Abu Dhabi Site Faced Harsh Conditions. *The New York Times*, May 18. https://www.nytimes.com/2014/05/19/nyregion/workers-at-nyus-abu-dhabi-site-face-harsh-conditions.html.
Kara, Siddharth. 2009. *Sex Trafficking: Inside the Business of Modern Slavery*. New York: Columbia University Press.
Lal, Chaman. 2011. Celebrate 'Indian Arrival' or 'Indian Deliverance'? *The Guardian*, October 25. http://www3.guardian.co.tt/news/2011/10/24/celebrate-indian-arrival-or-indian-deliverance.
Mangru, Basdeo. 2005. *The Elusive El Dorado: Essays on the Indian Experience in Guyana*. Lanham: University of America.
Moraley, William. 2005. *The Infortunate: The Voyage and Adventures of William Moraley, an Indentured Servant*. University Park: The Pennsylvania State University Press.
Moutoussamy, Laure. 2007. *Le 'Kooli' de morne Cabri*. Matoury: Ibis Rouge.
Sanadhya, Totaram. 1991. *My Twenty-One Years in the Fiji Islands; And, The Story of the Haunted Line*. Edited by John Dunham Kelly and Uttra Kumari Singh. Suva, Fiji: Fiji Museum.
Smoltczyk, Alexander. 2012. 2022 World Cup in Qatar: The Desert Dreams of German Architect Albert Speer. *Spiegel Online*, June 1. http://www.spiegel.de/international/spiegel/german-architect-albert-speer-plans-for-the-2022-world-cup-in-qatar-a-836154.html.

Index[1]

A
Abolitionists, 127
Aborigines Protection Services, The, 65
Achamma, 26, 36
  marriage of, 41, 51, 54
  migration of, 37, 40–41, 53, 259;
  labor of, 43
  See also Oral narratives
Achebe, Chinua, 149
Africa
  nations of, 7, 55
Africans
  as critical to Caribbean identity, 83
  depictions of, 13, 62–63, 72, 92–93, 92n12, 112, 119, 164, 218
  See also Africans, enslaved; Creole, people; Laborers, African
Africans, enslaved, 131n16, 161, 207
  Emancipation Day, 255
  and indentured laborers, 4, 7, 131n16, 207, 208

  narratives of, 16
  See also Laborers, African; Laborers, enslaved
Afro-Caribbean, 4, 22, 113
  Emancipation Day, 255
  and family, 130
  stereotypes, 98–99
  in *Those That Be in Bondage* (Webber), 91n10
  See also Africans
Afro-Cubans, 218–219
  See also Africans
Afro-Guyanese, 72, 121, 139, 168n14
  See also Africans
Afro-Trinidadians, 132
Agüero Sisters, The (García), 201, 204
  See also García, Cristina
Ahmad, Aijaz, 12
Aji culture, 151
Alcalá, Roberto del Valle, 137
Alienation, 148–150, 166, 171
Ali, Khalil Rahman, 95

---

[1] Note: Page numbers followed by 'n' refer to notes.

© The Author(s) 2018
A. Klein, *Anglophone Literature of Caribbean Indenture*, New Caribbean Studies,
https://doi.org/10.1007/978-3-319-99055-2

Allegory, 12
Allende, Isabel, 120
Altruism, 205, 210
Anarchy of Empire in the Making of U.S. Culture, The (Kaplan), 11
Ancestors
　female, 14, 18–19, 146, 150, 155–156, 165–166, 171, 176, 177, 199–200, 259
　in novels, 19, 105–106, 182, 185, 197–198, 200
　in poetry, 9, 18–19, 146, 150–152, 156, 177
　See also specific works
Anti-colonialism, 17, 48, 122
　and marriage, 41
　and women, 3, 48–49
Arkatis, 29, 29n3
Atteck, Helen, 12, 97
　See also Bound for Trinidad, An Historical Novel
Authenticity, 163
Autobiography, 16, 17, 31–32, 259–261
　of women, 33, 186
　See also Autobiography of Alice Bhagwandy Sital Persaud (Singh, Alice); *Autobiography of an Indian Indentured Labourer* (Khan); *Interesting Narrative of the Life of Olaudah Equiano, The*
Autobiography of Alice Bhagwandy Sital Persaud (Singh, Alice), 17, 26, 43–46
　gender in, 33–34
　See also Singh, Alice
Autobiography of an Indian Indentured Labourer (Khan), 16, 17, 20, 26, 29–32, 51–52, 186
　See also Khan, Munshi Rahman
Awoonor, Kofi, 149

B

Bahadur, Gaiutra, 44n11, 81, 114, 140, 182, 191–192
　Coolie Woman, 9, 182, 200n11
Bain, Kimberly, 134
　See also "Journey Across the Black Waters" (Bain)
Baksh, Anita
　on Mahadai Das, 157
　on "Per Ajie," 152
　on Singh, Rajkumari, 151
　on "They Came in Ships," poem, 160
Barbados Slave Code of 1661, 28
Beaumont, Joseph, 48, 65, 75
Beauvoir, Simone de, 213
Beecher Stowe, Harriet, 66
Beeharry, Deepchand, 20, 261
Bennett, Louise, 151
Bermuda, 28
Bhojpuri, 186, 190–191, 197
Birbalsingh, Frank, 123, 126
　on "Incarnation on the Caroni" (Manoo-Rahming), 173
Boehmer, Elleke, 184
"Boodhoo" (Mendes), 1–3
Bound for Trinidad, An Historical Novel (Atteck), 12, 97–99
Bowe, John, 257
Bragard, Veronique
　on "Ode to My Unknown Great-Great Grandmother" (Manoo-Rahming), 171
　on "They Came in Ships," poem (Das), 160
Brahmin, 34, 37, 39, 69, 123–125
　See also Caste; Religion, Hindu
Brathwaite, Kamau, 151
Brereton, Bridget, 177
Brighter Sun, A (Selvon), 20, 105n4
Britain, 6–7, 17–18, 29, 55, 122
　and China, 134, 138, 207–208
　colonization of Guyana, 122

INDEX   237

colonization of India, 122
exploitation of India, 104, 109, 167
as savior of India, 17, 104
slavery and, 65
British, depictions of, 72, 73, 77, 83, 126–129, 132, 134, 139, 172
British Guiana
   A. R. F. Webber in, 79–80
   British Guiana Immigration Ordinance, 1891, 81
   indentured laborers in, 42–43
   indenture in, 60, 61, 65, 67–69
   indenture legislation, 40, 45–46, 52
   in indenture literature, 13, 108
   Popular Party, 80
   Ruimveldt Riots, 62
   social hierarchies in, 79
   violence in, 69
   women murdered, 47
   See also Coolie, His Rights and Wrongs, The (Jenkins); *Guyana*; *Lutchmee and Dilloo* (Jenkins); *New Overseer's Manual* (Pearson); *Those That Be in Bondage* (Webber)
British imperialism, 3, 4, 12, 14, 38, 62, 64, 67, 126
   as beneficial, 74–75, 83, 86
   and Chinese, 134
   as civilized, 112–113
   as civilizing force, 66, 71, 73
   effect on Indian economy/social structure, 66, 67
   and feudalism, 67
   as feudalism, 108, 125
   and gender, 135–136
   Government of India Act of 1858, 69
   and India, 69
   in India, 125–126
   Indian Rebellion of 1857, 69
   justification for, 69, 127
   law in, 118–119
   as mutually beneficial, 127
   and patriarchy, 136
   Permanent Settlement Act of 1793, 66–67
   social hierarchies in, 85
Burnham, Forbes, 148, 157, 157n6, 163
   and National Security Act, 157n6
Burton, Antoinette, 33
Busha, 175
   See also Overseers

C
"Caged Soul" (Manoo-Rahming), 150
"Cane Piece Blues" (Lee), 174–177
   alienation in, 149, 150, 174
   ancestors in, 176, 177, 184–185, 199
   nationalism in, 175–176
   reception of, 174
   sugarcane in, 174–175
   women in, 150, 175–176
   See also Lee, Easton
Cannadine, David, 85
"Can the Subaltern Speak" (Spivak), *See* Spivak, Gayatri
Capitalism, 12, 67, 201
   "Beyond the Push and Pull Model," 67
   and imperialism, 206n15
Caribbean, 3, 137
   as birthplace of British imperialism, 65
   ethnic groups, 5
   independence of, 176
   postcolonial, 173
   post-independence movements, 146
Carnal Knowledge (Stoler), 11, 63, 206
   See also Stoler, Ann Laura
Carter, Marina, 27, 28, 50, 52n20, 114, 189

"Cast Aside Reminiscent Foreheads of
    Desolation" (Das), 158–160
  See also Das, Mahadai
Caste
  codified, 26
  in "Coolie Son" (Dabydeen),
    168–169
  erasure of, 39
  high, 12, 15, 37
  in India, 67, 108–109, 120,
    124–125, 195–197
  and *kala pani*, 10
  low, 37, 165
  untouchable, 124, 125
  in "Untouchable, The" (Dabydeen),
    169n15
  of women, 42, 44–45, 53
  See also Brahmin; *individual classes*
*Centenary History and Handbook of
  British Guiana* (Webber), 81
Césaire, Aimé, 184
Chamberlain, Mary, 130
Chengxun, Li, 38, 39
Chen, Willi, 20
Children
  abandonment of, 212–214, 217, 219
  as burden, 175
  and death, 13
China
  and Britain, 133, 138, 207
  gender roles in, 134–136, 182–183,
    203, 212–213, 212n20, 213
  indenture from, 31, 38, 39, 49,
    134–135
  indenture system, 134, 203, 207
  migration from, 135, 201n12,
    202–204, 206
  pre-Cultural Revolution, 204
  See also Chinese Cultural
    Revolution; "Journey Across
    the Black Waters" (Bain);
    Laborers, Chinese; *Last Ship,
    The* (Shinebourne); *Monkey

    Hunting* (García); *Pagoda, The*
    (Powell); Women, Chinese
Chinese-Caribbean, 20–21, 174
  ancestry of, 150
  poets, 145
  reaching across boundaries, 174
  women, 140
Chinese Cultural Revolution, 200,
  212–214, 219
Chitnis, Varsha, 27
Christianity, 6, 127, 128
  and imperialism, 38, 66, 69, 73
Civilization, 21–22
  marriage and, 55
  stagist view, 7, 55
Colonial
  legislation, 28
  paradigms, 176
Colonial anxiety, 17, 26–27, 47–48,
  52, 62–63, 84
  and intimacy, 63, 76
  Lutchmee and Dilloo (Jenkins) and,
    69
  See also Women, single
Colonial Desire (1995), 11
Colonialism
  abuses of, 123
  as beneficial, 17, 62, 79, 85, 91, 127
  and brutality, 12
  as civilizing influence, 12, 18, 27,
    60–61, 64, 69, 96–97, 126
  critique of, 120–121
  economic need, 127
  and gender, 3
  gender roles and, 260
  rationalization for, 127
  resistance to, 128, 137
  and women, 147
Colonial Question, The (Jenkins), 78
Coolie, His Rights and Wrongs, The
  (Jenkins), 2, 65, 67–69, 68n3,
  71n4, 71n5, 74–75
  See also Jenkins, Edward

INDEX 239

"Coolie Mother" (Dabydeen), 167–168
Coolie Odyssey (Dabydeen) collection, 162–163, 169
  Small, Jean on, 163
"Coolie Odyssey," poem (Dabydeen), 162–167, 172
  alienation in, 165–166
  ancestors in, 163–167, 185
  kinship in, 167
  women in, 162–165
Coolies and Cane (Jung), 9
  See also Jung, Moon-Ho
"Coolie Son" (Dabydeen), 168–169
Coolie Speaks, The (Yun), 9
  See also Yun, Lisa
Coolie Woman: The Odyssey of Indenture (Bahadur), 9, 182, 200n11
  See also Bahadur, Gaiutra
Corentyne Thunder (Mittelhölzer), 20, 61, 86
Counting House, The (Dabydeen), 107–122
  ancestors in, 105–106, 184–185
  as anti-colonial, 122
  as anti-national romance, 120
  class hierarchy in, 112–114
  colonial officials in, 118–119
  critical reception of, 108
  degradation of women, 113, 122–123
  domestic abuse in, 113
  ethnicity in, 116, 118–120
  female protagonist in, 106
  fractured timeline of, 14, 183
  gender in, 104
  Indian characters in, 123
  intimate relationships between English men/Indian women, 104, 139
  racial hierarchy in, 112–113, 118
  racial stereotypes in, 118–119
  sexual assault in, 114–116
  sexuality in, 112
  structure of, 14, 108–109
  women, abuse of, 113
  women in, 107, 140, 187–188
  See also Dabydeen, David
Creole, language, 36
  in David Dabydeen's poetry, 167
  Guyanese, 167
Creole, people, 9–10, 218–220
  depictions of, 84
  See also Cultural hybridization
Crosby, James, 25, 26
Cuba
  Armed Uprising of the Independents of Color, 218–219
  Chinese laborers in, 36, 38–40, 201–202, 209n16
  Cuban War of Independence, 211
  human trafficking in, 49, 135, 207
  literature of indenture, 4, 9, 200–201
  postcolonial, 204
  Race War, 218–219
  racial groups in, 218
  slavery in, 38, 39, 202–203, 207–208, 218
  Ten Years War (1868–1878), 211
  See also *Coolie Speaks, The* (Yun); *Dreaming in Cuban* (García); *Monkey Hunting* (García)
Cuban Revolution, 200, 211, 215–216, 219
  and America, 215–216
  Chinese contribution to, 211
  Cuban War of Independence, 211
Cudjoe, Selwyn, 64, 80, 80n7
Cultural hybridization, 9–10, 20, 21
  See also Creole, language; Creole, people; Race, mixed
Culture, evolution of, 7
Curry Flavour (Manoo-Rahming), 170

D
Dabydeen, David
  and ancestors, 146, 151, 152, 163, 171, 172, 176, 177, 183, 185, 259, 260
  background of, 121, 162
  "*Coolie Odyssey*," poem, 163–171
  and *Counting House, The*, 18, 64, 104, 107, 109–110
  Creole, 168, 168n14
  criticism of imperialism, 4, 12, 105–106, 108–109, 113, 118–120, 123–124
  on decolonization, 121n12
  in England, 148
  and Guyana, 120n11, 121, 169
  on India, 109–110
  and introduction to *Lutchmee and Dilloo* (Jenkins), 69, 73
  and lineage, 150
  mother of, 163n11
  poetry of, 8, 146, 161–170, 174; ancestors in, 146–147, 150; "Coolie Mother," 168; "Coolie Son," 168; "*Slave Song*," 162n10; "Untouchable, The," 169n15
  See also "Coolie Mother"; *Coolie Odyssey* (Dabydeen) collection; "Coolie Son"; *Counting House, The*
Das, Mahadai, 146–147, 158, 170
  ancestors, 14, 173
  background of, 156–157
  "Cast Aside Reminiscent Foreheads of Desolation," 158–160
  feminism of, 157
  "For Maria De Borges," 169, 169n16, 170; women's bodies in, 170
  gender and, 157
  on Guyana, 177
  I Want to Be a Poetess of My People, anthology, 156–158
  and Messenger Group, 156
  nationalism of, 10, 14, 19, 145, 146, 150, 156–159, 162, 166
  poems of, 147–148, 156–162
  "They Came in Ships," poem, 159–162; reception of, 159
  on women's bodies, 145–148
Decolonization, 121n12, 177
De Lisser, H.G., 93
Deliverance Day, 255–256
Des Voeux, William, 65, 96, 161–162
  hearings of, 94
Diaspora, 10, 13, 149, 163
  and dissolution of culture, 116
  double diaspora, 148–149
  embodied, 219
  gendered, 197
  postcolonial, 147
  See also specific countries
Diaspora, African, 131
Diaspora, Chinese, 4, 19–21, 27–28, 134–135, 176, 201–202, 206, 207, 210–211
Diaspora, Indian, 4–5, 21, 27–28, 129, 131, 152, 154, 166, 171, 176, 197, 202
Diaspora, South Asian, 28
  See also Diaspora, Indian
Domestic violence, 15, 21, 48–49, 54, 159
  in *Counting House, The* (Dabydeen), 113–114
  and gender imbalance, 5, 21, 93, 97, 113, 123, 140, 159n8, 191, 199, 258, 260
  in Guyana, 140

and marriage legislation, 27–28, 47, 52, 55, 136
and migration, 41
in *Silent Life, A* (Shah), 199
in *Swinging Bridge, The* (Espinet), 199
"wife murder," 48
Doolarie, 17, 21, 26, 36, 37, 42, 259
and domestic violence, 48–49, 54–55
marriage of, 50–51
See also Oral narratives
Dougla poetics, 9–10, 146
See also Cultural hybridization; Oral narratives
Douglass, Frederick, 16
Dreaming in Cuban (García), 201, 203

E
Education, 45, 86
of laborers, 16, 45, 55, 86, 190
of women, 5, 35, 45
Elect, The (Sharlow), 123
Emancipation Day, 255
Empire, *see* Imperialism
Equiano, Olaudah, 16, 31
See also Interesting Narrative of the Life of Olaudah Equiano, The
Eshel, Amir, 220
Espinet, Ramabai, 10, 182, 199
See also Swinging Bridge, The
Ethnicity, 6, 21, 134
and solidarity, 116, 117, 119–120, 131
tensions between, 116, 138
See also Race

F
Family, 3–4, 10–11, 130
effect of indenture on, 206
effect of repression on, 211
erosion of, 206–207, 216, 219

and slavery, 210
See also Kinship
Family Love in the Diaspora (Chamberlain), 130
See also Chamberlain, Mary
Fanon, Frantz, 81n8
on families, 206
Faruqee, Ashrufa, 52, 74–75, 94
Female, *see under* Women
Feminism, 3, 10, 64
post-indentureship, 10
Fertility, 146, 154, 156, 158, 165, 170, 172, 173, 175–177
Fiji, 260–261
Folklore, 187–188, 197
Foucault, Michel, 11, 108
Frere, William, 25
Friendship, 129–132
Fumagalli, Maria Cristina, 137
Futurity (Eshel), *see* Eshel, Amir

G
Gandhi, 196
García, Cristina, 3, 14, 19, 182, 184–185, 201, 259
Agüero Sisters, The, 201
background of, 200
on Cuba, 204–205
Dreaming in Cuban, 201
on family and nation, 211
Monkey Hunting, 3, 4, 14, 19, 176, 182–184, 200–220
nostalgia, 204
See also Agüero Sisters, The; *Dreaming in Cuban*; *Monkey Hunting*
García Márquez, Gabriel, 120
Gautam, Mohan, 32, 41
Gender, 18, 21, 33, 34, 129–131, 136n18, 260–261
and colonialism, 42, 260–261

Gender (*cont.*)
  imbalance of, 5, 6, 31, 61, 90,
    93–95, 97, 135, 159n8,
    201–202
  and land, 147
  oppression, 183
  ratio between men and women, 61
  and sexual assault, 21, 128–129
  as social construct, 212
  and violence, 258
Gender Negotiations among Indians in Trinidad, 1917–1947, 9
  See also Mohammad, Patricia
Gender roles, 5, 9, 31, 45, 48, 49, 55,
    110–111, 163, 194–196,
    199–200, 212–213, 260
  in China, 182, 212–213
  defiance of, 53–55, 114, 132–133,
    137, 159n8
  economic impact of, 189
  in *Jahajin* (Mohan), 185–186
  masculine, 193
  and migration, 6, 9
  and violence, 5–6
Genealogy, 146
  See also Chinese-Caribbean, ancestry of; Kinship
Ghosh, Amitav, 20, 261
Gladstone, John (historical), 107, 117–118
Global Horizons, 257–258
  See also Human trafficking
Globalism, 148, 177
Gopinath, Gayatri, on diaspora, 197
Gorney, Cynthia, 262
Government of India Act of 1858, 69
Gowricharn, Ruben, 31
Gramaglia, Letizia, 147
  on Mahadai Das, 157–159
Guantánamo Bay, 204, 215
Guha, Ranajit, 66
Guiana, 65

Guiana 1838: The Arrival, film (Jagessar), 139
Gulf Cooperation Council, 261
Guyana, 4–5, 14, 19, 31, 45, 120n11,
    121, 149, 162, 177
  abuse of women, 140, 159
  colonization by Britain, 122
  decolonization of, 121, 147
  Domestic Violence Act, 21, 140n20
  Human Rights Report, 2016, 140
  as husband, 159
  independence of, 80; Cuffy, 161;
    poetry of, 146
  nationalism in, 121
  National Security Act, 157n6
  People's National Congress (PNC),
    147–149
  politics of, 169
  postcolonialism, 157
  socialism, 149
  unrest in, 162
  women murdered, 140
  workforce, 140, 140n19
  See also British Guiana

H
Haggard, Henry Rider, 147
Haitian Revolution, 105n3
Hall, Stuart, 83
  on diaspora, 211
  "Negotiating Caribbean Identities," 83
Harris, Wilson, 91
Head, Bessie, 149
Heath, Roy, 20
  Shadow Bride, The, 20, 55, 65–66
Hegel, Georg Wilhelm Friedrich, 7
Hierarchy, 85
  legislation of, 26
  in literature of indenture, 12
  pervasiveness of, 17

racial, 63
seductiveness of, 62
social, 85–86
Hierarchy of class, 2, 12, 42, 44, 53, 55, 260
  in India, 253–254
  legislation of, 55
  in literature of indenture, 113, 120, 258–259
  and marriage, 55
  See also Caste
Hierarchy of gender
  in literature of indenture, 12, 61, 62, 139, 192, 258–259; India, 197; in Trinidad, 193
  See also Gender roles; Women, single
Hierarchy of labor, 8, 92–93, 98, 120
Hierarchy of race, 7, 12, 21–22, 63, 116, 177, 258–259
  damage of, 8
  as justification for indenture/slavery, 6, 55, 61
  legislation and, 55
  in literature of indenture, 70, 73, 78, 82, 86, 92–93, 92n12, 94, 98, 99, 113
  in Trinidad, 193
  See also White supremacy
History of Mary Prince (Prince), 29
Hoefte, Rosemarijn, 49, 51
Homophobia, 137
Homosexuality, 214
Hosein, Gabrielle Jamela, 10, 146
Hosein, Shaheeda, 39, 114
Human Rights Watch, 262
Human trafficking, 7, 256–258, 261
  malik, 256
  in the United States, 257–258
  See also Prostitution

I
"I am a Coolie" (Singh, Rajkumari), 151–152
Ideology, imperial, 3, 6, 11, 14, 22, 60, 64, 132, 206n15, 259
  abuses of, 256
  as beneficial, 13, 38, 47–48, 76
  benefits of, 86
  British, 61–62, 65
  and capitalism, 206n15
  as civilizing, 112–113, 259
  as civilizing force, 17–18, 66
  of colonizer-colonized relationship, 73–77
  critique, 18
  as damaging, 13
  defiance of, 136–137
  as destructive, 107
  and emigration, 126
  as evil, 126
  as exploitative, 259
  gender, 21
  gender ideologies, 21
  hierarchies, 3, 72
  as indifferent, 122
  justification for, 28, 63, 76
  legislation of, 28
  and marriage, 41
  and patriarchy, 136
  persistence of, 258
  resistance to, 54–55
  romanticized, 69
  and sexual relationships, 63
  See also Hierarchy; Hierarchy of class; Hierarchy of gender; Hierarchy of race
Immigration, see Migration
Imperial anxiety, 15, 27, 62
  See also Laws; Women, single
"Incarnation on the Caroni" (Manoo-Rahming), 3, 170–174
  ancestors in, 172–174

"Incarnation on the Caroni" (*cont.*)
kinship in, 10
See also Manoo-Rahming, Lelawattee
Indentured Labor, Caribbean Sugar (Look Lai), 9
See also Look Lai, Walton
Indenture, literature of, 1, 4, 7–9, 9n2, 19–21, 64, 182, 201–202, 259–261
and ancestors, 8, 14, 18–19, 105–106, 146, 151–158, 162–169, 176, 177, 182–183, 259
anti-colonial, 3, 18–19, 177
anti-national romance, 121, 177
autobiography, 16, 259, 261
Chinese, 20–21, 150, 200
hierarchy in, 12
Indian, 20, 150
by men, 14
narratives, 11, 17, 68, 187, 198; of women, 187–188
non-fiction, 17
novels, 8, 261
persistence of, 257–259, 262
poetry, 8, 18–19, 150–152, 259
post-colonial, 4
and race, 104
by women, 6, 14–15, 19, 62, 76, 113
Indenture, system of, 4, 18–20, 70–71, 78, 175, 259, 261
abolition of, 258
as beneficial, 68, 84
and British economy, 6, 65
British outlawing, 105
brutality of, 6
Certificate of Exemption from Labour, 37
China, 4, 9, 18, 20, 25, 134–135, 138, 174, 181, 202
as civilizing, 6
as civilizing mission, 6, 11, 38, 55, 63

contracts, 132, 189, 202, 257–258
as controversial, 105
criticism of, 259
and deception, 15, 37, 38, 65, 97, 126, 134, 165, 207
as destructive, 1–3
economic pressure, 37, 41
end of, 133, 256 (*see also* Deliverance Day)
as exploitative, 104
and family relationships, 206
gender oppression, 183
and gender roles, 5, 260
generational impact, 1–2, 183, 200, 259, 261
Gulf Cooperation Council, 261
kafala, 261
and labor shortage, 72
ongoing, 257
as positive, 4
recruiters for, 97
resistance to, 88, 256
role of, 260
ships of, 207
and slavery, 4, 7–8, 128, 139
violence in, 13, 183
women, 190; as doubly marginalized, 140
Independence movements, 184
See also Political movements; Political parties
India
and British imperialism, 69, 104
colonization by Britain, 122
culture of, 172
exploitation of, 104
famine, 67
as father, 159
feudalism in, 67
Government of India Act of 1858, 69
as idyllic, 109–110, 124, 196
Indian Rebellion of 1857, 69
in *Lutchmee and Dilloo* (Jenkins), 109

nationalism, 196
Permanent Settlement Act of 1792, 17, 66–67
postcolonial, 197
poverty in, 109
Indian Arrival Day, 173, 255, 256
Indian Emigration Act of 1883, 37, 40
Indian Rebellion of 1857, 69, 110
Indians
  and Caribbean identity, 83
  Caribbean population of, 31
  characterization of, 86–87, 90, 123
  education of, 86
  indenture, 9, 20, 21
  migration, 5
  nationalists, 137
  stereotypes of, 119
  textile market, 125
Indo-Caribbean, 5, 6, 17, 21, 187
  and *aji*, 151
  ancestors of, 150
  indenture of, 199
  literature, and *aji* culture, 151
  poets, 145
  in Trinidad, 173
  weddings of, 46
  women, 140
  See also Indians
Indo-Guyanese, 19, 21, 34, 114, 121, 139, 148, 152, 167
  depictions of, 167–170
  in "Per Ajie" (Singh, Rajkumari), 152–155
  women, 156–159
  See also Indians
Indo-Trinidadians, 187, 191
  See also Indians
Infourtunate, The (Moraley), 261
Interesting Narrative of the Life of Olaudah Equiano, The (Equiano), 16, 31
  See also Equiano, Olaudah
Intimacies of Four Continents, The (Lowe), 9, 63

See also Lowe, Lisa
"I See Bent Figures" (Singh, Rajkumari), 155
  ancestors in, 155–156
  labor, 154–156
  laborers bodies in, 155
  nationalism and, 156
  point of view of, 155
  See also Singh, Rajkumari
I Want to Be a Poetess for My People, anthology (Das), 156, 157
  indenture in, 157
  nationalism in, 157

J
Jackson, Joseph, 147
  on Mahadai Das, 157, 162
Jagan, Cheddi, 121
Jagessar, Rohit, 139
Jahahji-hood, 10
Jahaji bhai, 130
Jahaji-bhain, 187
Jahajin, 130, 199–201
Jahajin (Mohan), 19, 111n7, 176, 182, 185–199
  ancestors in, 183–189, 194, 197, 198, 200
  as auto-ethnography, 185–186
  diaspora in, 211
  female solidarity in, 187–188
  gender roles in, 186–189, 193–196
  generational violence in, 199
  hierarchy in, 197
  hierarchy of race in, 193
  indentured women in, 187
  marriage in, 194–196, 198
  and nostalgia, 186, 189–191, 194, 196–200
  oral narrative and, 186
  sexual assault in, 191–194
  textiles in, 196

Jamaica, 4, 10, 18, 21, 147–150
  Chinese music in, 10
  indenture, 4
  Jamaican Labour Party, 148
  in literature, 4, 133
  People's National Party, 148
  political violence, 148, 148n1
  post-colonial, 147–148
Jameson, Fredric, 12
Jane's Career (De Lisser), 93
Jenkins, Edward
  background of, 61, 64, 66
  and British empire, 11, 62, 66, 69, 78, 84, 104, 122, 259
  Colonial Question, 78
  and *Coolie, His Rights and Wrongs, The*, 65, 67, 68n3, 71n4, 71n5, 75
  criticism of indenture, 75, 77–79, 94n14, 259
  Ginx's Baby, 79
  and *Lutchmee and Dilloo*, 8, 13, 17, 69, 70, 104, 105, 109, 111, 126, 259, 260
  on relationships between British men/Indian women, 75
  support for indenture, 4, 13, 15, 63–64, 70, 72, 73, 91
  and violence, 111, 259
  See also Coolie, His Rights and Wrongs, The; *Lutchmee and Dilloo*
"Journey Across the Black Waters" (Bain), 13, 134
Jung, Moon-Ho, 9

K
Kafala, 261
Kakutani, Michiko, on *Monkey Hunting* (García), 203
Kala pani, 44, 146, 155, 160, 165, 171

  in "Incarnation on the Caroni" (Manoo-Rahming), 172
  ships, 207
Kala pani discourse, 10
Kandiyoti, Dalia, on *The Agüero Sisters* (García), 204
Kaplan, Amy
  Anarchy of Empire in the Making of U.S. Culture, The, 11
Kara, Siddarth, 256
Khan, Munshi Rahman, 12, 15–17, 26, 29, 33, 36, 186, 259
  caste and, 44
  education of, 29, 30, 39
  emigration of, 41
  on European women, 44–45, 47n17
  gender roles and, 54
  indenture of, 29–31
  marriage of, 41, 51, 52, 54, 55
  poems of, 30
  See also Women, laborers, in *Autobiography of an Indian Indentured Labourer* (Khan)
King Solomon's Mines (Haggard), 147
Kinship, 4, 19, 130, 206–207
  across time, 9, 10, 20
  of Chinese migrants, 205–206
  flexibility of, 260
  longing for, 167
  non-traditional families, 129
  past, 183
  poetics of, 3, 19, 146, 183
  in *The Swinging Bridge* (Espinet), 11
  See also Jahajin (Mohan)

L
Labor
  gendered, 110–111, 258
  systems of, 7, 55
  wage, 55–56, 62
Laborers

abuse of, 114, 175, 189, 207, 256–260
bodies of, 155
as children, 74–75
commodification of, 77–78
dehumanization of, 128, 160
education of, 16
exploitation of, 108, 120, 167
as men, 16
post-indenture, 130
power of, 192–193
ratio women to men, 201
recruitment of, 206–207
resistance by, 128, 208, 256
seasonal, 175, 176
suicide of, 134, 208, 215
unbound, 117
work of, 71n5, 155–156, 165, 181
Laborers, African, 12, 68
enslaved, 65
See also Africans, enslaved
Laborers, Chinese, 9, 12, 19, 21, 25, 26, 36–38, 63, 97–98
abuse of, 38–39, 202, 207, 215
broken families of, 205
contribution to Caribbean, 10
deception of, 134
dehumanization of, 133–134
education and, 39
and enslaved Africans, 207
marginalization, 20
migration, 5
music, 10
in poetry, 188
recruitment of, 206–207
return of, 133, 134, 174, 202, 211–212
and slavery, 4, 202–203
See also Monkey Hunting (García); *Pagoda, The* (Powell)
Laborers, enslaved, 260–262
and indentured Chinese laborers, 38, 39
rights of, 29
in Suriname, 31
Laborers, Indian, 4, 9, 13, 19, 20, 60, 62–66, 111, 190, 201–202
abuse of, 68
caste of, 125
depictions of, 13, 119–120
descendants of, 154–155
exploitation of, 106
in poetry, 146
resistance by, 69
sexual abuse of, 74
See also Jahajin (Mohan); Kinship
Laborers, Thai, 257–258
Laborers, women, 62, 188, 191
bodies of, 170
economic freedom of, 160
exploitation of, 176, 177, 259
financial independence of, 160, 260
independence of, 111, 160
as land, 147–148
as scapegoats, 6, 259
sexual assault of (*see* Sexual assault)
suffering of, 259–260
Labor shortage, 72
Lal, Chaman, 255
Language
English, 190
Hindi, 190
Last English Plantation, The (Shinebourne), 20
Last Ship, The (Shinebourne), 176–177, 181–182
ancestors in, 220–221
Laws
Barbados Slave Code of 1661, 28
British Guiana Immigration Ordinance, 1891, 81
codification of hierarchies, 27
Commission of Inquiry into the Treatment of Immigrants in British Guiana, 1870, 25
Domestic Violence Act (Guyana), 22

Laws (cont.)
Immigrants' Marriage and Divorce Ordinance, 1881 (Guyana), 52
to impose values, 26
National Security Act (Guyana), 157n6
Lazarus, Neil, 149–150
Ledent, Bénédicte, 137
Lee, Easton, 10, 18, 20, 21, 146, 177
background, 174–176
"Cane Piece Blues," 150, 174–176
poetry of, 174–176; "Cane Piece Blues," 174–175; *From Behind the Counter*, 174
in US and England, 148
Lee-Loy, Anne-Marie, 10, 20, 136
on Lee, Easton, 174
Le 'Kooli' de Morne-Cabri (Moutoussamy), 20, 261
Lineage, 146
See also Kinship
Lloyd, David Lloyd, 81n8
Look Lai, Walton, 9, 67, 126, 134
See also Indentured Labor, Caribbean Sugar
Lowe, Lisa, 9, 63
See also Intimacies of Four Continents, The
Lowenthal, David, on nostalgia, 185
Low, Gail, 108–109
Lutchmee and Dilloo (Jenkins), 8, 12, 65–79
as anti-national romance, 121
as critique of indenture system, 63, 69–73, 78–79
depiction of India, 109
feminism in, 64, 74
hierarchies in, 62, 63, 70
hierarchy of race in, 72–74, 76–77, 84
inspiration for, 66, 68
as justification for imperialism, 64–67, 69, 72–73, 75–76, 95, 104, 122

as justification of indenture system, 76
as novel of purpose, 66–67
on planters, 93
as pro-colonialist, 122
recruiters in, 126
as response to colonial anxiety, 69–70
structure of, 14
as supportive of imperialism, 13, 18, 61
See also Jenkins, Edward
Lysik, Marta, on *Monkey Hunting*, 203

M
MacDonald, Scott B., 170
Mahabir, Joy
on "Incarnation on the Caroni" (Manoo-Rahming), 172
on "Ode to My Unknown Great-Great Grandmother" (Manoo-Rahming), 171
Mahabir, Noor Kumar, 36, 37
Maharani, 26, 36–37, 43, 50, 53–54, 103, 140, 256, 259
defiance of gender roles, 53, 55, 103
and domestic violence, 48, 54
erasure of, 104
labor of, 43–44
marriage of, 49
migration of, 40
oral narrative of, 36–37, 40, 43
Maharani's Misery (Shepherd), 192
Malik, 256
Mangru, Basdeo, 258
Manoo-Rahming, Lelawattee, 3, 8, 14, 18–19, 146, 170–171, 176, 177
alienation of, 170, 172
ancestors, 14, 146, 171, 177, 185
background of, 170–171
in Bahamas, 148
"Caged Soul," 150
Curry Flavour, 170

"Incarnation on the Caroni," 172; ancestors in, 172–173; Indian culture in, 172; matriarchy in, 173
Indo-Caribbean roots of, 148
and lineage, 149–150
"Ode to My Unknown Great-Great Grandmother," 171–172
poetry of, 170–174
Mármol, José, 120
Marriage, 15, 17, 19, 25–55
and anti-colonialism, 41
as beneficial to women, 28, 29, 49–50, 88
as bondage, 217
bounty system for, 42
in British Guiana, 45
in "Cast Aside Reminiscent Foreheads of Desolation" (Das), 159
Christian, 52, 55
as civilizing, 27, 55
and class, 55
class differences, 54
between colonizer and colonized, 88–89
as control, 26, 39
and education, 45
forced, 204
See also Marriage, legislation of
Marriage, legislation of
Barbados Slave Code, 1661, 28
Immigrants' Marriage and Divorce Ordinance, 1881, 52
Indian Emigration Act of 1883, 37, 39
interethnic, 89, 260
in *Monkey Hunting* (García), 210
Muslim, 52, 55
pressure, 50–52
and race, 55
and religion, 15, 45–47, 52, 55
and slavery, 28–29

See also Laws
Martinique, 261
Marx, Karl, 77
Masculinity, 127
performance of, 260
Matikor ceremony, 186
Mauritius, 20, 27–28, 42, 50, 53, 261
bounty system of, 42
status of women in, 52n20
women laborers in, 51
Mawby, Spencer, 148n1
McClintock, Anne, 6, 147
on *King Solomon's Mines* (Haggard), 147
McKay, J. D., 69
McNeil-Lal Report of 1915, 110
Mehta, Brinda, 10, 146, 151–152
on "Caged Soul" (Manoo-Rahming), 150
on "For Maria De Borges" (Das), 169n16
on "Per Ajie" (Singh, Rajkumari), 152
Men
African, 63
bodies, 145
European, 62
Indian, 63; emigration of, 41–42; and protection of women, 48–49, 49n19
as laborers, 16
and protection of women, 49
Messenger Group, 156
Migrant workers, 261
human rights of, 262
mistreatment of, 262
Migration, 262
between 1838 and 1918, 4
of Chinese, 4–5, 134, 137–138, 176, 201–202, 207
and gender, 5, 9, 39, 41
of Indians, 4, 67, 126, 134, 176, 201, 255

Migration (*cont.*)
  mortality rates of, 207
  narratives, 68–69
  ships, 203n15
  of women, 190–191
  See also Diaspora; Diaspora, African; Diaspora, Chinese; Diaspora, Indian; Kala pani
Mill, James, 29
Misogyny, 113, 132, 164, 212
Mitchell, Robert, 40
Mittelhölzer, Edgar, 20, 61, 86
Mohammad, Patricia, 5, 36, 50, 61, 164n12
  and *Gender Negotiations among Indians in Trinidad, 1917–1947*, 9
Mohan, Peggy, 14, 19, 111n7, 182, 184, 203–204, 259
  background of, 186
  "Indians Under a Caribbean Sky," 191n6
  on postcolonial Trinidad, 204
Mohanty, Chandra, 111
Moiles, Sean, on *Monkey Hunting* (García), 203, 204, 208, 211, 216
Monkey Hunting (García), 3–4, 14, 19, 176, 182–184, 200–220
  altruism in, 205, 210, 216
  Chinese Cultural Revolution in, 212–214, 219
  Creole people in, 218–220
  critical reception of, 203
  Cuban independence and, 211
  Cuban Revolution, 219
  diaspora in, 219–220
  family in, 214, 216, 219
  gender in, 214–215
  gender roles in, 212–213
  generations in, 203–204, 218
  indenture and slavery in, 206–207
  marriage in, 210, 212, 217
  minimalism of, 203
  nostalgia in, 204–205, 208, 220
  pragmatic idealism in, 207, 208, 211n19
  racial solidarity in, 208, 260
  racism in, 215, 216
  religion in, 210
  sexual assault in, 210
  suicide in, 216
  time in, 203
  trauma, cycles of, 200
  trauma in, 213, 216, 217, 220
  United States in, 216
  Vietnam War in, 217
  vision in, 205, 214, 216
  women in, 202n13
  See also García, Cristina
Monkeys, 188n4, 208
  as Viet Cong, 216
Moraley, William, 261
Morton, Sarah, 111–112
Moutoussamy, Laure, 20, 261
Muslim, 25
Mythologies of Migration, Vocabularies of Indenture (Pirbhai), 9, 123
  See also Pirbhai, Mariam
My Twenty-One Years in the Fiji Islands (Sanadhya), 48, 261

N
Naipaul, Shiva, 105
Naipaul, V.S., 32, 105
Nair, Rukmini Bhaya, on *Jahajin* (Mohan), 185
NAR, *see* National Alliance for Reconstruction, Trinidad
Narain, Denise deCaires, 147
  on "Cast Aside Reminiscent Foreheads of Desolation" (Das), 159
  on Mahadai Das, 156, 157
Narratives
  hierarchies, 12

indenture, 69
 as interpretation, 36
 slave, 16
 and violence, 13
 written *vs.* oral, 35–36
 See also Indenture, literature of
National Alliance for Reconstruction (NAR), Trinidad, 131–132
Nationalism, 13, 81n8, 84, 120, 154, 156, 170, 175, 177
 in "Cast Aside Reminiscent Foreheads of Desolation" (Das), 159
 emerging, 13
 and fertility, 146, 154, 156, 158, 175, 177
 in indenture poetry, 155
 in India, 196
 and patriarchy, 136
 poetry of, 156–158
 and women, 146–147, 177, 259
Nationalist movements, 13
Neo-colonialism, 121, 121n12, 121n13
Neo-imperialism, 200, 215, 216
Nettleford, Rex, on *From Behind the Counter*, 174
New Overseer's Manual (Pearson), 69
New Slavery, The (Beaumont), 65
New York University, 261–262
 Abu Dhabi campus, 261–262
Non-fiction, 15, 17
Nostalgia, 183–184, 183n2, 184n3, 200, 204, 221
 of colonialism, 13–14
 in Cristina García's novels, 204
 cultural, 184
 as dangerous, 220
 as erasing, 187
 gendered, 191
 generational, 182
 of history, 221
 and memory, 184
 in *Monkey Hunting* (García), 220
 as negative, 186, 190, 191
 as positive, 183–184
 postcolonial, 185
 as seductive, 176, 185
Novels, 8, 17–18
 by women, 13–14
 See also Indenture, literature of

O

"Ode to My Unknown Great-Great Grandmother" (Manoo-Rahming), 171–173
 ancestors in, 171–172, 185
Ofry, Mohammed, 49
Oral narratives, 8, 9, 21, 26–28, 36–38, 171–173, 186, 259, 260
 of Chinese, 207
 of Maharani, 36–37
 See also Achamma; Doolarie; Maharani; Testimonials
Outar, Lisa, 10, 146
Overseers, 90, 175

P

Pagoda, The (Powell), 4, 18, 105, 133–139, 182
 condemnation of imperialism, 133
 critique of imperialism, 138
 ethnicity in, 138
 gender roles in, 132–134, 136
 hierarchies in, 138
 interracial relationship in, 105
 migration in, 138
 patriarchy in, 136
 sexual assault in, 133, 135
 sexuality in, 135–136
 whiteness in, 137
 See also Powell, Patricia
Pastrana, Juan Jiménez, 49
Paternalism, 140

Patriarchy, 3, 18, 28, 39, 113, 137,
    158–159, 259
  in China, 135
  in *Counting House, The*, 107
  in *Lutchmee and Dilloo* (1877), 74
  in marriage, 27
  in *Pagoda, The*, 136
  in *Promise, The*, 106, 107
Pearson, J. G., 69
Peepal Tree Press, 8
People's National Congress (PNC),
    148, 157
People's National Movement (PNM,
    Trinidad), 131
People's National Party (PNP,
    Jamaica), 131
People's Progressive Party, 132
"Per Ajie," 152–156, 158, 160
  ancestors in, 153–156
  Indian diaspora in, 151, 154
  Indian women in, 153
  Indo-Guyanese in, 154
  land as fertility in, 154
  Mehta, Brinda on, 152
  nationalism in, 154
  as optimistic, 154
  Poynting, Jeremy, 152
  sexual assault in, 153–154
  women's bodies in, 153
Persad-Bissessar, Kamla, 140
Persaud, Alice Bhagwandi Sital, *see*
    Singh, Alice
Phillips, Leslie, 59–60, 74
Pirbhai, Mariam, 9, 10, 106, 130
  on *Jahajin* (Mohan), 187
  *Mythologies of Migration,
    Vocabularies of Indenture*, 9,
    123
  on *The Promise* (Sharlow), 123
Plantations, 218
  abuse, 118–119
  corruption of, 127
  decline of, 62

hierarchical structure, 74
  managers of, 82, 83
  overseers of, 59–60, 75
  planters, 114, 124
Poetry, 8, 14, 18, 22, 145–177, 259
  alienation in, 148
  ancestors in, 105–106
  autobiographical nature of, 185
  language about women, 158n7
  from oral narrative, 36
  by women, 14
  women's bodies in, 145–146
  See also Indenture, literature of
Political movements, 19
  Black Power Revolution (Trinidad),
    170
  Negritude movement, 184
Political parties, 131–132
  Independent Party of Color (Cuba),
    218
  Jamaican Labor Party (Jamaica),
    148
  National Alliance for Reconstruction
    (NAR, Trinidad), 131–132
  People's National Movement
    (PNM, Trinidad), 131
  People's National Party (PNP,
    Jamaica), 132, 149
  Popular Party (Guiana), 79–80
Post-colonial governments
  replicating colonialism, 177
  as repressive, 157
Post-colonialism
  in African nations, 149
  in Guyana, 157
  and socialism, 149
Post-colonial literature, 147
  cynicism in, 149
Post-colonial states, 177
Post-indentureship feminisms, 10,
    133, 146, 157
  See also Dougla poetics; Kala pani
    discourse

Powell, Patricia, 4, 18, 105, 133, 135, 182
  motivations for writing *The Pagoda*, 138
  See also Pagoda, The
Poynting, Jeremy, 76, 78
  on *I Want to Be a Poetess of My People*, anthology (Das), 156–157
  on Mahadai Das, 156
  on "Per Ajie" (Das), 152
  on Rajkumari Singh, 151
Pre-capitalism, 12
Prince, Mary, 16, 29
Progression of civilization, 7, 21
Promise, The (Sharlow), 13, 16, 18, 120, 122–133, 138, 140
  ancestors in, 105–106
  British characters in, 96
  caste in, 124
  female protagonist of, 106
  gender in, 104
  imperialism as evil, 126, 127, 132
  India as idyllic, 124, 126–127
  reception of, 123
  sexual assault in, 128–130, 132
  sexuality in, 127, 132
  women in, 140
  See also Sharlow, Mohammed
Prostitution, 42, 135, 204, 217, 256
  See also Human trafficking
Puri, Shalini, 10, 10n4, 146

Q
Qatar, 262
Qichao, Liang, 8n2
Queue, 208

R
Race, 18, 21, 173, 260
  and imperialism, 22
  and marriage, 55
  mixed, 84–86, 91, 92 (*see also* Creole, people)
  and tension, 218
  tensions among, 258
  and violence, 21
  See also Hierarchy of race
Racial purity, 84–85
Racism, 72, 215, 257–258
  See also Hierarchy of race
Ramayana, 188n4
Rampaul, Giselle, 170
Rape, *see* Sexual assault
Reddock, Rhoda, 50
Relationship, intimate, 14–15
  between British man/Indian woman, 11, 18–19
  between colonizer and colonized, 3, 11–12
  as metaphor, 11, 12
  See also Sexual relationship
Religion, 18, 75
  Buddhism, 210
  Christianity, 45–46, 69, 210
  Hindu, 10, 15, 25, 27, 39, 172, 188n4
  and imperialism, 66
  Islam, 14–15, 25, 73
  and marriage, 15, 45–47, 52
  Santeria, 210
Remembering, 182
  and oppression, 187
  and trauma, 192
Revolutionary movements
  Armed Uprising of the Independent Party of Color, 218
Robinson, Cedric, 7
Rodney, Walter, 39, 148, 157n6, 162
Roopnarine, Lomarsh, 67–68
Rope, 1, 4, 7
  as metaphor for indenture, 1–2
  as metaphor for love, 1–2

Rose Hall Disturbances of 1913, 105n3
Routledge Reader in Caribbean Literature, The, 160
Royal African Company, 65
Ruimveldt Riots, 62
Russia, 62

S

Sanadhya, Totaram, 16, 48, 49, 125–126, 261
Sardar, 30, 30n5
Sarvan, Charles P., 108
Sati, 27, 29, 76
Schuessler, Jennifer, on *Monkey Hunting*, 203
Sea of Poppies (2008), 20, 261
"Search for Utopia, Desire for the Sublime: Cristina García's *Monkey Hunting*," 203
Seduction
  of hierarchies, 3, 62
  in intimate relationships, 3
  of persistence of class, 3
Selvon, Sam, 20, 105
Sembéne, Ousmane, 149
Sen, Sharmila, 106
Sexual assault, 18, 21, 107, 113, 124, 128, 133, 135, 192
  and class, 192
  See also Domestic violence
Sexuality, 134
  fluid, 135–136
  See also Gender roles
Sexual relationship, 104
  between British men/Indian women, 59–65, 74–75, 114, 117, 258; as symbolic of empire, 1, 62, 64, 84, 103–104, 119, 122, 125–129, 132, 139
  between colonizers and colonized, 60–63, 75, 114–116; with Indian women, 63, 64; McNeil-Lal Report of 1914, 74; 1871 Royal Commission, 74
  as exploitative, 60, 61, 108
  interracial, 260
  legislation of, 38
Shadow Bride, The (Heath), 20
Shah, Ryhaan, 182, 188n4
Sharlowe, *see* Sharlow, Mohammed
Sharlow, Mohammed, 12, 16, 18, 104, 104n2, 105–106, 120, 139, 259
  background, 123
  challenging imperial stereotypes, 123
  Elect, The, 123
  Promise, The, 122–133
  When Gods Were Slaves, 131n16
Shepherd, Verene, 191
Shinebourne, Jan Lowe, 20, 181
Shizen, Ren, 38–39
Silent Life, A (Shah), 182, 183, 188n4, 199–200
  ancestors in, 199–200
Singal, R.L., 32
Singh, Alice, 15, 36, 150, 151, 158, 259
  daughter of, 34
  diary of, 32–35, 54–55, 186
  education of, 35, 45
  grandmother of, 34
  husband of, 35
  marriage of, 46, 54
  social welfare projects of, 35
  See also Autobiography of Alice Bhagwandy Sital Persaud (Singh, Alice); Singh, Rajkumari
Singh, Alice Bahadur, *see* Singh, Alice
Singh, Rajkumari, 8, 18–19, 34–35, 160, 174
  and *aji*, 151, 152
  Alice Singh, mother, 151

background of, 150–151
on Guyana, 177
"I am a Coolie," 152
"I See Bent Figures," 155
Messenger Group, 151
nationalism of, 162
"Per Ajie," 152–155, 158
poetry of, 150–156
reception of, 151
on women's bodies, 145, 146
Slavery, 9, 128
abolition of, 55, 65, 68n3
Anti-Slavery Society, 65
autobiography of, 16, 29–30, 68, 127
Barbados Slave Code of 1661, 28
beginning of, 65
brutality of, 68, 114
and Chinese laborers, 4, 202, 207
as corrupting, 127, 132
in Cuba, 202–203, 207, 208
end of, 220
and family, 28, 130, 210
forms of, 203
Haitian Revolution, 105n3
and indenture, 3, 6–8, 29, 55, 65, 68n3, 126, 138, 139, 202
justification for, 29
and marriage, 28, 55
narratives of, 16
Royal African Company, 65
sexualized, 217
slave codes, 16, 28
in Suriname, 44n13
See also Emancipation Day
Small, Jean, 163
Smith, Sidonie, 34
Socialism, 86, 149, 201
in London, 86n9
Solidarity, 10, 123, 131, 132, 139, 161, 260
across time, 10
racial, 208, 218
Sommer, Doris, 13, 120
Spanish colonialism, 65, 201

Speer, Albert, Jr., 262
Spivak, Gayatri, 6, 27, 76
Still Cry, The (Maharani), 36
See also Maharani
St. Lucia, 65
Stoler, Ann Laura, 11, 63, 206
Stowe, Harriet Beecher, 66
Sugarcane, 65, 174–176, 190, 215, 219, 261
Sugar factories, 181
Sugar's Sweet Allure (Ali), 95–99
British superiority in, 95
empire in, 99
gender imbalance in, 97
indenture in, 95, 97
pluralism in, 96
racial hierarchy in, 95, 98
Suicide, 208, 215–217
Supremacy, British, 64, 96
See also Hierarchy of race;
Ideology, Imperial; White supremacy
Surinam, *see* Suriname
Suriname, 4, 15, 26, 29, 32, 45, 49
indentured Indians in, 29
and monarchy, 44n13
slavery in, 30, 44n13
women in, 51–52
Swinging Bridge, The (Espinet), 10, 182, 183, 200
ancestors in, 199, 200
and kinship, 10
sexual assault in, 199

T
Technology, 66
Testimonials, 8, 16, 17, 26, 36, 38
See also Oral narratives
Textiles, 196
That Others Might Live (Beeharry), 20, 261
They Came in Ships (Das) anthology, 156

"They Came in Ships," poem (Das), 156, 158–162
  abuse of women in, 159
  ancestors in, 156, 163, 166
  bodily fluids in, 161
  citations of, 159–160
  dehumanization of laborers in, 160
  ethnic solidarity in, 161
  eyes in, 160–161
  history in, 161
  Indian women in, 159–160
  reception of, 159–160
  voices in, 161
"Third World Literature in the Era of Multinational Capitalism" (Jameson), 12
Those That Be in Bondage (Webber), 8, 13, 17, 18, 61–63, 76, 79–95, 165, 217
  Afro-Caribbeans in, 91–93, 91n10
  audience of, 93, 93n13
  bondage in, 82
  British Guiana in, 83
  characterization of Indians in, 86–87
  coloured class in, 81
  critique of indenture system, 90
  hierarchy of labor in, 92
  hierarchy of race in, 81, 83, 84, 92–93
  mixed race in, 92
  racial stereotypes, 82
  rebellion in, 88
  support for indenture, 64
  See also Webber, A.R.F.
Tinker, Hugh, 7
Trinidad, 131–132
  Bhojpuri, 186, 190–191, 197
  Black Power Movement, 148
  Black Power Revolution, 170
  Chinese migration, 202
  Chinese population, 20–21
  decolonization of, 170
  economy of, 122
  girls' education in, 45
  government of, 170
  Immigrants' Marriage and Divorce Ordinance, 1881, 52
  indenture in, 37, 37n8, 40–41, 204, 220
  indenture literature of, 14, 18–20, 183
  Indian marriage, 52
  Indian population, 20, 31, 173
  Indo-Caribbeans in, 3, 148
  migrants, Chinese, 134–135
  National Alliance for Reconstruction, 131–132
  in "Ode to My Unknown Great-Great Grandmother" (Manoo-Rahming), 171
  People's National Movement (PNM), 131, 170
  Persad-Bissessar, Kamla, 140
  politics of, 131–132, 148, 204
  slavery in, 122
  Williams, Eric, 21, 148, 170
  women in, 191
  women murdered, 47
  women's wages, 50
  See also Achamma; "Boodhoo" (Mendes); *Bound for Trinidad, An Historical Novel* (Atteck); *Brighter Sun, A* (Selvon); Doolarie; *Gender Negotiations among Indians in Trinidad, 1917–1947*; "Incarnation on the Caroni" (Manoo-Rahming); Jahajin (Mohan); "Journey Across the Black Waters" (Bain); Maharani; Manoo-Rahming, Lelawattee; "Ode to My Unknown Great-Great Grandmother" (Manoo-Rahming); *Promise, The* (Sharlow); *Swinging Bridge, The* (Espinet)

INDEX 257

Trinidad and Tobago, *see* Trinidad
Tumbridge, Mark, on *Monkey Hunting*, 209n16

U
Uncle Tom's Cabin (Beecher Stowe), 66
Under the Southern Cross (McKay), 69
United Arab Emirates (U.A.E.), 261, 262
United States, 11, 62, 262
 and Cuba, 204
 slavery in, 68n3

V
Vietnam, 200
Vietnam War, 200, 203, 215–217
 American departure from, 217
Violence
 generational, 199
 in indenture narratives, 13, 16, 36
 against laborers, 28, 77, 189
 political, 149
 racial, 21
 religious, 75n6
 See also Domestic violence; Sexual assault

W
Ward, Abigail, 147–148
 on "Coolie Odyssey," poem, 167–168
 on *Jahajin* (Mohan), 187, 194
Watson, Julia, 34
Wayward Reproductions (Weinbaum), 11
Webber, A.R.F., 4, 6, 12, 13, 17, 18, 61–63, 66, 76, 79, 80, 90, 126, 259
 on Africans, 92n12
 background of, 64, 79
 biography of, 64
 Centenary History and Handbook of British Guiana, 81
 critique of indenture system, 90
 and Guyanese independence, 18
 on immigration, 81–82
 mixed race of, 64, 79
 politics of, 80–81
 and Popular Party, 80–81
 See also Those That Be in Bondage (Webber)
Weber, Elizabeth E., 8n2
Weinbaum, Alys Eve, 11
Whiteness, 9, 137
White, passing as, 92, 137
White supremacy, 7, 9, 55, 74
 See also Hierarchy of race
Williams, Eric, prime minister, Trinidad, 170
Wilson, Janelle, 183n2
Women, African, 6, 12
 See also Dougla poetics
Women, as possessions, 12, 15, 25, 42–43, 51–53, 55, 59–60, 74–75, 112, 128–130
Women, as wives, 16, 110
Women, bodies of, 18, 19, 145–148, 150, 171, 177
 as land, 147–148, 162
Women, British, 132
Women, Chinese, 3, 5
 as animals, 213
 migration of, 134, 201–202
 sexual assault of, 135
 trafficking of, 49
Women, Indian
 as animals, 12, 74, 128, 132, 153, 210
 as bearers of culture, 5, 6, 18, 61, 107, 115, 124, 140, 159n8, 177, 193
 in Caribbean culture, 10

Women, Indian (*cont.*)
  caste, 42–43
  as children, 12
  control of, 38, 61, 114, 140, 159
  depictions of, 13, 106–107
  domestic abuse of, 159n8
  and gender roles, 194–196
  legislation of, 26–29
  migration of, 40, 152–153
  murder of, 93, 258
  as representation of India, 18, 83, 104, 106, 128–129, 139–140
  as representation of nation, 146, 259
  resistance of, 53, 55
  as scapegoats, 63, 94–95
  sexual assault of, 28, 29, 114, 191, 192
  sexualization of, 259
  silencing of, 200
  violence against, 94
  virtue of, 48, 49n19
Women, Indo-Caribbean, 34
  depictions of, 106
Women, Indo-Guyanese
  bodies of, 168
  depictions of, 159, 167–168
Women, laborers
  abuse of, 96, 191
  in *Autobiography of an Indian Indentured Labourer* (Khan), 32
  bodies of, 145–146
  doubly marginalized, 140
  economic independence of, 5, 160
  exploitation of, 74, 120
  independence of, 111–112, 114–115
  mistreatment of, 48
  murder of, 5, 47–48, 97, 140
  pay discrimination against, 49, 51
  as representation, 6
  as scapegoats, 5, 6
  sexual exploitation of, 259
  stereotypes of, 163
  work of, 49
Women, silencing of, 137, 259
Women, single, 13, 15–17, 27, 43, 47–48, 51–52, 110, 110n6, 190, 259
  pressure to marry, 50–53
  as scapegoats, 47–48
Women, South Asian, 3
Wright, Danaya, 27

Y
Young, Robert J.C, 11
Yun, Lisa, 9, 25, 26, 36, 38–39, 207
  on Chinese merchants, 209n16
  on migrant ships, 207
  on resistance, 208
  testimonies of Chinese laborers, 205–206
  See also Coolie Speaks, The

The manufacturer's authorised representative in the EU is Springer Nature Customer Service Centre GmbH, Europaplatz 3, 69115 Heidelberg, Germany. If you have any concerns regarding our products, please contact ProductSafety@springernature.com

Printed and bound by CPI Group (UK) Ltd, Croydon, CR0 4YY
23/03/2026
02076679-0008